RARE

'Famous American composer and lyricist Stephen Sondheim was fond of saying "Opportunity is not a lengthy visitor." Take advantage of things presented to you.

I doubt Rakesh had ever heard of Stephen Sondheim, but he certainly took that advice to heart. Faster than you could say 'liberalisation', he had snapped up stakes in assorted businesses, backed hungry entrepreneurs and mentored dozens of turtles. A larger-than-life persona, swashbuckling personality, and a what-you-see-is-what-you-get image endeared him to millions of investors.

Politicians to punters listened to his every pronouncement. The story of his life, as written, is truly the history of Modern Dalal Street.'

—Ramesh Damani, Investor

NANDINI
VIJAYARAGHAVAN

RARE

INVESTING THE RAKESH JHUNJHUNWALA WAY

WESTLAND
BUSINESS

WESTLAND
BUSINESS

Published by Westland Business, an imprint of Westland Books, a division of Nasadiya Technologies Private Limited, in 2025

No. 269/2B, First Floor, 'Irai Arul', Vimalraj Street, Nethaji Nagar, Alapakkam Main Road, Maduravoyal, Chennai 600095

All photographs, except as otherwise credited, courtesy of the Jhunjhunwala family collection; select photographs by Ritika Shaiva. Reproduced from *Rakesh Jhunjhunwala: The Man Who Believed in India* Ashoka University, 2023, with permission from the publisher.

Images from Titan Company and GCMMF reproduced with permission.

ISBN: 9789371972048

10 9 8 7 6 5 4 3

Typeset by Jojy Philip

Printed at Manipal Technologies Limited, Manipal

Contents

Foreword

BHASKAR BHAT
Former Managing Director, Titan Industries

THERE ARE STORIES THAT SHIMMER QUIETLY, AND THEN THERE are stories that blaze a trail across the sky—stories that inspire, instruct and ignite the imagination of an entire generation. The life and legacy of Rakesh Jhunjhunwala belong, without doubt, to the latter category.

As I turn the pages of *Rare: Investing the Rakesh Jhunjhunwala Way*, I am reminded of the bustling energy of Dalal Street, the relentless optimism that powers India's markets, and the extraordinary journey of a man who dared to dream big, and then dream even bigger. The book keeps taking me back to the memorable times Rakesh and I had together, whether sipping JW Blue Label at his Malabar Hill home or having fun singing and making merry with family and friends in Lonavala or merely eating ghar ka khana in his office in Nariman Point. Never was there a moment of boredom when I was with him, and this book brings alive RJ's skill at investing, his whims and fancies, his sharp intellect, his weaknesses and above all his love for India.

This is not just a book about investing. It is a book about a confident and daring India—about the spirit of enterprise, the courage to take risks, and the humility to learn from failure. It is about the power of conviction, the value of relationships, and the joy of giving back. It is about the magic that happens when intellect meets intuition, and when hard numbers dance with human stories.

Rakesh Jhunjhunwala's life is a testament to the fact that fortune favours not just the brave, but also the curious, the patient and the ever-learning. He was a man who could see patterns where others saw chaos, who could spot opportunity in adversity, and who never lost sight of the human heart that beats beneath every balance sheet.

What makes this book truly special is its breadth and depth. It takes us behind the scenes—into the living rooms where family debates shaped young Rakesh's worldview, into the trading rings where fortunes were made and lost, and into the boardrooms where decisions changed the destiny of companies. It is rich with anecdotes, data and insights, but above all, it is rich with humanity.

With well-researched content, the author has woven together the threads of history, economics, psychology and personal narrative with the skill of a master storyteller. We meet not just the investor, but the son, the husband, the father, the mentor, the friend. We see laughter, the arguments, the midnight snacks, the setbacks, and the triumphs. We learn about the importance of integrity, the dangers of hubris, and the enduring value of optimism.

For every reader—whether you are a seasoned investor, a student of business, or simply someone who loves a good story—there is something here to cherish. You will find practical wisdom, timeless principles, and the gentle reminder that, in the end, it is not just about the wealth we accumulate, but the lives we touch and the legacy we leave behind.

As you embark on this journey through the pages of *Rare*, I invite you to do so with an open mind and an open heart. Let the story of Rakesh Jhunjhunwala inspire you to think boldly, act wisely and believe in the extraordinary possibilities that lie within each of us.

Because, as this book so beautifully reminds us, rare fortunes are not just built in markets—they are built in minds, in families and in the spirit of a nation that is forever on the rise.

Mumbai
October 2025

Foreword

Amit Goela
Partner, RaRe Enterprises

AS RAKESHJI'S ASSOCIATE/PARTNER FOR OVER THIRTY YEARS, I am both deeply honoured and delighted to introduce *Rare: Investing the Rakesh Jhunjhunwala Way*. Rakesh Jhunjhunwala was an extraordinary investor who, through his sheer intellectual heft, ability to express and back his opinion fearlessly, and force of personality, achieved the almost-impossible task, not only making serious wealth for himself and his family but also transforming Dalal Street into 'a respectable place for professional investors and brokers'. Rakeshji's role in the evolution of Dalal Street from a technologically archaic traders' den during India's pre-liberalisation era (before 1991) when he started his career, to the vibrant market at par with those of developed economies it is now is significant.

There could not be a better person than Nandini Vijayaraghavan to write this book. Nandini, armed with a CFA and degrees in Economics and Finance from Tufts University and London Business School and prior experience of having written two books and tracked Indian markets and personalities for over two decades, paints a vivid picture of Rakeshji's life and times.

Rare: Investing the Rakesh Jhunjhunwala Way is a well-researched bilingual story that takes a step back and chronicles India's business and regulatory environment when Rakeshji started his career, how he successfully built his flagship investment firm RaRe Enterprises, his influences, peers, the choices he made and the consequences of these choices. Readers will find the first section of the book, which narrates the story of Dalal Street and the business of investing in the late eighties and early nineties, absolutely fascinating. It will be of great interest to all those who have joined the profession in the last fifteen to twenty years.

I label the book as bilingual because while the book is narrated in English, it uses copious amounts of data—macroeconomic, market related and company specific—to weave an engaging tale. In adopting a bilingual narrative and drawing parallels, the book underscores the nuances of investing and the risks investors are exposed to. While shedding light on Rakeshji's investing style and thought process, the chapter on his risk management philosophy nudges readers to introspect, research and devise an investment strategy that works for them.

The book also covers what Rakeshji believed were mistakes of his career. Doing this alerts investors to the fact that the best of investors make mistakes and what needs to be done so that mistakes do not derail the lives and livelihood of their families.

The lives and careers of humans are both a function of their decisions and the environment they live in. There are few people who leave indelible imprints—both positive and negative—in the sands of time. *Rare: Investing the Rakesh Jhunjhunwala Way* tells the story of a human who improved the lives of thousands of people as a family man, investor, entrepreneur and philanthropist.

The book is both an account of Rakeshji's investment career and of India's contemporary business history, which will appeal to entrepreneurs, professionals, seasoned and novice investors and students alike.

Mumbai
October 2025

Introduction

WHY WRITE AND PUBLISH A BOOK ON RAKESH JHUNJHUNWALA (RJ) in 2025, when at least four books have already been published on one of India's most renowned investors? What more is there to say?

Let's get the facts out of the way.

This book, *Rare: Investing the Rakesh Jhunjhunwala Way*, has at least five distinguishing aspects. First, it traces the trajectory of RJ's portfolio of listed equity investments, specifically in those entities in which he held at least a 1% stake. While other books cover his individual investments, the chapter titled 'Lies, Damned Lies and Statistics' describes how his major equity investments performed as a whole. This is important, as share prices of a portfolio's constituents seldom rise and fall in symphony, and the timing of investors' decisions to buy, sell and hold securities affects their portfolios' performance and ultimately their wealth.

Second, RJ's six private equity (PE) investments that listed between 2015 and 2024 are chronicled in the chapters 'Jackpot!' and 'Janus Stock'. RaRe Enterprises, the investment firm RJ founded, was the PE backer for six businesses—Baazar Style Retail, Concord Biotech, Inventurus Knowledge Solutions, Metro Brands, Nazara Technologies, and Star Health and Allied Insurance.

Third, a brief account of the films he produced is included. Film production had a negligible impact on RJ's wealth, but it sheds light on his personality. Fourth, the book narrates the performance of RJ's listed equity and PE investments during two periods—from 31 December 2015 up to his demise on 14 August 2022 and the phase spanning 15 August 2022 and 31 December 2024.

The least discussed aspect of RJ's investment style is his risk management. A bird's eye view of RJ's risk management, which is a critical skill and process that separates the grain from the chaff, is provided in the chapter 'Arthur Road Jail and Mahalaxmi Race Course'.

However, RJ's life is not just a story about him. It is about the environment, his associates and family that shaped him; it is about India, the opportunities the country affords and the roadblocks it presents.

Our Fascination with Wealth and the Wealthy

Most people around the globe are more likely to remember the names of the wealthiest persons in their countries and the world, actors and sportspersons than the recipients of the Nobel Prize and the Fields Medal. Such is the allure and clout of wealth, films and sports. The fame that accompanies wealth, I suppose, in part, reflects the aspiration of many to become wealthy themselves or at least improve their standard of living.

It is this widely prevalent aspiration that may have resulted in the pantheon of several religions consisting of one or more gods of wealth. The Aztecs worshipped Tezcatlipoca while the ancient Egyptians deified Bes. The Romans and Greeks sought the blessings of Pluto and Plutus respectively. The Chinese revered Caishen and Guan Gong. Hindus prayed to and continue to venerate Ganesha, Lakshmi and Kubera. I am yet to come across a civilisation whose pantheon did not include a god or goddess of bounty.

The Hindu conception of wealth seems among the most broad-based and balanced. We continue to venerate the octet or eight manifestations of Lakshmi (Ashta Lakshmi), who is believed to preside over eight sources of fortune—enlightenment, money, harvests, livestock, progeny, bravery, victory and knowledge. Contemporary dictionaries, conversely, define wealth as abundance, affluence, cash, property, prosperity, revenue, riches, richness, security, treasure and worth.

Those aspiring to become rich may be divided into two categories—entrepreneurs who try to build businesses and investors who seek to build a portfolio of financial investments. Financial investments include equities, bonds, mutual funds and allocations to hedge funds and private equity partnerships; this is a non-exhaustive list. Their careers intertwine, though. Entrepreneurs who become affluent invest in financial assets. Investors lend and subscribe to the equity of enterprises floated by entrepreneurs. For example, Warren Buffett's investment vehicle Berkshire Hathaway owns a 6% stake in Apple as of May 2025.

The wealthy may be broadly classified into two categories, though almost all own large financial investment and property portfolios. The first category derives its wealth from founding and/or owning controlling stakes of large businesses like Tesla's Elon Musk, Amazon's Jeff Bezos and Meta's Mark Zuckerberg. The second group of wealthy became affluent by managing their own money and that of their clients. According to *Forbes* magazine's April 2024 estimates, eight of the hundred richest people in the world—Warren Buffett, Stephen Schwarzman, Ken Griffin, Masayoshi Son, Jeff Yass, David Tepper and Steve Cohen—predominantly derive their wealth by managing financial investments.

India has just two financial investors among its hundred richest citizens—Radhakishan Damani (ranked sixth, with a net worth of $31.5 billion or ₹2,68,908 crore) and Rekha Jhunjhunwala (ranked twenty-eighth with a net worth of $9.3 billion or ₹79,392 crore) as of April 2025.[1] The Damani family's stake in the listed retail chain Radhakishan founded, Avenue Supermarts, is around ₹2,12,455 crore or 79% of his net worth. Financial investments worth ₹56,453 crore constitute around 21% of Damani's net worth and is at par with the wealth of the forty-fourth richest Indian—Nusli Wadia, the chairman of the Wadia group, of which Britannia Industries is the flagship entity. Damani is a rare entrepreneur-cum-active-investor.

This puts Rekha, the wife of this narrative's protagonist, RJ, in a unique position. She is the sole pureplay financial investor among India's richest, a position bequeathed to her by her late husband.

RJ passed away on 14 August 2022 due to heart failure. He was a first-generation investor, and an outspoken one at that. A significant chunk of his investments was in listed equities, which makes a large portion of his portfolio highly traceable. The transparency of a part of RJ's portfolio has motivated amateurs to track his every move and emulate him. But is what's good for the goose good for the gander? That's what we are setting out to explore.

Show, Don't Tell

Born in 1960, RJ began his career as an investor in 1985. This was a time before liberalisation, when the markets were very different from what we see today. This was also when Harshad Mehta, born in 1954, was active on Dalal Street, to be joined a few years later by the 1966-born Ketan Parekh. All three men began their careers in the pre-liberalisation (before 1991) and pre-digital era; an era characterised by stifling regulation, scarce capital, minimal computerisation and conspicuously absent emails. The trio were bestowed the epithet 'Big Bull'. Yet, their careers panned out very differently. Understanding each one, as well as the impact that they had on the market and on retail investors, is crucial to getting to know RJ and his investment philosophy, strategy and career.

The chapter 'Catalysts' describes the state of India's capital markets and banking sector in that era, thus setting the context of the field in which they worked. 'Growmore' outlines Mehta's career, while 'Pentafour Bull' delineates Parekh's. RJ makes a cameo appearance in the latter two chapters as Mehta's, Parekh's and RJ's paths crossed.

The impact of Mehta and Parekh on India's capital markets did not end with the former's demise in 2001 and the Securities and Exchange Board of India (SEBI) debarring the latter from the markets for fourteen years in 2007. In July 2022, the Mehta family, helmed by Harshad's brother, Ashwin, alleged that the government-appointed custodian had sold the shares it had seized at throwaway prices, resulting losses of over ₹20,000 crore! 'Growmore' examines the accuracy of this claim. Barely three years after SEBI's ban on Parekh operating in capital market ended, he came under the regulatory scanner again in January 2025. 'Growmore' and 'Pentafour Bull' assess the impact of Mehta and Parekh on India's capital markets after 1993; the year journalists Sucheta Dalal and Debashis Basu published their critically acclaimed bestseller, *The Scam: From Harshad Mehta to Ketan Parekh*.

The three chapters—'Catalysts', 'Growmore' and 'Pentafour Bull'—are essential to understand the money-making opportunities in that era and the choices the three Big Bulls made.

A key difference between RJ and the other 'Big Bulls' was that he consciously professionalised RaRe Enterprises, an unlisted entity that invests in listed equities and is also a PE backer. The performance of the traceable components of RaRe Enterprises' business after RJ's demise is analysed in 'The Show Goes On'.

The Psychology of Investing

An investor needs to assess the current and potential impact of quantitative and qualitative factors—the macroeconomy, political and regulatory environment, the industry in which their investees operate, investee-specific factors, sentiments of other investors and extant condition of capital markets—to decide whether to buy, sell or hold securities. Investing is thus an art and a science. Yet another factor that determines the success and sustainability of investors is mindset or motivation. What drives investors? A desire to accumulate wealth or fame, a sense of accomplishment, a wish to facilitate the growth of investees? Much as our myths define what wealth means to us, they also warn us of its potential ill effects.

The Hindu god of wealth, Kubera, once invited the Devas for a sumptuous banquet at his palace. He visited Mount Kailasa, the abode of Lord Shiva and his consort Goddess Parvati, to invite the divine couple to the feast. Shiva and Parvati expressed their inability to attend the event but assured Kubera that their son Ganesha would be present. On the appointed day, the Devas flocked Kubera's opulent palace. So did Ganesha, who was then just a boy. On reaching the palace, Ganesha declared that he was hungry and demanded that he be fed right away. Kubera ushered Ganesha to the dining area and instructed his cooks to feed the boy. Much to the bewilderment of those assembled, Ganesha devoured the food cooked for the hundreds of guests! Kubera ordered his retainers to procure food from the neighbouring villages, which too was inadequate to satiate Ganesha's hunger. Ganesha then wolfed down the raw groceries at the palace and started gobbling down the gold coins and jewellery in Kubera's treasury. A distraught Kubera rushed to Kailasa and sought refuge in Shiva and Parvati, who then gave him a fistful of rice. When the once arrogant and now chastened Kubera offered this rice to Ganesha, the divine offspring ate it and was finally satiated.

Greek and Roman legends narrate the story of King Midas of Phrygia, an ancient district of Anatolia in present-day Turkey. Midas found the wandering Silenus, a satyr and companion of Dionysus, the god of fruitfulness and vegetation. Silenus, pleased with the king's hospitality, granted him a boon. Midas, in his greed for wealth, wished for all objects he touched to turn into gold. But he did not realise the perils his boon posed: while every petty rock he touched turned into a gold ingot and made him wealthier, so did the food he touched, almost starving him to death. The ruler's daughter Marigold also turned into an inanimate golden statue on embracing her father. Dionysus released the repentant Midas from the boon that was in reality a curse by having him bathe in the Pactolus River. The presence of alluvial gold in that stream is attributed to this legend.

Hubris and greed, as with Kubera and Midas, have brought about the downfall of many an entrepreneur and investor. Did RJ possess these traits? Was he aware of them? How did he manage them? What were his strengths and weaknesses? How did RJ's traits influence the performance of his investment portfolio? *Rare* attempts to illuminate RJ's personality by analysing his interviews, assessing his interactions with investees during results announcements and his investment decisions. While I have followed RJ's investment style and investments for over two decades, I sadly never had the opportunity to meet him. His interactions with the media and voice bytes that have now become investing mantras offered me insights into the investor's character and personality. The chapter titled 'Thus Spake RJ' is a compendium of RJ's quotes, with explanations wherever required, to enable readers to independently assess his personality and investment persona.

The Analytical Aspect

Investing is a multidisciplinary process that draws from numerous bodies of knowledge, including finance, economics, politics and psychology. The interdisciplinary nature of investing is evident in one of the critically acclaimed books in the recent times—*Debt: The First 5000 Years*, by David Graeber, an anthropologist. Authors of business books analyse macroeconomic and industry trends and financial statements, scrutinise judiciary and regulatory orders, read brokerage and credit rating reports, newspaper columns and magazines articles, watch hundreds of YouTube videos, and interview those associated with the subject of their book as part of their research.

Business book authors are usually academics, journalists and bankers/analysts. These professionals deploy their experience and tools of the trade while writing. The differences in narrative styles and analysis are best understood by juxtaposing the works of journalists, such as Anita Raghavan's *The Billionaire's Apprentice* and Gregory Zuckerman's *The Man Who Solved the Market*, with those of academics, such as Chris Miller's *Chip War* and Niall Ferguson's *The Ascent of Money* and bankers, as with Michael Lewis' *The Big Short* and Liaquat Ahamed's *Lords of Finance*.

As an analyst by profession and an avid reader, I have adopted a hybrid research method, which comprises first-hand analysis of the market and industry data and financials of RaRe Enterprises' investees and an evaluation of the historical, social, personal, regulatory and political factors that shaped RJ. Appendices 1 to 6 provide snapshots of the data-based analysis and information that aided the narration of this chronicle. I am grateful to Amit Goela, R. Balki, Bhaskar Bhat, Rajiv Agarwal, Ramesh Damani, Rekha Jhunjhunwala, Renuka Ramnath, Uday Kotak, Utpal Sheth, Vishal Gupta and Venkat Eshwara, whose insights allowed me a deeper understanding of Rakesh Jhunjhunwala, the human being and investor.

GCMMF (Amul) and Titan Company graciously permitted me to incorporate their topicals and print advertisement respectively in *Rare*. Maha Iyer and his colleague Suraj S. created two beautiful charts for this book—'Sensex's Forty Year Trajectory' and 'Sensex & CRR Trends'. Thank you, Maha and Suraj.

I am indebted to my reviewers for their honest and incisive feedback. Thank you, Arun Arumugam, Shijo George, Siddharth Vijayaraghavan and V.S. Kumar. Raj Jayaram, a reviewer of my previous book, *Unfinished Business: Evolving Capitalism in the World's Largest Democracy*, does not feature in the aforesaid list. When I informed Raj that Westland Books had commissioned me to write a book on Rakesh Jhunjhunwala, he quipped, 'Everyone thinks they know everything about RJ. I hope you discover a fresh angle.' I hope I have. Sadly, Raj is no longer in our midst.

A thoroughfare that RJ often frequented, especially at the beginning of his career, one that enables investors who look for viable businesses to deploy their monies and enterprises that seek financing at competitive rates transact, and embodies capital markets in India, is Dalal Street. It is apt that this narrative begins with a chronicle of Dalal Street.

Part 1

Big Bulls and Mr India in Dalal Street

1

Dalal Street

A Brief but Affectionate History

THE AMERICAN CIVIL WAR, WAGED BETWEEN 1861 AND 1865, triggered a series of events that led to the founding of the world's tenth oldest and Asia's first stock exchange in India. The war disrupted American cotton exports to Britain, which instead started sourcing raw cotton for its cloth mills from the jewel in its crown, India. Indian cotton exports more than doubled in five years, from 5,28,000 bales in 1860 to 1.2 million bales in 1865. Tales of traders extracting cotton by tearing apart mattresses and pillows and filling cushions with coir fibre instead underscore the huge demand for the commodity, which earned the moniker 'white gold'. Traders invested the profits they earned by selling cotton in the share market. So did investors, who financed equity purchases with money borrowed from banks. Market participants also used 'time bargains', which are now known as forward contracts, to bet on rising prices. These factors propelled the rise of share prices to stratospheric levels after the outbreak of the American Civil War.

Table 1.1: The American Civil War Fuelled Share Price Mania

Company	Share Price (₹)		Return (%)	
	1861	1865	4-Year	Annualised
The Back Bay Reclamation	5,000	50,000	900	78
The Port Canning Share	1,000	1,10,000	10,900	224
Asiatic Bank	200	460	130	23
Bank of Bombay	500	2,850	470	55
Colaba Land Company	10,000	1,20,000	1,100	86
Elphinstone Press Company	46,000	1,35,000	193	31
Apollo Press	12,000	20,000	67	14

Source: BSE, The Temple of Wealth Creation.

The cotton traders, investors and banks believed that the ensuing bull run would last forever. They ignored the warnings of the naysayers who opined that the share price appreciation did not reflect the performance of the underlying companies, and was hence unsustainable. The investors' irrational exuberance is evident from the Elphinstone Press Company's stock quoting at ₹1.35 lakh in 1865, which is just 10% lower than the most expensive Indian equity as of January 2024, the tyre maker MRF (previously known as Madras Rubber Factory), whose share price was ₹1.50 lakh. The equivalent of ₹1.35 lakh in 1865, assuming an annual inflation of 5%, was over ₹30 crore in January 2024.

The naysayers included Bartle Frere, the governor of Bombay, and Cowasji Jehangir Readymoney, a director on the board of the Bank of Bombay. On 16 November 1864, Frere, who had observed several government employees investing in the share market, issued a circular that advised civil servants of the risks during the 'present period of excitement'. The elderly and sick Readymoney, who believed that the Bank of Bombay would collapse like the Union Bank of Calcutta had in 1848 should it continue financing share purchases, resigned. He was replaced by Premchand Roychand, who had built a reputation as a formidable investor. Roychand would later be appointed as a board member of the Bombay Stock Exchange

Frere attempted to pass the Wager's Bill to clamp down on the time bargains. Investors, including Roychand, and over 250 British firms vehemently protested as they believed that the government was clamping down on a profitable activity. However, Frere persuaded the Bombay Legislative Council to pass the bill and despatched it in November 1864 to Viceroy John Lawrence for assent. The bill was curiously lost in transit between Shimla and Calcutta. By the time Lawrence signed the bill in mid-1865, thereby making it a law, it was too late.

The American Civil War ended in April 1865, resulting in a decline in cotton prices, as buyers expected the United States to resume exporting the commodity. This in turn resulted in a crash in the Indian stock market, with share prices of several companies trading below their 1861 levels. The Backbay Reclamation share price nosedived by over 96% from ₹50,000 to below ₹2,000. The Bank of Bombay's plunged by 97% from ₹2,850 to ₹87. Investors tried to sell their shares in shell companies, albeit unsuccessfully. Several merchant princes of Bombay, including Behramji Hormusji Cama, Rustomji Jamsetji Jejeebhoy and Kharshedji Furdunji Parekh faced financial distress. The city's population also declined by 21% from 8,16,000 people in 1864 to 6,44,000 in 1872 due to the 'migration from Bombay of the swarms of adventurers and labourers from all parts of India and from abroad who were attracted to the city by the speculative enterprises and the high prices of labour which marked the season of unexampled prosperity'.[1] The market crash clearly had deep and lasting implications on the city and the country at large.

Under a Banyan Tree

The government, in response to this event, enacted the Special Legislation Act XXVIII of 1865 to handle the large-scale collapse of companies in a timely and efficient manner. The liquidations lasted till 1872. Scarred by the 1865 crash in share prices and the seven-year downturn that ensued, the Bombay merchants decided to focus on listing productive enterprises such as mills, presses and mining companies, and to refrain from taking shell companies public. Alongside this, cotton mills and dockyards were established in the city and transportation facilities improved, bolstering Bombay's business environment. Finally, in 1875 merchants from Bombay's diverse communities, including Parsis, Muslims, Jains, Marwaris, Maharashtrians, Gujaratis, Baniyas and Brahmins joined hands to form the Native Share and Stock Brokers' Association to facilitate the organised trading of equities and debt. Their Articles of Association explicitly stipulated that 'no other person except natives of India shall be admitted as members of the said association'. It is indeed impressive that Indian merchants should collaborate to incorporate the predecessor of the Bombay Stock Exchange (BSE) when India was still a British colony and stipulated that membership was restricted to natives. Only in 1911, thirty-six years after the incorporation of the Native Share and Stock Brokers Association, Sir Sorabji Pochkhanawala would incorporate the first bank wholly owned and managed by Indians—the Central Bank of India.

The Bombay Stock Exchange website (www.bseindia.com) states that the first office of the Native Share and Stock Brokers Association was under a banyan tree. The first managing committee comprised twelve members, all Indians, including Premchand Roychand. The association had 318 members in its year of founding, 1875; the new members were charged a membership fee of ₹1. The first stock exchange building was rented from Bai Motibai Wadia, who charged a monthly rental of ₹130; the association struggled to pay the rent. Fast-forward forty-five years to 1920; the number of members had grown by 50% to 478, despite membership fees skyrocketing to ₹48,000! Such was the demand for membership.

In 1895, Sir Dinshaw Maneckji Petit, the first baronet, a Parsi merchant who founded India's first textile mill, owed the association ₹14,857. To settle it he tendered twenty-five shares of his company, Victoria Manufacturing Co. Ltd., that were then trading at ₹690 each. The association raised ₹17,250 by selling these shares, returned the excess ₹2,393 to Sir Petit and used the ₹14,857 repayment to buy its own building. The edifice, which was located at the junction of Mumbai Samachar Marg, Ambalal Doshi Marg and Dalal Street, was named after Sir Dinshaw M. Petit.

Sir Petit's legacy is not limited to textile mills and the Bombay Stock Exchange. His grandson, Fali, went on to become Sir Dinshaw Maneckji Petit, the third baronet, and married J.R.D. Tata's elder sibling, Sylla. Fali's sister Ratanbai Petit, aka Ruttie, married Muhammad Ali Jinnah; their offspring Dina married the chairman of Bombay Dyeing, Neville Wadia. The nuclear scientist Homi J. Bhabha was the first baronet's great grandson.

The performance of the Native Share and Stock Brokers Association and the facilities and safeguards it offered to its members during the early years aren't available in the public domain. However, the rest of the country was impressed with the benefits of an organised marketplace to transact financial securities, and followed its footsteps. The Ahmedabad Share and Stock Brokers' Association was established in 1894 followed by Calcutta (1908), Madras (1920), Lahore (1934), Uttar Pradesh and Nagpur (1940), Hyderabad (1944) and Delhi (1947).

The Epochal Budget

Between 1946 and 1961, the number of stock exchanges in India remained unchanged at seven, while the number of listed companies rose from 1,125 to 1,203. The book value of listed companies' capital almost trebled from ₹270 crore in 1946 to ₹753 crore in 1961. But the market value of the listed companies' capital or market capitalisation (market cap) grew by just 33% during this fifteen-year period, translating to a compound annual growth rate (CAGR) of 1.92%, from ₹971 crore in 1946 to ₹1,292 crore in 1961.

Two watershed events that left indelible imprints on India's socio-economic and political landscape was the country's independence on 15 August 1947 and the liberalisation of the economy that Dr Manmohan Singh's 24 July 1991 budget ushered in. The 1991 budget had a much more significant impact on India's capital markets than its independence.

The profile of the capital markets underwent a sea change in the four-year period following the 1991 budget. The number of stock exchanges inched up from twenty in 1991 to twenty-two in 1995, while the number of listed companies grew by 38% from 6,229 in 1991 to 8,593 in 1995. The book value of listed companies' capital grew by 86% from ₹32,041 crore in 1991 to ₹59,583 crore in 1995. Market cap more than quadrupled at a CAGR of 44.30% from ₹1,10,279 crore in 1991 to ₹4,78,121 crore in 1995![2]

Government oversight of capital markets grew in tandem with their rising significance. The first step towards this was outlined in the Constitution of India, which came into existence on 26 September 1950 and decreed that stock exchanges and future markets came under the purview of the central government. The Securities Contracts (Regulation) Act of 1956 was put in place to regulate the contracts executed in Indian capital markets and stock exchanges. A special body was established in 1992 to regulate capital markets: the Securities and Exchange Board of India (SEBI). The basic functions of SEBI are '... to protect the interests of investors in securities and to promote the development of, and to regulate the securities market...'.[3]

Alongside government regulation, stock exchanges developed indices to track the performance of markets. On 1 January 1986, BSE constituted India's first stock index. Deepak Mohoni, a stock analyst, coined the name 'Sensex', which is a portmanteau term of the words 'sensitive' and 'index'. The Sensex comprises stocks issued by thirty of India's largest and financially strongest companies. This large cap index was initially constituted as a 'full market capitalisation' index but, on 1 September 2003, shifted to the 'free-float capitalisation methodology'. Full float market capitalisation is the product of the aggregate shares issued by an entity and its share price. Free float market capitalisation is the number of shares readily available in the market multiplied by the share price; this metric ignores locked-in shares such as those owned by promoters, insiders and governments.[4] The change was to align BSE's methodology with that of major index providers, including MSCI and Financial Times Stock Exchange (FTSE).[5]

The maxim 'change is the only constant in life' is applicable to index constituents too. As entities waxed and waned in scale and financial strength and India's economy evolved, Sensex's composition changed. This is applicable to all indices, which are by definition meant to represent the profile and performance of the sectors they track. Only six entities have remained constituents of Sensex during the thirty-eight-year period spanning 1986 and 2024—Hindustan Unilever, Larsen & Tubro, Mahindra & Mahindra, Reliance Industries, Tata Motors and Tata Steel (Table 1.2).

Sensex's changing composition is a reflection of the changes in the Indian economy and the universe of large cap stocks. Stocks issued by financial institutions, including banks, public sector undertakings (PSUs, referred to as state-owned entities or SOEs

Table 1.2: S&P BSE Sensex Constituents for Select Years

	1986	**2010**	**2024**
1	ACC	ACC	Asian Paints
2	Bharat Forge	BHEL	Axis Bank
3	Bombay Dyeing	Bharti Airtel	Bajaj Finance
4	Ballarpur Industries	DLF	Bajaj Finserv
5	Ceat Tyres	Grasim	Bharti Airtel
6	Century Spinning	HDFC	HCL Technologies
7	Food Specialties (now Nestle)	HDFC Bank	HDFC Bank
8	Great Eastern Shipping	Hero Honda	Hindustan Unilever
9	GSFC	Hindalco	ICICI Bank
10	Glaxo	Hindustan Unilever	IndusInd Bank
11	Gwalior Rayon (Grasim)	ICICI Bank	Infosys Ltd
12	Hindustan Aluminium (now Hindalco)	Infosys	ITC Ltd
13	Hindustan Lever (now Hindustan Unilever)	ITC	JSW Steel
14	Hindustan Motors	Jaiprakash Associates	Kotak Mahindra Bank
15	Indian Hotels	Larsen & Tubro	Larsen & Tubro

	1986	2010	2024
16	Indian Rayon	Mahindra & Mahindra	Mahindra & Mahindra
17	ITC	Maruti Udyog	Maruti Suzuki
18	Kirloskar Cummins	NTPC	Nestle India
19	Larsen & Tubro	ONGC	NTPC
20	Mahindra & Mahindra	Reliance Communications	Power Grid Corporation of India
21	Mukand	Reliance Industries	Reliance Industries
22	Pieco Electronics (now Philips)	Reliance Infrastructure	State Bank of India
23	Premier Automobiles	State Bank of India	Sun Pharmaceuticals
24	Reliance Industries	Sterlite Industries	Tata Consultancy Services
25	Siemens	Sun Pharma	Tata Motors
26	TELCO (now Tata Motors)	Tata Consultancy Services	Tata Steel
27	Tata Power	Tata Motors	Tech Mahindra
28	Tata Steel	Tata Power	Titan Co
29	Voltas	Tata Steel	Ultratech Cement
30	Zenith	Wipro	Wipro

Source: www.bseindia.com & BSE Sensex is Now 25, Press Information Bureau, 6 January 2010

elsewhere in the world) and software companies are conspicuous by their absence among the thirty stocks that initially constituted Sensex in 1986. This is because listings surged in India after the 1991 budget and further accelerated during the tenure of the Atal Bihari Vajpayee-led National Democratic Alliance (NDA) alliance (1998–2004). The Vajpayee-led government was the first to set up a disinvestment ministry with Arun Shourie as minister and divested stakes in twelve PSUs.[6]

India's largest bank, the State Bank of India, listed in 1995, while the country's largest private sector banks, HDFC Bank and ICICI Bank, floated their initial public offerings (IPOs) in 1995 and 1997, respectively. The largest mortgage lender, HDFC Limited, was listed in a lacklustre IPO that was undersubscribed in 1978 and was not included in Sensex till much later. The three public sector behemoths—ONGC, NTPC and Power Grid Corporation of India—listed in March 2004, October 2004 and September 2007, respectively. Sensex, as of 2024, includes four software majors—Infosys (which listed in 1993), Tata Consultancy Services (TCS) (2004), Wipro (1946)* and Tech Mahindra (2006).

Sensex has also had among its ranks the equities market equivalent of fallen angels—bonds that were once rated investment grade but have since been downgraded to junk category due to a deterioration in financials and debt servicing ability. Jaiprakash Associates, which was a Sensex constituent in 2010, later became a member of the 'Dirty Dozen', India's largest corporate defaulters. Two embattled constituents of the now-in-shambles Anil Dhirubhai Ambani Group (ADAG), Reliance Communications and Reliance Infrastructure, were included in Sensex in 2010 as well .

---

* Wipro was incorporated in December 1945 as Western India Vegetable Products Limited and listed in 1946.

The Rise of the National Stock Exchange

Even as BSE was growing from strength to strength, some quarters opined that the stock exchange, on account of being a monopoly, had become 'imperious'. In January 1990, the union ministry of finance constituted a committee to study and recommend reforms to overhaul the Indian stock exchange ecosystem under the stewardship of the former Unit Trust of India (UTI) chairman, the 'Big Bull' Manohar J. Pherwani. The Pherwani Committee submitted its report the following year, recommending the setting up of a National Stock Exchange (NSE), which would be accessible to investors across the country and oversee a computer-networked national stock exchange system. The committee opined that the challenges of a lack of sufficient liquidity and poor service to small investors would not be solved by setting up new exchanges but by integrating the then existing nineteen exchanges.

Despite the proliferation of stock exchanges in India, BSE was a clear and dominant market leader that accounted for around 70% of the stock market activity. The Pherwani Committee suggested that NSE complement and not compete with BSE by limiting its activities to the listing of medium-sized companies. The committee recommended that NSE facilitate the listing and trading of bonds and debentures, businesses it felt were ignored by BSE and regional exchanges.

Another reason for incorporating a new exchange was BSE's powerful broker lobby. As Debashis Basu and Sucheta Dalal wrote, '… brokers controlled the stock exchanges; there was no sanctity to settlements; defaults were frequent; and investors were hapless victims with no recourse'.[7]

In 1992, SEBI asked market intermediaries to register themselves with the regulator and pay registration fees, which caused a furore. G.V. Ramakrishna (GVR), SEBI's second chairman (1990–1994) met brokers at BSE's trading ring to explain SEBI's stance and listen to the brokers' viewpoints. No consensus was reached at the end of the rather contentious two-hour meeting. GVR then formally wrote to the finance ministry recommending the setting up of NSE.[8]

BSE understandably opposed the Pherwani Committee's recommendation. Its executive director, M.R. Mayya observed, 'This is not in consonance with the trend the world over. A national stock-market system is administered by the country's leading exchange.' BSE's president, Hemendra Kothari, disputed the committee's inference. He remarked, 'The NSE will only result in fragmenting the existing market, which will lead to less competition and greater volatility.'[9]

Notwithstanding BSE's protests, NSE was incorporated in 1992 and was recognised as a stock exchange by SEBI in April 1993. It launched the wholesale equity and debt market segments and started electronic or screen-based trading between 1993 and 1994. The NSE's flagship large cap index, the Nifty50, was launched on 22 April 1996.[10]

The presence of two national stock exchanges and the emergence of screen-based trading resulted in dwindling clientele and diminished liquidity for the regional stock exchanges. The Calcutta and Hyderabad Stock Exchanges shut down in 2013, followed by Ahmedabad and Cochin in 2014, Madras in 2015 and Delhi in 2017.[11]

NSE's focus on technology since inception enabled it to evolve into the world's largest derivatives exchange, in terms of the number of contracts traded, for the fifth year in succession in 2023. Contracts traded at the NSE between January to March 2024 were a staggering 30.48 billion, which is more than five times the trades executed at the second largest exchange, BSE, which reported 5.91 billion trades. But BSE is catching up with a year-on-year growth of 4,696.4% vis-à-vis NSE's still robust 48%. International exchanges lag behind NSE and BSE, with the São Paulo-based B3 (reporting 2.06 billion contracts), Chicago

Mercantile Exchange (817.82 million) and Dalian Commodity Exchange (508.65 million) ranked third-, fourth- and fifth-largest derivative exchanges in the three months ending March 2024.[12]

NSE's rise, however, was marred by the co-location scandal from a decade earlier. In late January 2015, Sucheta Dalal, one of India's most renowned business journalists, received an envelope from Singapore through snail mail. It contained a letter dated 14 January 2015 addressed to B.K. Gupta, a deputy general manager in SEBI's market regulation department, and was copied to Dalal. The writer of the letter, who wished to remain anonymous, contended that a set of traders had earned exponential and unfair profits by rigging NSE's algorithmic trading (algo trading) platform that engaged in high frequency trading (HFT) and the use of co-location servers. The letter alleged that NSE insiders were involved in this front running—an illegal practice whereby a broker who possesses material non-public information that would affect the price of a stock trades the stock before the news is disseminated to the public.

SEBI concluded its investigations by penalising NSE to the tune of ₹624.89 crore plus 12% interest per annum for five years. NSE's chairman, Ravi Narain, and CEO, Chitra Ramkrishna, were ordered to disgorge 25% of their salaries from the previous five years and were barred from associating with market institutions for five years. While Ramkrishna had quit NSE in 2016 citing personal reasons, Narain resigned in 2018 over the co-location investigations.[13] Ramkrishna was arrested in March 2022, and the Delhi High Court granted bail to her in February 2023.[14] A decade has passed since the uncovering of the co-location scandal, and NSE's expansion plans continue to face regulatory roadblocks.

Two IPOs

Both BSE and NSE announced their intention to float IPOs in 2016 and filed their prospectuses. By this time, NSE's revenues and post-tax profits had overtaken those of BSE. In the financial year ending 31 March 2016 (FY2016),* NSE's ₹2,450 crore revenue was more than thrice that of BSE's ₹658 crore. NSE's post-tax profits were an impressive ₹975 crore, which was more than six times that of BSE's ₹160 crore![15] Notwithstanding NSE's impressive financial performance, the co-location scandal scuttled its listing plans.

BSE floated a ₹1,243 crore IPO in January 2017 at a price of ₹806 per share.[16] It was an offer for sale (OFS), wherein the then shareholders sold their stakes; BSE's receipts from the IPO were nil. NSE had also intended its IPO to be an OFS.[17] BSE's IPO was well received; it garnered subscriptions equivalent to 51.22 times the IPO size and listed on NSE on 3 February 2017. The share generated a handsome listing day 'pop', that is, the share price appreciated by 32.65% to ₹1,069.20 on listing day.[18] BSE's share price has more than trebled since its listing to ₹2,783 on 17 May 2024, delivering an annualised return of 18.54%.

The still unlisted NSE has consolidated its lead over BSE. By FY2024, NSE's ₹16,354 crore revenue was ten times BSE's ₹1,618 crore. NSE's ₹8,306 crore post-tax profits were almost eleven times BSE's ₹772 crore. As of end-2024, BSE's shareholders comprise institutional and retail investors. NSE's trading members and their associates held a 43.80% stake in the unlisted exchange, followed by LIC (10.72%) as of 31 March 2024. Four state-owned insurance companies—General Insurance Corporation of India, New India Assurance, National Insurance and Oriental Insurance—together hold a 6.81% stake. The balance is held by several domestic and overseas institutional investors and individuals. Rakesh Jhunjhunwala's mentor, Radhakishan Damani, owns 7.82 million shares, which is equivalent to a 1.58% stake.[19]

---

* The Indian financial year (FY) is the twelve-month period beginning 1 April and ending on 31 March of the subsequent calendar year

Though NSE has emerged as a market leader in facilitating derivative trading and is financially larger and stronger than BSE, the market cap of the entities listed in both exchanges is comparable, as most companies in India are listed on both exchanges. One exception is BSE, which is listed on NSE. As per the data on the stock exchanges' websites, the aggregate market cap of entities listed on BSE and NSE as of 28 March 2024 was ₹387 trillion ($4.65 trillion) and ₹381 trillion ($4.57 trillion), respectively. India's ten largest listed companies account for 23.05% and 23.41% of BSE's and NSE's market cap, respectively. These ten entities are Reliance Industries, TCS, HDFC Bank, ICICI Bank, Bharti Airtel, State Bank of India, Infosys, Life Insurance Corporation of India, ITC and Hindustan Unilever.

While BSE and NSE are the largest exchanges in India, they are not the only two that facilitate the trading of financial instruments. The other SEBI-approved exchanges are Metropolitan Stock Exchange, NSE International Exchange, Indonext and India International Exchange. Fuelled by the accelerated growth of the Indian economy following the 1991 reforms, improved performance of corporates and financial institutions and the continuing trend of new businesses floating IPOs, both BSE and NSE went from strength to strength. India's market cap grew by almost sixteen times at a CAGR of 13.42% from $225.65 billion in 2000 to $3.60 trillion in 2022. The ratio of market cap to gross domestic product (GDP) has more than doubled from 48.17% in 2000 to 105.47% in 2022. The robust growth in market cap of India's listed entities is certainly impressive. But are high growth and large market cap the major determinants of a stock's attractiveness as an investment proposition?

Stock exchanges characterised by sound governance, strong financial profiles and efficient technology platforms are prerequisites for capital markets to thrive. These are the hygiene factors. For capital markets to flourish, the pricing and yield on transacted securities ought to be reasonable. This is where we need to change track from an anecdotal chronicle of Dalal Street to quantitative metrics. There is a danger in accepting data as gospel truth. But as the following examples of GDP and market cap—two metrics investors often use in decision-making—illustrate, data ought to be used with caution. A data-driven chronicle of India's capital markets follows, preceded by a discussion of the merits and demerits of the metrics used for analysis.

The Limitations of Measurement Metrics

In her seminal work *GDP: A Brief but Affectionate History*, British economist Diane Coyle pointed out that while GDP, invented during World War II, is a qualitative measure of a country's size and its change is designated as a nation's growth, the metric is not devoid of drawbacks. Readers may be surprised to learn that GDP is a subjective metric influenced by political and social factors. In 2010, Ghana changed the base year in its calculations from 1993 to 2006, resulting in a 60% increase in GDP and its elevation from a low-income to a lower-middle-income country.[20] Similarly in 2014, Kenya announced that its economy was 25% larger than previously estimated as its most profitable industries—communications and property—were not considered in earlier calculations, which used 2001 as the base year.[21]

Coyle highlights the several drawbacks of GDP. These include its failure to measure innovation and the value of the environment, such as having clean rivers and lakes and unpolluted forests. The metric measures only those activities that occur in the marketplace and which may be priced. A household growing vegetables in its premises and the value of owning a home vis-à-vis renting are not included in GDP. Further, GDP does not measure the service economy. For instance, GDP statistics do not fully reflect the value of the 'sharing economy' and the rise of services like Uber and Airbnb. Yet another drawback of national income estimates is that they only measure the provision of goods and services and their use, and not the reasons for their use. For example, the rebuilding of homes and industries in the aftermath of the 2004 Indian Ocean tsunami resulted in a significant rise in consumption, which would show as a spike in the GDP. GDP does not measure unpaid activity like housework; how sustainable an economy is; the size of informal, cash-based or illegal activities; income distribution; or human and social capital.[22]

Notwithstanding the aforesaid disadvantages, Coyle concludes, 'Economic growth is not everything, but it supports the existence of many highly-valued social goods, and so it is crucial that we measure it.'[23]

Market cap, akin to GDP, is a useful metric not devoid of limitations. First, whether the rise in market cap is on account of a broad-based share price rally or a steep rise in a few large cap stocks is not evident. Second, the absolute value of market cap and its trends does not indicate if a country's stock market is cheap, expensive or fairly priced, in relation to comparable nations or the historical values of price-earning, price-to-book-value or enterprise-value-to-EBITDA ratios. Third, neither does a bull market guarantee the profitability and viability of its constituents nor does a bear market herald an economic and financial apocalypse. In other words, it is quite possible in the short to medium term for a company's performance and its market cap to be uncorrelated, as the latter is also influenced by the global and national macroeconomy, investor sentiments and other idiosyncratic factors. Fourth, changes in the prices of equities and number of listed stocks, which in turn is a reflection of listings, buybacks and delistings, underpin the market cap trend. However, the market cap metric does not reveal the relative shares of changes in the prices of equities and the number of listed stocks.

This non-exhaustive list of market cap's drawbacks does not diminish its importance as an indicator of the size and momentum of a nation's capital markets, and is a key input for the computation of numerous valuation and return metrics that form the cornerstone of sensible investing.

Bulls, Bears and Item Numbers

The aggregate market cap of companies listed on Indian stock exchanges is $4.23 trillion as of 19 May 2024—the fourth largest in the world. The US is ranked first, with its listed entities together reporting a market cap of $54.58 trillion, followed by China ($6.82 trillion) and Japan ($4.76 trillion). The trajectories of the stock exchanges of these nations have been anything but smooth. Sensex's trajectory is a case in point. Sensex has appreciated a whopping 600 times from 123.54 points in January 1980 to 72,482.78 points by end-April 2024, according to data published on the BSE website. This translates to a CAGR of 15.55%. Events like good monsoon, market manipulation, a rise in commodity prices and reforms initiated by the government have fuelled bull runs and, in turn, share price rallies. Cyclical downturns, both country-specific and global, discovery of market manipulation and missteps like demonetisation have caused equity markets to crash.

A key factor, in addition to economic, political, industry- and company-specific events, that has propelled Sensex's exponential rise is interest rates. During the 44.25 years spanning January 1980 to March 2025, RBI's cash reserve ratio (CRR)—the benchmark interest rate that forms the basis of interest paid on deposits and charged on loans—has declined from a peak of 15% that prevailed between August 1994 to October 1995 to 4% in March 2025. Lower borrowing costs make it more viable for companies to borrow money to finance capital expenditure and results in higher profits, which, in turn, propels share prices and indices. As is evident from Figure 1.2, the CRR and Sensex have moved in diametrically opposite directions since January 1980.

Figure 1.1: Sensex's Forty-Four Year Trajectory

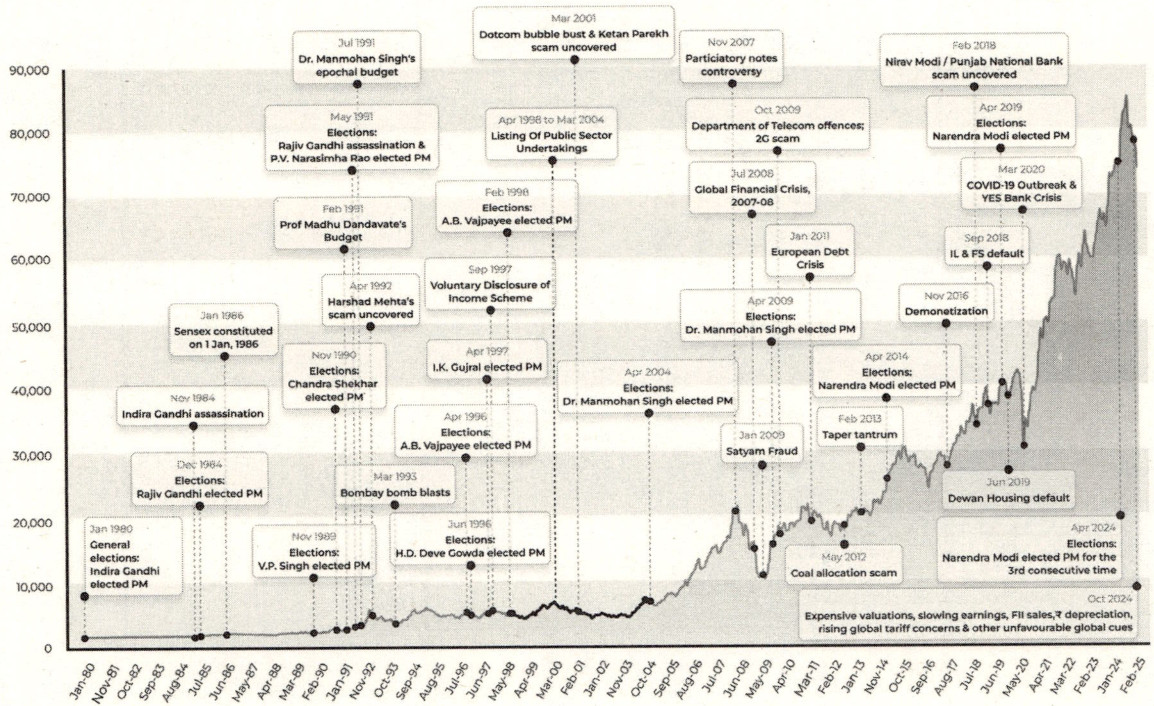

Source: bseindia.com

Figure 1.2: Trend in CRR and Sensex

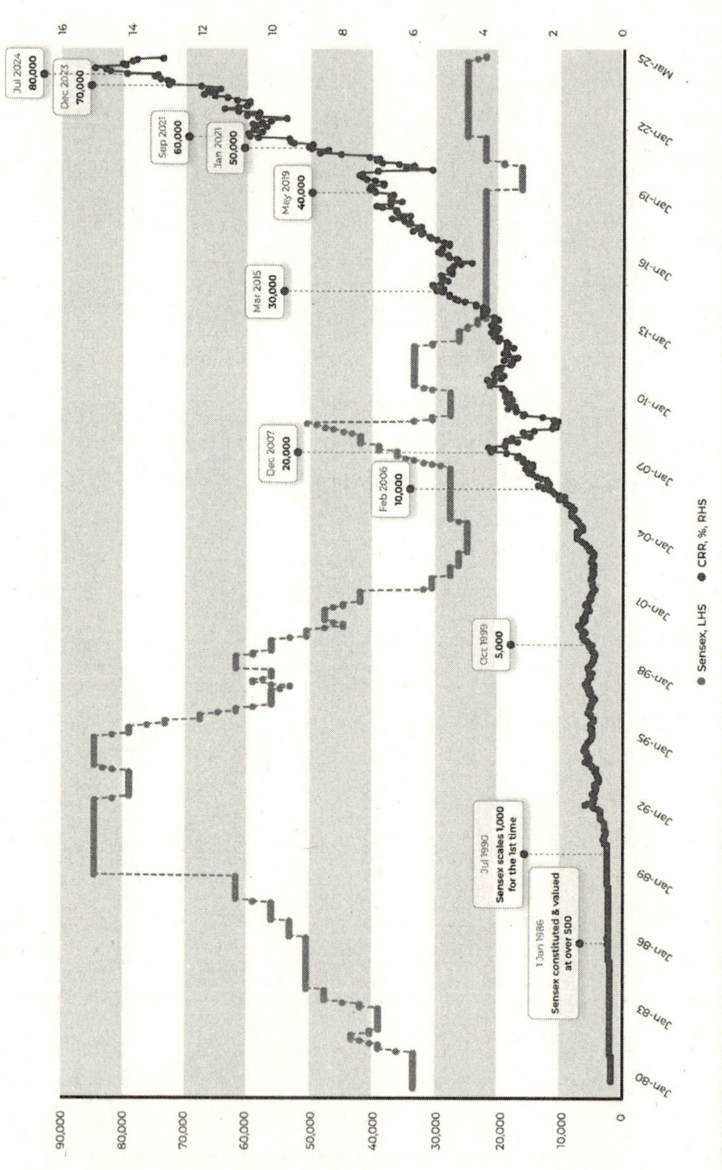

While the exponential growth of Indian entities' market cap has been widely discussed, the behaviour of two other metrics that are among the key parameters investors ought to consider hasn't. These are the price earnings (PE) ratio and dividend yield. The PE ratio is the price of a stock divided by earnings per share. The trend of the PE ratio over time and in comparison, with that of other countries, is an indicator of how expensive or cheap a nation's stock market is.

India's PE ratio has risen from 15.21 times in 2000 to 23.24 in 2023, and is the second-highest in the world, after the US, among ten countries, of which seven are developed nations (the US, Australia, France, Canada, Japan, Germany, the UK, and Italy) and three are emerging economies (Brazil, China and India).

One but not the sole outcome of a high and rising PE ratio is an abysmal dividend yield, which is the dividend per share divided by its price. The dividend yield shows how much a company pays out in dividends every year relative to its share price. The dividend yield of an index is the sum of dividends paid by the index's constituents divided by market cap. This value is akin to the interest paid on a fixed deposit. The key difference is that interest is a contractual payment the borrower makes to the lender, the non-payment of which is termed as default and has legal consequences. The payment of dividend is non-contractual; companies that issue shares have the option to skip or reduce dividend payments. MSCI India's dividend yield has declined from 1.52% as of December 2000 to 1.22% in December 2022. Further, it is the lowest among the ten aforesaid countries at 1.11% in April 2024 (Table 1.3).

Investors, both in India and globally, believe that certain events, like elections and IPOs, have the potential to generate quick and large profits. Elections become particularly significant, as investors tend to categorise political parties as friendly, neutral or antagonistic towards businesses, and who comes to power will eventually determine the fate of the markets.

Table 1.3: India's High Capital Gains Is Tempered by High Share Prices and Low Dividend Yields

As of 31 December	Market Cap		PE Ratio	MSCI India Index Dividend Yield (%)
	US$ Bn	% of GDP		
2000	225.65	48.17	15.21	1.52
2001	148.77	30.65	10.71	2.12
2002	172.19	33.44	10.68	1.86
2003	308.99	50.85	14.86	1.41
2004	415.54	58.60	13.24	1.78
2005	624.74	76.15	15.65	1.32
2006	895.27	95.22	17.62	1.11
2007	1,961.86	161.24	23.27	0.69
2008	791.31	66.00	9.19	1.76
2009	1,367.31	101.89	16.70	0.94
2010	1,762.46	105.18	16.05	1.12
2011	1,244.60	68.27	11.79	1.51
2012	1,390.42	76.08	14.16	1.42
2013	1,265.06	68.13	14.17	1.36

As of 5 March 2024	PE Ratio	MSCI Dividend Yield (%)
United States	25.86	1.33
India	24.14	1.11
Australia	20.06	3.98
France	19.54	2.78
Canada	17.44	3.00
Japan	16.13	2.06
Germany	14.77	2.99
United Kingdom	14.52	3.79
Italy	11.03	4.59
China	9.63	2.47
Brazil	7.65	7.16

As of 31 December	Market Cap		PE Ratio	MSCI India Index Dividend Yield (%)
	US$ Bn	% of GDP		
2014	1,686.71	82.72	15.98	1.48
2015	1,745.17	82.96	17.09	1.38
2016	1,746.30	76.10	15.85	1.47
2017	2,555.99	96.40	18.52	1.30
2018	2,282.31	84.44	17.27	1.51
2019	2,286.92	80.65	18.84	1.26
2020	2,595.46	97.15	23.88	1.09
2021	3,598.38	114.22	22.52	1.00
2022	3,603.48	105.47	21.45	1.18
2023	4,202.43	115.50	23.24	1.22
2024	4,891.74	125.14	23.77	1.16
March 2025	4,137.73	98.82	23.31	1.22

Source: data.worldbank.org, https://worldperatio.com/, and https://en.macromicro.me/collections/5738/msci-index-dividend-yield/48221/msci-dividend-yield

Shyam Sekhar, an investor and founder of the Chennai-headquartered wealth management firm, ithought, likens elections to the 'item numbers' of commercial Indian cinema. Sekhar observes, 'We have been tracking elections from 1991. Many times, we have been spot on; sometimes we have been wrong. The irony is even when we were spot on in our prediction, the market may have punished us. It could be operation success but patient dead with respect to your investment and trading … So, what's all this excitement about elections? It's our need for excitement, our need for action, our egos wanting to grandstand on social media on what we think will happen. So is it productive? From my experience, not really … Whatever be the outcome, it is not going to matter in the long run to my investment. My experience tells me that … Elections come and go; economy continues to grow. Businesses which are more efficient tend to give superior performance during phases of higher economic growth … Buy businesses at the right valuation using volatility as an opportunity.'[24]

Sensex's short- and long-term returns vindicate Sekhar's observation. But this data must be interpreted with caution due to insufficient sample size. Sensex dipped on the counting and results announcement day of India's union elections in four instances since 1991. The steepest decline was in 2004 when the Manmohan Singh-led UPA was voted to power, followed by 2024 when the Narendra Modi-led Bharatiya Janata Party (BJP) emerged as the single largest party albeit with a significantly lower seat share, 2019 when the BJP was voted to power for a second time, and in 1999 when the Vajpayee-led NDA came to power. In 2019 and 2024, Sensex recovered and appreciated by 2.69% and 6.86% during the election month, probably because of the continuity offered by the BJP government. In 1999 and 2004, Sensex declined further during the election month. But this was a short-term phenomenon.

The eighteen-month period (December 1989 to June 1991) during which V.P. Singh and Chandra Shekhar were prime ministers and the Sensex rose by 47% is an outlier, which may be ignored, as Harshad Mehta was active then. Sensex, which had registered the sharpest decline on a counting day and election month since 1991 when the Dr Singh-led UPA was voted to power in May 2004, delivered the highest annualised return during the subsequent five years—25%. If Sensex performance were the sole metric that determines the central government's efficacy, then Dr Singh's first term (May 2004–May 2009) is the most successful, followed by P.V. Narasimha Rao (June 1991 to May 1996: 24%) and Rajiv Gandhi (December 1984 to December 1989: 21%).

That the Sensex's long-term return following general elections was predominantly positive should not be interpreted as the index always delivering positive long-term returns. There have been thirty-seven months in the forty-four-and-a-half years spanning January 1980 and June 2024 when the Sensex traded at a level lower than it did five years ago. These were between February and March 1997, October 1998 and July 1999, March and July 2001, September 2001, December 2001, January 2002, March and November 2002, January and May 2003, and September to November 2012.

Sensex appreciated during seven of the nine general elections that took place between 1991 and 2024. The flagship index also appreciated during ten of the eleven prime ministerial tenures during the forty-four-year period spanning January 1980 to May 2024. The trend is not surprising, as Sensex encapsulates the performance of the largest and most liquid companies in the world's second fastest growing major economy—India.

Listing day 'pop' is the profit made by investing in IPOs; we shall see later in the book examples of listing day pop earned by investors, including Rakesh Jhunjhunwala—the Big Bull who is the subject of this book. Indian equities are an appreciating though expensive and low dividend-yielding asset class. It is in

Table 1.4: Short- and Long-Term Returns of Sensex Following General Elections

	Counting Day	*Election Month Change*
1991	1.10%	2.82%
1996	1.50%	10.64%
1998	2.70%	12.34%
1999	-0.20%	-9.26%
2004	-11.10%	-14.86%
2009	17.30%	50.64%
2014	0.90%	8.18%
2019	-0.80%	2.69%
2024	-5.74%	6.86%

Source: Sreedev Krishnakumar & Ashokamithran T. 'How did the Indian stock market react to elections in the past?', *Hindustan Times*, 24 May 2024

Prime Minister	*Tenure*	*Election to Election Change*	
		Gross	*Annualised*
Indira Gandhi	Jan 1989–Oct 1984	117%	17.68%
Rajiv Gandhi	Dec 1984–Dec 1989	154%	21%
V.P. Singh & Chandra Shekhar	Dec 1989–Jun 1991	84%	47%
P.V. Narasimha Rao	Jun 1991–May 1996	293%	24%
A.B. Vajpayee, Deve Gowda & I.K. Gujral	May 1996–Feb 1998	-3%	-2%
A.B. Vajpayee	Mar 1998–Oct 1999	23%	13%
A.B. Vajpayee	Oct 1999–May 2004	7%	2%
Dr Manmohan Singh	May 2004–May 2009	207%	25%
Dr Manmohan Singh	May 2009–May 2014	67%	11%
Narendra Modi	May 2014–May 2019	64%	10%
Narendra Modi	May 2019–May 2024	88%	13%
Narendra Modi	From June 2024	n.a.	

Source: Election Commission of India & www.bseindia.com

this asset class that multiple Big Bulls, including RJ, made their fortune and consequently captured the imagination of their peers, the masses and, in some instances, the government. They also came under the regulatory scanner. Investing is a high stakes game that may entail high rewards but is also accompanied by significant risks. Several events and factors enabled these men to make Dalal Street their playfield and the quarry they could mine for gold.

What brought RJ to investing? What were the initial decisions that laid the foundations of his wealth? What allowed him and his wife Rekha to join the ranks of India's wealthiest? We shall examine this in the subsequent chapters.

2

The Early Years

R. BALKI, THE CHAIRPERSON OF ONE OF INDIA'S LEADING advertising agencies Lowe Lintas circa 2009, was at a charity event organised by ICICI Bank. Balki had recently directed his first full-length Hindi feature film, *Cheeni Kum*. The film, in which Amitabh Bachchan and Tabu played the lead roles, was both a commercial and critical success. A portly, bespectacled man walked up to Balki at the event, and remarked, 'I really loved *Cheeni Kum*. We both must work together.' The man then handed Balki his business card, which read 'Rakesh Jhunjhunwala'. The film-maker, who describes himself as not being financially savvy, had no clue who RJ was and how the duo may collaborate. He returned to his office and handed over the business cards he had collected to his assistant for filing.

RJ's presence at the high-profile event was not just a reflection of his meteoric rise but would have been considered improbable given the circumstances of his birth. RJ was born in present-day Telangana on 5 July 1960 to Radheshyam, an income tax officer, and Urmila, a homemaker.[1] RJ's limbs were paralysed at the time of birth and he was diagnosed with meningitis; he was visually impaired. A doctor discovered a tumour in the child's spine, which was the cause of these conditions. The surgery to remove it was successful, and RJ's physical impediments vanished. RJ was the youngest of four kids; his siblings were Rajesh, Sudha and Neena. He joined school in second grade. It is unclear when the family moved, but RJ completed his schooling at Hindi Vidya Bhavan, Marine Lines, Mumbai.

Radheshyam and his friends often met and discussed stocks at their home. RJ was a curious child, and these discussions piqued the young boy's curiosity. When he asked his father what caused stock prices to fluctuate, Radheshyam advised his son to follow the news. Two publications helped RJ to understand stock markets. The first was a pamphlet from the International Labour Organization, on the interpretation of financial statements. The second was a research note by Standard Chartered Bank, which predicted capitalism would prevail in the then socialist India. These would be formative influences for RJ.

Rajesh recalled, 'As a schoolboy, he [RJ] loved playing table tennis and cricket, but he was also serious about studying and was very good at it. He was a hard worker and voracious reader from a young age. He developed an interest in the stock market early on, and never shied away from expressing his opinion on it. I remember a party we had at our home once, when he was in Class 8 or 9. Our father worked in the revenue services and many of the guests were senior government officials. The conversation turned to the stock market and the economy. Everyone was giving their views when Rakesh spoke up, "All of you have talked. Now listen to me." And he proceeded to tell everyone exactly what he thought about the stock market. He couldn't have been more than fifteen then! In his first year in college, he wrote an article in the Hindi women's magazine *Sarita* about the stock market and recommended the Sesa Goa stock. Everybody laughed at him at the time, but he had the last laugh as the company became super successful.'[2]

Discussions were encouraged in this closely knit Marwari Bania family. Radheshyam was a diehard socialist and RJ was a dyed-in-the-wool capitalist. Discussions often morphed into heated debates. An exasperated Urmila forbade parleys during family meals. By 1979, Radheshyam was promoted and transferred to Bangalore. The recently married Rajesh, who was by now a practising chartered accountant, his wife Vinita and RJ continued living in Mumbai. Radheshyam sent money to Mumbai every month from which RJ received ₹50 as pocket money. Rajesh supplemented this with another ₹50 from his salary. RJ reminisced later, 'I think that ₹50 is worth more than fifty lakhs.'[3]

On completing his schooling, RJ secured an undergraduate degree in commerce at Sydenham College, Mumbai. Uday Kotak, the founder of Kotak Mahindra Bank, was one year his senior both at school and college and a lifelong friend. Two other titans of the financial services industry graduated from Sydenham College several years before Kotak and RJ—Vallabh Bhansali and Deepak Parekh. Kotak would have a career in tandem with RJ's, though vastly different as we shall see. RJ then enrolled for the chartered accountancy course and simultaneously worked as an articles clerk at Bansi Mehta & Associates, an audit firm founded in 1958. The Mumbai office of Bansi Mehta & Associates is located in Marine Lines. Enrolling as an articles clerk is a prerequisite for completing the chartered accountancy course in India.[4] In 1985, RJ secured the chartered accountancy accreditation, a rigorous course he insisted left all those who pursued it shattered.

When RJ was studying to be a chartered accountant, he spent a lot of time with his sister Sudha and brother-in-law Ashok Gupta at their home in Hyderabad. He would play cards with Ashok's friends every evening. One day, a card player's wife offered to buy RJ a return ticket to Mumbai. She complained that her husband worked all day, played cards with RJ all evening and returned home only to sleep for a few hours. The card soirees may have declined in Hyderabad after RJ returned to Mumbai. But RJ and his friends played cards during weekends in Mumbai and headed to Macau and Genting to play before his kids were born.[5]

RJ's love for food and passion to entertain others is legendary. He loved all kinds of cuisine—Chinese, Indian, farsan (Gujarati snacks), etc. Golden Dragon, Shamiana and Shalimar were some of his favourite restaurants in Mumbai. Rekha Jhunjhunwala recalled, 'Rakeshji loved the Gujarati thali at Shree Thaker Bhojanalay. The restaurant is located on the first floor of an old building at Kalbadevi. When he was unable to walk up the narrow flight of stairs, he arranged for the thalis to be delivered at home.' RJ was fond of chicken, eggs, ghar ki roti, dal and fried bhindi. As the Jhunjhunwala family is vegetarian, RJ would eat chicken at restaurants.[6] His daughter, Nishtha, remembered, 'My dad and I were so similar in nature that we even had the same scheduled time for our late-night snacks. At 3 a.m. sharp, I would see my dad open his bedroom door just as I was opening mine, only to ask, "What do we want to have tonight?" There were times when we even snuck out of the house after my mom was asleep, and drove all the way to Sofitel to have chicken tikka and butter chicken with cheesy garlic naan.'[7]

RJ loved whisky too. Black Label, Blue Label, Royal Salute and King George V were his preferred labels. He occasionally had martinis. RJ's favourite cigarette brand was 555.

More importantly, RJ loved to feed people. He was a gracious and warm host. Amit Chandra, the chairperson of Bain Capital India, reminisced, 'I distinctly remember that one of the best meals our family had during the COVID-19 lockdown was him sending over Mutuswami's full course of south Indian food for all of us!'[8] RJ arranged for Mutuswami's catering for the inauguration of his office at Nariman Bhawan in 2004 and insisted that Renuka Ramnath, the founder-CEO of Multiples Asset Management, partake of the lunch.[9] Whenever Bhaskar Bhat, the former CEO of Titan Company, visited Mumbai, RJ would call him a day ahead and ask what he would like to eat at his home. Bhat fondly recollects Rekha packing his favourite kulfi for him when he visited the couple's Mumbai residence.[10]

Initiation

RJ had saved ₹5,000 from running a small crown caps business, which was his equity to embark on a career as an independent investor on Dalal Street.[11] While Radheshyam encouraged independent thinking and curiosity, Urmila fretted that RJ's career choice may greatly diminish his marriage prospects, given that this wasn't a secure job with a stable income. RJ was undeterred—he quipped that she would have one less daughter-in-law to worry about. Radheshyam, who had by 1985 risen to become the commissioner of income tax, informed RJ that he could live rent-free in his parents' house but would have to raise his own capital to invest. He cautioned RJ, 'Don't forget you're going to play with fire. Be responsible. Never cheat anybody. Remember, your word is your bond. May god bless you … Aspire but do not envy.' This was an important piece of advice, given that now the onus of raising money was on the young man. RJ remarked, 'I had rich friends. My father advised (me) not to envy rich friends.'[12]

Rajesh came to RJ's rescue. He informed his clients about RJ's keen interest and expertise in stocks. Two of his clients lent RJ money to invest. An affluent woman lent ₹2.5 lakh against the security of the stocks he purchased, and one Mr Mendoza extended an unsecured loan of ₹5 lakh. In a March 2011 interview with Ramesh Damani, yet another renowned stock picker and presenter of CNBC TV18's 'Wizards of the Street' show, RJ revealed, 'I went to his house to give him some security against the money, but he refused to take it. I told him, "Mr Mendonza, you have no idea what you are doing. I am in the stock market." But he said, "Rakesh, I trust you."' RJ divulged in the same interview that he was still paying Mr Mendoza 24% interest.[13]

Tata Tea was among RJ's earliest investments. In 1986, he purchased 5,000 shares of Tata Tea at a price of ₹43 apiece and sold these shares three months later, when the share price had more than trebled to ₹143. His pre-tax profit was a sizable ₹5 lakh.[14]

RJ started visiting the BSE building at Dalal Street daily to better understand stock markets. He was not a member of BSE and hence not allowed to enter the trading ring. He would stand outside the ring every day and watch the goings-on. He was careful not to mention to anyone that his father was an income tax commissioner. In the 1980s, when tax rates were high and compliance abysmal, the very mention of an 'income tax officer' would make people suspicious and fearful, and RJ persona non grata.

It was on Dalal Street that RJ met his mentor Radhakishan Damani (R.K. Damani) and three other prominent investors—Ramesh Damani, Nemish Shah and Kamal Kabra.[15] The two Damanis are not related. Ramesh Damani would, decades later, become the chairperson of the R.K. Damani-founded D-Mart, one of India's most successful listed retail chains. Nemish Shah would join hands with Vallabh Bhansali to incorporate the ENAM group, one of India's leading homegrown investment houses.

RJ observed in an interview with journalist Shekhar Gupta, 'After my father, I have learnt the most from Radhakishan Damani. He is a broad numbers man, unlike Nemish Shah. From Radhakishan Damani, I learnt two plus two equals twenty-two. From Nemish bhai, I learnt two plus two equals four. I learnt the importance of basic research, basic information.'[16] R.K. Damani's personal mores resonated with RJ, who admitted, 'Damani taught me (to respect) parents and be patient. Damani is an original thinker; (he) does not get carried away by others' opinions. Constant interactions will help us understand a person's bias. Damani was an expert in that. He will listen without arguing … My role models are the Tatas, Azim Premji and Radhakishan Damani.'[17]

In 1987, RJ married Rekha. In a tête-à-tête with *The Economic Times*, Rekha stated, 'Actually, Rakesh's marriage alliance came for my cousin … But the person who had brought the proposal told Rakesh to meet me—the rest is history!'[18] Their wedding was solemnised at the Mahalaxmi Race Course campus. RJ's two nephews, Kunal Jhunjhunwala (Rajesh and Vinita's son) and Vishal Gupta (Ashok and Sudha's son) were the two bindayaks. In Marwari weddings, the bridegroom and a young boy or bindayak twin their outfits. The bindayak accompanies the groom in the wedding rituals. Vishal Gupta would later join RaRe Enterprises and become RJ's confidant.

Rekha hailed from a family that was more affluent than RJ's. Nevertheless, she effortlessly assimilated with RJ's joint family. Rajesh, RJ and their wives lived with Radheshyam and Urmila, who had returned to Mumbai by the time RJ and Rekha were married. RJ has mentioned in multiple interviews that though Rekha owned a car before marriage, she had no qualms about using public transport when travelling with RJ or her in-laws.

At the time of their wedding, the Jhunjhunwala family did not employ a chauffeur. Rekha would drive RJ to office every day and also the family to holidays in Lonavala and Matheran, though RJ knew how to drive. 'He [RJ] was so absent-minded, he would pay no attention to the road. One day he put the car on the divider. His driving used to make me so nervous, I preferred to drive,' observed Rekha.[19]

Vishal reminisced, 'Like most Indian kids, I used to visit nana-nani's home during summer vacations. They used to live in Walkeshwar then. In the evenings, we all would pile into one car and Rekha mami would ferry us to Marine Drive. Though RJ knew how to drive, he seldom did. We also used to visit Matheran and Lonavala during summer holidays.'[20]

RJ acknowledged, 'Rekha is my biggest supporter, after my parents.' RJ's affection for Rekha was evident in the name he chose for his investment firm—RaRe Enterprises, 'RaRe' being a portmanteau formed with the first two letters of the couple's names. Rekha reciprocated this sentiment; she describes RJ as a 'family man' and admitted, '[He] makes me feel special. Whenever he invests, he makes a token investment in my name.'

The couple's first child, daughter Nishtha, was born in 2003. Their sons, twins Aryaman and Aryavir, were born in 2009. RJ confessed in a 2016 tête-à-tête with Bollywood actor Katrina Kaif, 'I experienced the greatest joy of my life thirteen years earlier at the age of forty-three and after seventeen years of marriage, when my princess was born. I have never experienced greater joy in life, meeting the most beautiful woman, having the largest number of drinks, making most money in the stock exchange, than meeting my children.

'Our circle of friends are normal people. Rekha and I do not want our kids to know how much money we have. Kids travel by economy. I don't want them to get a sense of superiority. I want my kids to have my brains, Rekha's character ...'[21]

'Vadhare vadhare levanu, ghatare ghatare bechvanu'

RJ made his first profit by investing in Tata Tea. He purchased Tata Tea shares in 1986, when they were trading at ₹43 apiece. In three months, the share price trebled.[22]

By 1989, RJ had accumulated ₹15 lakh, and he asked his father for a loan of an equivalent sum to grow his investment portfolio. Radheshyam once again declined. It was then that RJ decided to embark on share trading to earn the requisite capital to build his investment portfolio. So, what is the difference between share trading and investing? Investing and trading are two different methods of attempting to profit in capital markets. Investors generally seek larger returns over an extended period through buying and holding securities. Traders, by contrast, take advantage of both rising and falling markets to enter and exit positions over a shorter time frame (usually from less than a day to a week), taking smaller, more frequent profits. While successful traders earn gargantuan profits, it is a high-risk activity. I am yet to meet or read or hear of a trader (RJ included) who has not incurred losses.

RJ's description of his trading activities underscores the highly risky, unpredictable and potentially profitable nature of this business: 'My net capital employed in trading is ₹1 lakh. Even if I make one crore, you cannot imagine my return on equity. Everything else is borrowed and I pay interest on it. Trading is based on pure leverage. You want to trade, you trade. You want to invest, invest. Don't confuse the two. Trade is for creating the capital. Investing is for growing the capital. In trading, risk is extreme. In investment, risk is not extreme.'

RJ reveals that he made trading profits in three phases. First, between 1989 and 1992, when Sensex almost quadrupled from 666 to 2,615 points. The second phase was between 2003 and 2007, when the index grew six-fold from 3,384 to 20,287 points. The 2007–2008 global financial crisis (GFC) caused stock markets around the world, including India's, to crash. The index's recovery and 60% growth thereafter between 2009 and 2011 from 9,721 to 15,455 points was the third phase during which RJ made trading profits. RJ admits that he did not make any trading income between 1994 and 1999 when Sensex rose by almost 46% from 3,437 to 5,006 points.[23]

Even an astute trader like RJ was unable to profit from all four phases of rising markets. This is because traders need to read the market's mood and momentum correctly, whereas investors analyse entities' fundamentals and outlook. Though RJ's description of trading, '*Vadhare vadhare levanu; Ghatare ghatare bechvanu*' (Buy when the market is rising and sell when it is falling) makes the activity sound simple, mood and momentum are more difficult to predict than fundamentals and outlook.

A stock with which RJ was able to practise this maxim was Sesa Goa, a firm engaged in the exploration, mining and processing of iron ore. The Anil Agarwal-helmed Vedanta Resources would acquire a majority stake in Sesa Goa in 2007. RJ, while addressing Flame University's students in 2009, mentioned, 'One Mr Bajaj used to extol the virtues of Sesa Goa just as I used to talk non-stop about Tata Power. Mr Bajaj mentioned that iron ore prices were fixed six months in advance and that Sesa Goa had secured a 26% price rise. Further, the exchange rate movements would increase the company's earnings. I was convinced and purchased three lakh shares at ₹32 apiece. Mr R.K. Damani was not convinced and he had shorted the stock. In six months, Sesa Goa's share price dipped to ₹25 before rising to ₹65 and further to ₹2,200.'[24] A short, or a short position, is created when a trader sells a security first with the intention of repurchasing it or covering it later at a lower price. A trader may decide to short a security when they believe that the price of that security is likely to decrease in the future.[25] RJ's decision to buy Sesa Goa shares despite his mentor R.K. Damani's intention to short it reveals two attributes that characterise successful investors—conviction and independent judgement.

Breakthrough

RJ's breakout moment dawned when V.P. Singh's finance minister, Madhu Dandavate, tabled the union budget in March 1990. In a February 1990 column titled 'Mood in Share Market Turns Downbeat', *India Today* reported that the stock markets, which turned bullish in December 1989 when V.P. Singh became the prime minister, started declining from January 1990 onwards. Investor sentiment turned negative due to expectations of a stiff tax hike and the government receiving 'complaints about certain institutions using their clout in the markets to bring about an "artificial" rise in the values of particular scrips'. A proposal to set up a board to recommend names of top personnel in banks and financial institutions was interpreted as the government's dissatisfaction with incumbents. The share price of Reliance Industries declined by ₹9.50 in a single fortnight.[26] Rumours were rife that a tax on education would be introduced in the budget.

RJ narrated this incident too while addressing Flame University's students in 2009. He highlighted the importance of research in warfare and investing, and went on to mention that had Hitler invaded the UK instead of Russia, the Axis powers may have won World War II. When RJ did some research, he realised that education came under the purview of states, and hence the union government did not have the power to tax the sector. Besides, he was convinced that Prime Minister V.P. Singh, though a Thakur, was business-friendly; he was the one who had abolished estate duty. So, he remained invested in the market, which reacted positively to the budget. Sensex rose 15% in a single month from 676 points on 28 February to 781 on 31 March 1990. RJ disclosed that his net worth zoomed from ₹1 crore to ₹20 crore. He mentioned that the one thing Rekha had asked after marriage was an air conditioner. RJ purchased air conditioners for his entire family in March 1990.

Locking Horns

RJ had struck gold amidst the quicksand-like political environment and precarious economic situation. V.P. Singh and Chandra Shekhar occupied the prime minister's chair for less than a year each, and P.V. Narasimha Rao replaced the latter in June 1991. By June 1991, India's foreign exchange reserves dipped below $1 billion and were inadequate to meet three weeks of imports. Between 4 and 18 July 1991 India pledged gold with the Bank of England and the Bank of Japan to raise a $405-million foreign currency loan. The RBI undertook a two-step devaluation of the rupee against major currencies by around 9% on 1 July 1991 and another 11% two days later.[27]

On 24 July 1991, Finance Minister Dr Manmohan Singh presented a budget that ended the licence-permit raj and overhauled the import–export policy. The budget slashed import licencing and promoted exports and optimal import compression. The Indian industry was now exposed to overseas competition. The epochal budget also rationalised duty structures, with the peak customs duty declining from 220% to 150%.[28]

The bull run which began amidst the political uncertainty accelerated when the Narasimha Rao-led minority Congress government ushered in relative political stability and Dr Singh tabled the landmark budget, which transformed India into one of the fastest-growing major economies. Sensex, which had touched 1,000 points on 25 July 1990, went on a rampage thereafter, quadrupling to 4,285 points by end-March 1992. But it was not just the strength of Indian democracy to weather political instability, macroeconomic reforms and Dr Singh's groundbreaking budget that fuelled the bull run. The financial engineering the founder of Growmore Research and Asset Management, Harshad Mehta, resorted to played a significant role.

On Friday 24 April 1992, Sucheta Dalal published an explosive column in *The Times of India* titled 'The Pied Piper of Dalal Street' that brought to light Mehta's modus operandi. Sensex crashed by 12.77% on 28 April 1992. As of 2024, this is the second-highest single day decline in Sensex, the highest being the 13.15% drop on 23 March 2020 fuelled by the declaration of a nationwide lockdown to counter the COVID-19 outbreak. However, RJ did not lose money in this crash. He had entered into short positions in anticipation of the unravelling of the stock market.

So, why did RJ build a short position when the markets were so optimistic? This is my conjecture. Clearly, the country's political and economic situation did not warrant a bull run. The economic situation was worsening with the GDP growth decelerating from 9.6% in 1988 to 5.9% in 1989, 5.5% in 1990 and to an abysmal 1.1% in 1991. The GDP growth in 1991 is India's fifth lowest to date since 1961; the economy shrunk by 5.8% in 2020 due to the COVID-19 pandemic, 5.2% in 1979, 2.6% in 1965, and 0.6% in 1972.[29] Given that the licence-permit raj was still prevalent in India, banks and corporates were unlikely to have performed well by focusing on their international business to offset lackadaisical domestic performance. While it took *The Times of India* and Sucheta Dalal to enlighten the nation at large about Mehta's machinations, Dalal Street regulars must have heard murmurs.

This incident highlights RJ's twin strengths and the skills investors must develop to be successful—knowledge and network. RJ visiting the BSE building on Dalal Street and observing the goings-on at the periphery of the trading ring every day not only enhanced his understanding of share trading but also facilitated the building of a network that would alert him to the goings-on at the market place as speedily as possible in the pre-digital era.

3

Catalysts

WHEN RJ EMBARKED ON HIS CAREER AS AN INDEPENDENT investor in the 1980s, he was preceded by Harshad Mehta and followed by Ketan Parekh in a few years. India's banking sector and capital markets during the 1980s were very different from what they are in 2025. It was an era characterised by draconian regulation, limited capital, and outdated technology and communication. Hence, investors operating in that era had more leeway to decide whether or not to play by the book. This choice in turn determined their career trajectories, the performance of the counterparties, especially banks that transacted with them, and the fate of the investments of the tens and thousands of retail investors who emulated them.

An understanding of India's financial landscape in the years leading to the liberalisation initiated by the 1991 epochal budget is essential to understand the motivations and actions of various stakeholders—the government, domestic and foreign banks, and investors. Listed banks need to balance the twin, and at times conflicting, objectives of protecting depositor interests and maximising shareholder returns. Regulators across the world require banks to maintain a certain percentage of their deposits as reserves to repay deposits in a timely manner should there be a run on the bank. The RBI stipulates banks maintain a cash reserve ratio (CRR) with the central bank and a statutory liquidity ratio (SLR) in their own vaults. The RBI pays zero interest on banks' CRR balances and the return on SLR investments, which comprises cash, gold and government securities, is usually lower than the banks' cost of funds. Hence, the regulatorily imposed safeguards of CRR and SLR depress banks' profits.

Between 1985 and 1992, the SLR ranged from 36.5% to 38.5%, while the CRR rose from 9% to a peak of 15% between July 1989 and 16 April 1992. The RBI also stipulated additional reserve requirements of CRR on incremental domestic deposits.[1] This meant that for every ₹100 banks received in deposits, they could lend not more than ₹46.50–54.50 between 1985 and 1992. As of July 2024, the CRR and SLR are less than half of the values of these metrics between 1985 and 1992 at 4.50% and 18.50%, respectively, enabling banks to lend ₹77 for every ₹100 of deposit mobilised.

Beleaguered Banks

The lending operations of the banks were highly regulated as well, with banks having to comply with priority sector lending (PSL) norms. This involved lending to the agricultural sector, amongst others. Indian agriculture was and continues to be beset by several challenges, including small landholdings, outdated farming practices, water scarcity and vulnerability to droughts, soil degradation and land erosion, climate change and natural disasters, limited access to technology and research, and market volatility and price fluctuations.[2] While farmer distress is a real concern in India, farm loan waivers have vitiated the credit culture. The central government has enacted farm loan waivers twice (1990–91 and 2008–09) and state governments frequently announce loan waivers before elections.[3] Hence, lending to the agricultural sector has not been a viable proposition for most banks. PSL's profitability and loan quality have improved since the early 1990s, with the government expanding its scope to include lending to micro, small and medium enterprises (MSME), social infrastructure and renewable energy projects, export credit, education, and affordable housing loans. This has resulted in a reduction of banks' non-performing loans and a corresponding improvement in asset quality.

The regulatory restrictions imposed both on the borrowing and lending operations of the bank was made worse by crony capitalism. Politicians frequently directed banks to lend to shaky and even dubious businesses helmed by their acolytes—a practice known as 'telephone banking'. Needless to say, most of these loans were never recovered.

Matters were exacerbated by the absence of a money market, where debt securities may be traded. Journalists Sucheta Dalal and Debashis Basu observe, 'RBI's participation in the money markets could have been a corrective mechanism. Unfortunately, its role, unlike several leading central banks, ended with the issue of central loans.'[4]

Basu and Dalal also narrate how ignorance and outdated technology depressed the profits of public sector banks. In 1986, employees of India's largest bank, the State Bank of India, were reportedly unaware of the difference between bond coupon and yield—basic information that every banker needs to have. A bond's coupon is the rate of interest it pays annually. A ₹1,000 bond with a coupon rate of 6% pays ₹60 in interest annually and a ₹2,000 bond with a coupon rate of 6% pays ₹120 in interest annually. A bond's yield is the return it generates.[5] For example, let's assume the government issued a ₹1,000 bond of ten-year tenor with a coupon rate of 6% on 1 January 1990 and another ₹1,000 bond of the same tenor with a coupon rate of 8% on 1

January 1991. The price of the 1990 bond would fall to below ₹1,000 on 1 January 1991 because of the higher coupon on the second bond. Conversely, if the government issued a ₹1,000 bond of ten-year tenor with a coupon rate of 4% on 1 January 1991, the price of the 1990 bond would rise above ₹1,000 on 1 January 1991 because of the lower coupon paid by the bond issued in January 1991.

This knowledge lacuna resulted in SBI being manipulated by foreign banks in the 1980s. 'Their strategy was simple: sell securities with longer maturity to SBI (say, 7.5% coupon rate of 1997 maturity) and buy securities with shorter maturity (say, 6.75% of 1992). Why would SBI buy them? Because they fetched it higher (7.5%) current yield than the bonds it sold (6.75%). The deal, brokers argued, helped SBI step up the yield of its portfolio. The yield step-up trick, of course, rested on ignoring a crucial point: effective yield ... A quick look at bond tables would show that in 1986, when the current coupon rate was 11.5%, a 6.75% 1992 bond would be priced at Rs 83.50 to give 10.5% yield. If the bank were to exchange this for a 7.5% bond of 1997 maturity, it would similarly look up the bond table and find that the price is just Rs 79.25. The exchange, therefore, left it richer by 0.75% on current yield but poorer by Rs 4.25 on price.' Further, SBI was unaware of the existence of bond tables and used to perform the calculations by hand. It was only after a broker introduced G.G. Vaidya, who was then working in SBI's treasury and would go on to become its chairman in 2000, to bond tables did the exploitation of foreign banks end.[6]

SBI's profitability was affected not just by ignorance and outdated technology but also a 'coupon-hike scam'.

The Coupon-Hike Scam

SBI incurred losses on account of ignoring a key market development—the dates when the government announces interest rates—while investing in SLR securities. Following the 1991 budget and as directed by the International Monetary Fund, which was providing financial assistance to India, the government decided to align the subsidised coupon or interest paid on government securities with the higher market rates. Basu and Dalal observe, 'If you guessed correctly that the interest rate was about to go up, or better still, knew when it would happen, you could draw up a contract to sell the securities before the hike.' Why? When the coupon paid on a tranche of securities rises, the prices of securities that pay lower coupons decline. So, security holders will profit from selling securities paying lower coupons ahead of an interest rate hike and buying them back at lower prices after the hike. This investment strategy reverses the 'buy low, sell high' maxim.

By September 1991, Indian Oil Corporation (IOC) had placed a whopping ₹4,307 crore it had raised as dollar-denominated debt as deposits with the SBI, which was then required to make SLR investments. Hence, SBI purchased ₹550 crore government securities from a set of banks and brokers on 20 September 1991 for delivery a fortnight later on 5 October, which was two days after RBI was scheduled to announce the new interest rates. SBI had purchased securities at a higher price and had contracted to sell the same at a lower price fifteen days later!

On 7 August, SBI had written to the RBI requesting that that the two institutions enter into a ready forward transaction for ₹1,000 crore of central government loans that paid 11.5% interest. On 27 September, a week after SBI had concluded the guaranteed loss transaction involving ₹550 crore securities, RBI declined SBI's request. On 19 September, a day before SBI purchased the ₹550 crore securities that paid a coupon of 11.5%, the Tamil Nadu government had written to all banks requesting them to subscribe to its loans that paid 12% interest. Why the SBI chose to invest in securities that paid a lower coupon when it had the option to purchase higher interest-bearing securities is a mystery.

SBI had purchased on 20 September the ₹550 crore securities at their face value of ₹100.83 and their price had declined to ₹97 by the 5 October delivery date, resulting in the bank incurring a ₹22 crore loss in two weeks!

IOC's deposits with SBI had surged to ₹5,272 crore by end-February 1992. To meet the resultant SLR requirements, SBI purchased securities on 15 and 16 March for delivery on 18 March, when a rate hike was scheduled on 17 March. Basu and Dalal report,

> These deals were not investigated, nor were the brokers and counterparty banks questioned. There is enough circumstantial evidence to raise the suspicion that some banks and brokers knew about the 17th March coupon-rate increase. There was a major row between RBI and the ministry of finance over the 17th March rate increase. RBI had been stalling it but the ministry was keen on pushing it through. Eventually, the governor told the finance minister to take his own decision. For the first time in many decades, the announcement of a coupon-rate increase came from the ministry, not from RBI. The chief of a foreign bank, later forced to leave the country, knew about this row between RBI and the ministry. He may have even 'advised' the ministry that since the market was expecting a hike since January, the hike should come later rather than sooner, so that 'speculators are taught a lesson.' Did this do-gooder bank chief know exactly when the rate would be hiked?[7]

While Harshad Mehta may not to have participated in the 'coupon-hike scam', he did use ready forward deals and portfolio management services to his advantage.

Portfolio Management Scheme (PMS)

In 1986, the government permitted PSUs to issue tax-free bonds to finance their sizable and growing capital expenditures. The inability of the liquidity-strapped banks to meet the PSUs' funding requirements was a contributory factor. The government permitted PSUs to issue tax-free bonds that paid 9%, 13% and even 17% interest. The attractiveness of PSU bonds as an investment option is evident when compared to the interest rates on fixed deposits (FD) paid by banks in 1986: 8.50–9% for FDs of one-to-three-year maturities, 10% for three to five years, and 11% for over five years.[8] By 1991, PSUs had issued over ₹20,000 crore bonds. As the deployment of the funds raised through bond issues occurred in a phased manner, PSUs had accumulated sizable cash balances. PSUs also availed of US dollar-denominated loans to finance imports; this was and continues to be standard market practice. The depreciating Indian rupee resulted in the effective dollar cost of borrowing rising to a steep 25% in 1987. IOC alone had ₹4,000 crore of dollar-denominated debt with a potential loss of ₹600 crore in one year.

The PMS, which was announced by the RBI in 1987, allowed banks to accept deposits from institutions, without setting aside monies to meet SLR and CRR stipulations. The rules governing PMS stipulated that the minimum tenor of deposits was one year, clients had to stipulate the investments banks made on their behalf, the returns on PMS deposits had to be aligned with market rates, and banks were forbidden from guaranteeing a fixed rate of return. Further, foreign banks were barred from offering PMS to PSUs.

The PMS provided a way for banks to earn profits without being fettered by stringent CRR, SLR and PSL regulations. PSUs availing of PMS could earn a return on their idle cash balances, and the profits from their PMS investment would help defray a part of the high interest costs of their dollar denominated borrowing.

Harshad Mehta used the bank receipts and PMS to emerge as a Big Bull on Dalal Street. Given that he was a contemporary in RJ's early years, his rise and the techniques he deployed to influence the market form a fascinating study in comparison and contrast. Mehta's story is narrated in the following chapter.

4

Growmore

IN 1990, HARSHAD SHANTILAL MEHTA PAID ₹26 CRORE ADVANCE taxes, thereby becoming India's highest individual tax payer and probably the first stockbroker in independent India to top the list. *India Today* reported that 'any broker would give his trading arm for [Harshad Mehta's reach]: top billing with the Ambanis, lunches with ITC Limited executives, a line into the chief executives suite of nearly all banks in India—local and multinational – and friendships with industrialists from Raunaq Singh to Dilip Piramal'.*[1]

Mehta aspired to buy the fourteen-storey building in which his office occupied one floor—Maker Chamber V located in India's then most expensive real estate enclave, Mumbai's Nariman Point. The offices of Reliance Industries spanned five storeys of Maker Chamber IV. It took far less time for Mehta to move his firm, Growmore Research and Asset Management Limited, from

* Raunaq Singh was the CMD of Apollo Tyres and Dilip Piramal, as of 2024, is the chairman of India's largest luggage manufacturer, VIP Industries. Dilip's nephew Anand is married to Mukesh Ambani's daughter, Isha.

an inconspicuous office in a building called Bharat Bhavan at Kalbadevi, Mumbai's cotton and yarn trading centre, to Maker Chamber V, than Dhirubhai Ambani did to relocate Reliance Industries (which was incorporated as Reliance Commercial Corporation) from Masjid Bunder to Nariman Point.

Mehta and Dhirubhai shared similarities, though. Both were first-generation entrepreneurs born in modest families far away from Mumbai. While Dhirubhai was born in Chorwad in Gujarat, Mehta's birthplace was Raipur in Madhya Pradesh. The two men were also united by a fierce ambition and unwavering focus to reach the top echelons of their professions and to amass wealth. Reliance Industries' motto is 'Growth is Life', while Mehta named his enterprise Growmore Research and Asset Management. Interestingly, the Adani group's watchword is 'Growth with Goodness'.

The 1954-born Mehta secured admission in the bachelor of commerce course at Mumbai's Lala Lajpat Rai College, primarily thanks to his cricketing abilities. Sucheta Dalal and Debashis Basu, in their book *The Scam: From Harshad Mehta to Ketan Parekh* observe, 'In an unusual combination that typifies most of Mehta's actions, he was a left arm leg spinner and a right hand batsman.'[2] Mehta scrapped through with a passing grade to graduate with a B.Com degree in 1977. He joined New India Assurance that year as a clerk, with a monthly salary of ₹600. After trying his hand at several businesses, including purchasing rough diamonds, polishing and selling the gemstones, Harshad and his brother Ashwin, who was then working at Unit Trust of India, decided to try their hand at the stock market. The siblings, whose lunch break was for an hour, wrapped up their meal in fifteen minutes and rushed to Dalal Street. There they observed the traders and jobbers buying and selling stocks in the trading ring by the open outcry method. Jobbers match buyers and sellers of stocks by gesticulating and calling out quotes. Mehta was consumed by a burning desire to trade stocks.

Mehta's first job at Dalal Street was that of a jobber. He had convinced stockbroker P. Ambalal to give him a badge. According to Ashwin, Harshad evolved from a novice jobber incurring heavy losses to one of the most skilful in the industry. However, a jobber does not earn enough money to invest in stocks. So, Mehta adopted a four-pronged strategy to become rich. To raise capital, he brokered ready forward transactions between banks. Mehta used the cash banks credited to his account to purchase shares. He then collaborated with certain promoters of the companies he invested in and select stockbrokers to ensure the share prices of the stocks he invested in rose exponentially. He sold some of these stocks, whose prices had appreciated considerably, to mutual funds. Mehta's dizzying rise was underpinned by the profits earned from share sales and the cash banks continued crediting into his account.

So, were all of Mehta's activities above board? Why was Sensex's dizzying one-year rise from 1,168 points in the end of March 1991 to 4,285 points in March 1992 attributed to Mehta? Why was he arrested?

The Bank Receipts Scam

Let's begin with how banks conducted inter-bank transactions. Banks extended and availed of short-term secured debt amongst themselves through ready forward (RF) deals. The security or collateral for these RF deals was government securities. RF deals involved borrowing banks selling government securities to lending banks and buying them back on expiry of the loan tenure at a slightly higher price. These deals were high-volume transactions. Before the advent of the dematerialisation of securities, the physical movement of the collateral—that is, the government securities—between the borrowing and lending banks was a cumbersome task. So, the borrowing bank issued a banker's receipt (BR) confirming it owned the collateral to the lending bank, against which it availed of debt.

Yet another market practice, though disallowed by the RBI, was that banks issued cheques favouring brokers and not the borrowers at the time of loan extension and lenders during repayment. The high volume of daily transactions resulted in cheques being issued in the names of brokers, who would then aggregate and make the necessary payments.

Tainted stockbrokers, including Mehta, who by 1987 had become a money market dealer, spotted an opportunity in facilitating RF transactions. Certain brokers purchased stocks with the monies banks credited to their accounts for BR-backed transactions, which was illegal. This illegality was complicated by multiple transgressions. First, certain banks issued BRs for securities they did not own. Second, certain bank employees falsely recorded in banks' account books that RF deals were squared, that is, the loans were repaid when no repayments occurred. Third, bank officials diverted monies to brokers' accounts under the guise of entering into RF transactions. Fourth, banks flouted RBI norms by extending unsecured loans to brokers.

There appears to be no wrongdoing in the second prong of Mehta's strategy—purchasing shares. The third aspect of his modus operandi—collaborating with companies' promoters to artificially inflate share prices—is a form of insider trading. But there were no laws to check insider trading in India during the late 1980s and early 1990s. Mehta popularised the 'replacement cost theory' to justify the exponential increase in the share prices of the stocks he invested in. He argued that stocks of a manufacturing company ought to be valued at a price equivalent to the cost of building a similar enterprise in the current period. Hence, the sharp rise in share prices was a reflection of the company's assets being revalued. The fourth dimension of Mehta's operations was selling the shares at inflated prices to mutual funds.

When the wrongdoing of the brokers, banks and bank employees was uncovered, share prices crashed and investors in mutual funds witnessed a sharp depreciation in the market value of their holdings. The third and fourth dimensions of Mehta's business—colluding with promoters to inflate share prices and selling these overpriced shares—is referred to as 'pump and dump', an activity now illegal in India and most other countries.

The diversion of monies banks routed through money market dealers for the purchase and sale of government securities was one of the three malpractices that was prevalent in Indian capital markets during the late 1980s and early 1990s. The second was the misuse of PMS that we explored in the previous chapter.

The Buccaneer Bankers

The PMS, which ought to have been a win-win proposition for banks and PSUs, deteriorated to banks, especially foreign banks, winning at the expense of PSUs.

Basu and Dalal report, 'To get a PSU to park its money with banks, a standard 2% kickback was paid – often through brokers. Brokers have even bypassed companies and struck deals with parent ministries. Foreign banks employed close relatives of various government officials who could influence the investment decisions of the PSUs. When the business became rampant in the 1990s, even nationalised banks paid kickbacks to get PMS money. How have the banks accounted for this? Partly by granting advances to firms controlled by politicians and their backers and then writing off that money as bad loans over a period of time.'

Some of the rules set by the government and their lax enforcement were to blame. The pecuniary rationale for the RBI stipulating a minimum investment tenor is unclear. If an effectively administered PMS offered products of less than one-year tenor, this could have reduced the negative carry PSUs suffered from the non-deployment of tax-free bond proceeds. It would have also moderated the skyrocketing effective borrowing costs of their dollar-denominated borrowings. Banks and PSUs colluded to mask PMS investments of less than a one-year as cash management services (CMS). Canbank Financial Services (Canfina, a Canara Bank subsidiary engaged in merchant banking) masked and marketed PMS as 'Financial and Investment Advisory Services', while Standard Chartered Bank (Stanchart) named these Corporate Cash Deployment Services.

Citibank offered PMS to the PSUs using Vijaya Bank as a front. It also skirted the rule that forbade guaranteeing returns on PMS schemes by offering 'assured', 'benchmark' and 'indicative' returns. Banks not only engaged in the aforesaid actions that flouted rules or, much worse, were illegal but they also acted to the detriment of their clients.

Power Finance Corporation (PFC) had issued ₹300 crore bonds that paid 17% interest. Citibank and Canfina brokered a deal with PFC by which the duo subscribed to the bonds, and PFC in turn invested in Citibank's PMS, which offered a return of just 14.25% amidst a bull market, when corporate debentures paid 16%. In 1987, government-owned banks and insurance companies were allowed to set up mutual funds. Insurance companies, SBI, Canara Bank and Bank of India (BoI) were among the public sector financial institutions that did so. Harshad Mehta subscribed to ₹20 crore or close to 41% of BoI Mutual Fund's Boinanza scheme, whose corpus was ₹49 crore. Boinanza in turn agreed to purchase the shares Harshad Mehta asked it to buy. The subsidiary of BoI, which was then wholly government-owned, was abetting Mehta's pump and dump schemes.

Despite RBI prohibiting foreign banks from offering PMS to PSUs, three foreign banks (Stanchart, HSBC and Citibank) and Canfina accounted for ₹32,255 crore or 83.4% of the total funds under PMS and similar schemes (₹38,675 crore) between January 1991 and June 1992.[3]

The Unravelling

In April 1992, SBI, as part of a regular internal scrutiny, discovered that Mehta owed the bank money to the effect of ₹500 crore. The bank later revised the figure to ₹660 crore. A brokers' strike and the stock market remaining closed for several days prevented Mehta from squaring his exposure. The news leaked to the press. On Friday, 24 April 1992, Dalal, who was then a journalist with *The Times of India*, published a scoop titled 'Pied Piper of Dalal Street'. On Tuesday, 28 April, Sensex crashed by 12.77% or 570 points to 3,870 from 4,440 on 27 April. This was the index's second steepest single day crash as of 2024, with the most precipitous one-day crash following the COVID-19 outbreak, when the large cap index shed 13.15% or 3,935 points on Monday, 23 March 2020, to end at 25,981 from 29.916 on Friday, 20 March. RJ, in the 20 January 2021 'Off the Cuff' episode, stated that he was among the 'bears' who had bet that the index would decline sharply in 1992.[4]

SBI demanded repayment from Mehta, who in turn approached an institution Growmore regularly transacted with and which was RBI's wholly owned subsidiary for money—the National Housing Bank (NHB)! Manohar Pherwani, NHB's chairman, headed the Unit Trust of India (UTI) till 1989. The exponential growth in UTI's investments under Pherwani's watch had earned him the nickname 'Big Bull'. *India Today* reported, 'Promising to deliver a BR later, Mehta persuades NHB to issue a cheque to ANZ Grindlays. ANZ credits this to Mehta. This is not legal, but is said to be common practice.'[5] NHB issued nine account payee cheques aggregating ₹506 crore favouring Mehta to ANZ, which promptly deposited the amounts in the broker's account.[6]

Though Mehta was able to repay SBI, the mess in SBI's books and the market crash caught the regulators and law enforcement agencies' attention. Soon, the Central Bureau of Investigation (CBI) accused the broker of conspiracy, criminal breach of trust and cheating under provisions of the Indian Penal Code. RBI began the scrutiny of the treasury transactions of seventeen public and private sector banks and three foreign banks—Citibank, ANZ and Stanchart.[7] Mehta was not the sole broker who was under the lens; there were twenty-three more.

The Janakiraman Committee Report

RBI appointed a 'Committee to Enquire into Securities Transactions of Banks and Financial Institutions' led by one of its deputy governors, R. Janakiraman. This committee, which is popularly known as the Janakiraman Committee, tabled six reports between May 1992 and April 1993. The committee concluded, 'In most banks the IBA* guidelines were observed only in their breach. In particular, BRs were not issued on security paper or in the prescribed form and more significantly were not exchanged with actual scrips but were returned for cancellation on reversal of the original transactions or even against independent transactions of equivalent value. There are several instances where BRs were treated as negotiable instruments and transferred by endorsement and even instances when in support of purchases, BRs issued not by counterparty banks but by "third parties" were accepted.'[8]

The Janakiraman Committee identified eighteen banks, comprising twelve domestic and six foreign institutions, that had engaged in improper RF transactions and attributed the 20% or ₹865 crore in investment income the eighteen banks reported in FY1992 to these deals (Table 4.1). Domestic banks, led by SBI, dominated India's banking landscape. Their investment income grew by 15% to ₹4,782 crore in FY1992. The close to 94% growth in investment income reported by the foreign banks, though eye-popping, is off a low base. Notwithstanding the low base effect, it is indeed suspicious that the six foreign banks together almost doubled their investment income in a single year. Citibank, ANZ

* IBA: Indian Banks Association.

Grindlays, Bank of America and Stanchart led the charge in the explosive growth of the foreign banks' investment income.

Table 4.1: Investment Income of Banks That Engaged in Improper RF Transactions

	FY1991	FY1992	Increase in Investment Income	
			₹ Crore	%
Domestic Banks [A]	**4,154.94**	**4,781.95**	**627.01**	**15.09**
State Bank of India	1,854.71	2,028.50	173.79	9.37
Punjab National Bank	520.56	645.44	124.88	23.99
Bank of India	452.74	530.46	77.72	17.17
Canara Bank	439.18	504.08	64.90	14.78
Bank of Baroda	381.58	453.55	71.97	18.86
Union Bank of India	255.37	305.33	49.96	19.56
Oriental Bank of Commerce	104.35	125.90	21.55	20.65
Corporation Bank	60.99	77.91	16.92	27.74
The Federal Bank Ltd.	27.90	38.51	10.61	38.03
The Bank of Rajasthan Ltd.	26.94	33.80	6.86	25.46
The United Western Bank Ltd.	16.13	20.51	4.38	27.15
Bank of Madura Ltd.	14.49	17.96	3.47	23.95
Foreign Banks [B]	**254.72**	**492.90**	**238.18**	**93.51**
ANZ Grindlays Bank	92.34	144.94	52.60	56.96
Citibank N.A.	50.38	128.27	77.89	154.61
Standard Chartered Bank	43.93	81.24	37.31	84.93
Bank of America	22.91	66.94	44.03	192.19
Hongkong & Shanghai Banking Corporation	39.41	58.83	19.42	49.28
ABN Amro Bank N. V.	5.75	12.68	6.93	120.52
Total [A] + [B]	**4,409.66**	**5,274.85**	**865.19**	**19.62**

Source: Janakiraman Committee Report

The committee report also highlighted the nexus between banks and brokers that gave the latter group access to vast sums of money. It estimated that during the fourteen-month period between 1 April 1991 and 23 May 1992, banks had engaged in 87,271 transactions that involved securities with a face value of ₹12.86 lakh crore (₹12.86 trillion). Banks transacted with each other directly for just 42.16% of the transactions, which the committee opines is an optimistic estimate. The report notes, 'Out of the transactions shown as direct, there were many transactions with "routing" banks where the counterparties were in fact the brokers. Besides, in some banks although the bulk of these transactions were shown as direct, these were in fact entered into through brokers.' More than half, that is, 57.84% of transactions were routed through brokers. The largest brokers were Hiten P. Dalal, who facilitated 9.92% of the transactions, followed by Mehta (5.35%) and Somayajulu & Co. (3.76%). Notwithstanding their limited market presence in India, foreign banks accounted for 56.57% of the transactions. Citibank topped the league table with a market share of 16.74%, followed by Stanchart (14.63%), Bank of America (12.41%), ANZ Grindlays (7.31%) and American Express Bank (5.38%).[9]

Mehta's client roster was indeed impressive and included India's largest bank to date, SBI, and its two subsidiaries, State Bank of Saurashtra and SBI Capital Markets; NHB; ANZ Grindlays; and UCO Bank. Hiten P. Dalal collaborated with Stanchart and, through another broker A.D. Narottam, worked with Bank of Karad and Metropolitan Co-operative Bank. Stewart and Company and C. Mackertich colluded with Citibank, while Hiten P. Dalal and C. Mackertich joined hands with Canfina.[10]

The Janakiraman Committee estimated the banks' problem exposure to be ₹4,024 crore, of which investments made by banks for which they held no securities or BRs accounted for 56% or ₹2,263 crore (Table 4.2). Two banks—Bank of Karad and Metropolitan Co-operative Bank—had issued BRs worth ₹1,473 crore or 37% of the problem exposure, for which there 'appeared to be no security backing'. RBI liquidated both banks. Miscellaneous transactions effected by Stanchart, Canbank Financial Services and Andhra Bank Financial Services, to the tune of ₹288 crore, accounted for 7% of the gross problem exposure.

Table 4.2: Banks Gross Problem Exposure

	₹ Crore
Total value of investments made by banks for which they do not hold any securities, SGL transfer forms or BRs (1), [A]	**2,262.57**
National Housing Bank	1,271.20
State Bank of Saurashtra	174.93
SBI Capital Markets	121.36
Standard Chartered Bank	506.61
Canbank Financial Services Ltd	188.47
Total exposure against BRs/SGL transfer forms issued by Bank of Karad or Metropolitan Co-operative Bank (for which there appears to be no security backing) [B]	**1,473.47**
Canbank Financial Services	438.66
Canbank Mutual Fund	102.97
Standard Chartered Bank	931.84
Other Items [C]	**288.41**
Standard Chartered Bank	43.69
Canbank Financial Services Ltd	39.60
Andhra Bank Financial Services	205.12
Gross Problem Exposure [A] + [B] + [C]	**4,024.45**

(1) SGL - Subsidiary General Ledger
Source: Janakiraman Committee Report

The custodian's report released on 8 January 2016 reported that Mehta's ₹16,045 crore liabilities were more than nine times his ₹1,724 crore assets. Statutory dues such as interest, claims and penalties of ₹11,175 crore accounted for 70% of his liabilities, while his dues to banks and financial institutions amounted to ₹4,662 crore or 29%. The market value of shares he owned as of 30 September 2015 was reported to be ₹1,028 crore or 60% of his assets. Bank deposits worth ₹640 crore formed another 37% of his assets.[11]

Repercussions

On Monday, 9 November 1992, the CBI arrested Mehta and his brothers, including Ashwin, for allegedly misappropriating more than 2.8 million shares of about ninety companies, including Associated Cement Companies (ACC) and Hindalco, through forged share transfer forms.[12] The arrest occurred around three months after the Janakiraman Committee had completed its third interim report in August. Mehta, who was initially released after 107 days in custody, was given a hero's welcome.

For three years after his 1992 arrest, Mehta appears to have avoided Dalal Street. But he did not remain quiet. On 16 November 1993, barely a year after his arrest, Mehta accompanied by his brother Ashwin and two high profile lawyers—Ram Jethmalani and his son Mahesh—convened a press conference at Mumbai's Taj Mahal Hotel and announced that he had paid the then Prime Minister P.V. Narasimha Rao a bribe of ₹1 crore. He also filed an affidavit to this effect. The Prime Minister's Office denied the charge.

Between 1995 and 2001, the never-say-die Mehta attempted three comebacks. Basu and Dalal note, 'Twice he had allegedly introduced benami shares into the market, paralysing the system.'[13] The third time, he proffered investment advice that was publicised by newspapers. SEBI's investigations revealed that Mehta was also rigging the prices of stocks using a front of seven companies and eighteen brokerages. Three companies whose share prices benefitted from Mehta's machinations were the T.P. Gopalan Nambiar-helmed BPL, Venugopal Dhoot's Videocon Industries and the Anil Agarwal-led Sterlite Industries. Nambiar's son-in-law, BJP politician and three-time member of Parliament, Rajeev Chandrasekhar, oversaw BPL's telecom business during this time. Nine years after Mehta's first arrest, on 19 April 2001, SEBI permanently debarred him from operating in capital markets. BPL, Videocon and Sterlite were debarred for four, three and two years, respectively.

On 9 November 2001, the CBI arrested Mehta again for diverting money from the PSU Maruti Udyog Limited (MUL) to his own accounts and misappropriating nearly ₹2,500 crore.[14] Mehta did not get bail and succumbed to a cardiac arrest on 31 December 2001 at the age of forty-seven.

Image credit: GCMMF

Mehta was not the sole person to be incarcerated in the aftermath of the securities scam. In 2001, stockbroker Bhupen Dalal became the first person to be convicted. There were several charges pending against Dalal, but a ₹78 crore cheque bouncing case resulted in his conviction.[15] In 2014, Dalal was again convicted with another stockbroker, Haresh Dalal, and industrialist T.B. Ruia. A fine of ₹5 lakh was slapped on him, and he was directed to pay ₹38 lakh compensation to the state and was also imprisoned for a year.[16] In January 2019, Hiten Dalal,

Figure 4.1: SEBI's Press Release on Debarring Mehta from Capital Markets

भारतीय प्रतिभूति और विनिमय बोर्ड
Securities and Exchange Board of India

प्रेस विज्ञप्ति
PRESS RELEASE

संपर्क प्रभाग, सेबी भवन, बांद्रा कुर्ला कॉम्प्लेक्स, बांद्रा (पूर्व), मुंबई - 400 051
Communications Division, SEBI Bhavan, Bandra Kurla Complex, Bandra (E), Mumbai – 400 051
दूरभाष / Tel: +91-22-26449000 ईमेल / email:press@sebi.gov.in वेबसाइट /website: www.sebi.gov.in

Apr 19, 2001 Press Releases

Press Release

April 19, 2001
Ref.No.PR 71/2001

Investigations were carried out by SEBI into the alleged price manipulations in the scrips of BPL , Videocon and Sterlite,in 1998. Investigations were completed in three stages. In the first stage, it was brought out that a set of brokers and sub brokers acting on behalf of a common set of clients who were acting as a front for Shri Harshad Mehta cornered large chunk of shares of Videocon, BPL and Sterlite. This cornering led to price manipulation. The scrip prices rose substantially. Pursuant to these investigations, 17 brokers (10 of BSE and 7 of NSE) were suspended for periods ranging from one to three years. Several other brokers were given lesser punishment. Secondly, the President of BSE was asked to relinquish the office. The Vice President of BSE resigned following investigations. Later investigations were completed against Harshad Mehta and BPL, Videocon and Sterlite by October, 1999. Show cause notices were issued to them in December, 1999. Once the notices were issued , SEBI was required to hear these cases in quasi judicial manner. The parties asked for inspection of the documents. Later on they also asked for cross examination of witnesses which prolonged the proceedings. After giving them the opportunity of final hearings in the month of March/April,2001. The following 4 orders have been passed by SEBI today :

1. SEBI has permaneantly debarred Harshad Mehta under Section 11 and 11B of SEBI Act, read with Regulation 11 of SEBI (Prohibition of Fraudulent and Unfair Trade Practices for dealing in securities) Regulations, from dealing in securities. His prosecution has also been ordered under section 24 of SEBI Act.
2. BPL Limited has been debarred from accessing capital market for a period of 4 years under section 11 and 11B of the SEBI Act. Prosecution proceedings of the company through 5 of its directors/ officials has been ordered under section 24 of SEBI Act for violation of SEBI Act and SEBI(Prohibition of Fraudulent and Unfair Trade Practices for dealing in securities)Regulations..
3. Videocon International Ltd.. has been debarred from accessing capital market for a period of 3 years under section 11 and 11B of the SEBI Act. Prosecution proceedings of the company through 3 of its directors/ officials has been ordered under section 24 of SEBI Act for violation of SEBI Act and SEBI(Prohibition of Fraudulent and Unfair Trade Practices for dealing in securities)Regulations..
4. Sterlite Industries Ltd. has been debarred from accessing capital market for a period of 2 years under section 11 and 11B of the SEBI Act. Prosecution proceedings of the company through 3 of its directors/ officials has been ordered under section 24 of SEBI Act for violation of SEBI Act and SEBI(Prohibition of Fraudulent and Unfair Trade Practices for dealing in securities)Regulations..

who had brokered a higher volume of securities transactions than Mehta, was sentenced to two years' jail for using spurious BRs issued by Bank of Karad and Metropolitan Co-operative Bank to defraud Stanchart.[17]

Pherwani resigned as chairman of NHB in early May 1992, weeks after *The Times of India* reported the scam. On 21 May, Pherwani's family members found him dead. 'The journalist [R.C. Murthy, then chief of bureau at *Business Standard*] got a phone call and rushed to the house at about 8 am … Pherwani's body looked blue, he [Murthy] remembers. It was cremated at 11.30 am the same day with the face covered instead of being kept open in the normal Hindu way. The death was ascribed vaguely to a heart attack. Murthy and many others believe Pherwani committed suicide.'[18]

In August 2009, UCO Bank's former chairman and managing director, K. Margabandhu, and general manager, R. Venkatakrishnan, were sentenced to six months' rigorous imprisonment.[19] The bank had extended ₹50 crore clean credit that is, a loan without a collateral, to Mehta, and at the time of the loan's maturity, purchased shares worth ₹49.50 crore from the broker to facilitate his repayment. Further, NHB had lent ₹40 crore on call to UCO Bank on 6 April 1992, which was credited to Mehta's account.[20]

Bengaluru-based Fairgrowth Financial Services was floated by the former chairman of Canara Bank, B. Ratnakar, who passed away before the scam broke out. Fairgrowth, which was incorporated in July 1990 and was an aggressive enterprise even during Ratnakar's lifetime, struggled to borrow money during the months running up to the scam. Its managing director, K. Dharmapal, and executive director, R. Lakshminarayanan, confessed to having borrowed money from Andhra Bank Financial Services, NHB and Bank of India by providing false receipts for securities Fairgrowth did not possess.[21] Dharmapal passed away in April 1999. Lakshminarayanan and R. Srinivasan, a senior vice president in Fairgrowth, were sentenced to four years' rigorous imprisonment in July 2018.[22] India's then commerce minister P. Chidambaram and his wife, Nalini, were shareholders in Fairgrowth. P. Chidambaram resigned in July 1992.

Technocrat V. Krishnamurthy, former chairman of SAIL Ltd and Maruti Udyog, chair of a committee on public sector divestment, and member of the Planning Commission, was accused of accepting a ₹32.74 lakh loan (which CBI later said was a bribe) from Harshad Mehta and of having arranged a ₹70 lakh bank loan for a company his two sons ran. Krishnamurthy clarified that the loan had been arranged before he joined the Planning Commission. He was arrested and held in a two-bedroom flat at the CBI complex in New Delhi for three weeks.[23] After six years, a court ruled that the CBI had no case.[24]

The Economic Times observed, 'The Raj Rajrathnam (of Galleon Group hedge fund) insider trading case, was wrapped up in about three years' time. The Societe Generale unauthorised trading case of 2008, involving rogue trader Jerome Kerviel, was tied up in over two years' time. Back home, the Satyam scandal was settled in a record three years' time.' When the 1992 securities scam came to light, 76 criminal cases and over 600 civil suits were filed against Mehta and his family. There were 27 cases pending against the stockbroker at the time of his death. Lawyers informed *The Economic Times*, "It's normal for civil cases to go on for 30–40 years ... The Harshad Mehta case had a bearing on the banking system and stock markets, and should have got resolved expeditiously."'[25]

The glacial pace at which the courts adjudicated the case enabled Harshad Mehta's brother Ashwin, who had secured a degree in law in 1979, to obtain a licence in 2013 and start practising as a lawyer.[26]

The Mehta Family's Claim

In July 2022, Mehta's wife Jyoti launched a website, https://www.harshadmehta.in/. In the overview section of the website, Jyoti alleged that Mehta had died of medical negligence. The website also states,

> Much before the claims against us got finalised and knowing fully well that they were false and highly exaggerated but the Custodian yet supported and secured the release of Rs.3285.46 Crores in favour of the IT department and Rs.1716.07 Crores in favour of the banks and thereby fully met the entire demands of tax and the entire principal sum of the decrees obtained by the banks.... To meet these patently illegal demands, the Custodian prematurely sold our appreciating Blue Chip shares at throwaway prices and thereby inflicted upon us huge losses of Rs.20,677.28 Crores the details above losses are provided in the enclosed chart.[27]

Jyoti is reportedly a homemaker. So, it would not be incorrect to assume that the Mehta family, including Ashwin, participated in creating the content for this website.

Appendix 3 provides the aforesaid chart, which is a downloadable pdf file. According to this chart, Mehta had invested in eighteen companies that the custodian sold in twenty-eight tranches. For example, the custodian sold 16.26 million shares of ACC in October 2003 and close to 5,44,000 shares in July 2011. These two transactions of ACC share sales constitute two tranches. This chart offers interesting insights to investors.

First, the only small cap stock among the eighteen stocks Mehta had invested in was Revathi Equipment, which changed its name to Semac Consultants in July 2023. All other stocks are large caps and include blue chips such as ACC, Ambuja Cements, Hindustan Unilever, Larsen & Tubro, Mahindra & Mahindra and Reliance Industries. The eighteen stocks listed in the chart is a non-exhaustive list of Mehta's equity holdings. Second, the chart claims that the custodian sold these stocks at 'throwaway prices', thereby realising ₹1,616 crore cash, and that the market value of these stocks would have appreciated more than twelve-fold to

₹19,896 crore by 31 August 2021. Further, the dividends paid by these stocks between 2003 and 2021 amounted to ₹2,420 crore. Hence, the Mehta family suffered a loss of ₹20,677 crore, which is the ₹19,896 crore market value as of 31 August 2021, plus ₹2,420 crore dividend receipts minus ₹1,616 crore sale proceeds realised by the custodian.

As I scanned the chart, the investment in Castrol India caught my eye. As per the chart, the 4,08,245 shares that the custodian sold in July 2011 would have grown 400-fold to 16,32,98,000 shares! But another tranche of 1.18 million Castrol shares the custodian sold in 2003 would have grown eight-fold to 9.47 million shares. I examined the history of Castrol's bonus issues. The lubricant manufacturer had declared 1:1 bonus issues in April 2010, September 2012 and December 2017. Hence, the 4,08,245 shares the custodian reportedly sold in July 2011 would have increased to 1.63 million by August 2021 and not 163.29 million as reported on the website. I used the share price data on the BSE and NSE websites to estimate the sale proceeds and market values.

I realised that there were errors in this chart. First was an addition error. A linear summation of the cash the custodian reportedly realised by selling the eighteen stocks is ₹1,695 crore and not ₹1,616 crore. Second, the dates of sale of the two tranches of Bharti Telecom shares have been input as numbers. Hence, it is not possible to ascertain the date of sale and sale price. Third, the date of sale of Revathi Equipment shares is input as 2004–2005; an exact date has not been provided.

Using the share price date available on the BSE and NSE websites and excluding the sale proceeds of Bharti Telecom and Revathi Equipment shares, the sale proceeds realised by the custodian is around ₹4,041 crore. The difference between my estimate of ₹4,041 crore and Mehta family's computation of ₹1,616 crore is primarily on account of a typographical error. The estimated sale proceeds from selling 186.84 million Ambuja

Cement shares in August 2011 is around ₹2,506 crore and not ₹25.06 crore.

Similarly, the market value of the eighteen stocks would have appreciated to around ₹36,575 crore by 31 August 2021, which is 84% higher than the ₹19,896 crore reported by the Mehta family. The under-reporting of the market values of three stocks—L&T, Ambuja Cements and Bharti Telecom—account for most of the difference. The market value of Mehta's holdings in L&T would have been around ₹12,440 crore on 31 August 2021 and not ₹3,119 crore as reported. Similarly, Ambuja Cement's market value was ₹7,850 crore and not ₹79 crore, and Bharti Telecom's market value was higher at ₹1,289 crore that the reported ₹924 crore. One trait of Mehta's that emerges while reading *The Scam: From Harshad Mehta to Ketan Parekh* is that the stockbroker was not good at book-keeping. The errors in the calculations provided on the website seem to back this. Computing the dividend receipts of these eighteen stocks between 2003 and 2021 is a tedious affair. I am not masochistic and hence skipped the exercise. My workings are in Appendix 4.

We have no means of knowing all the constituents of Mehta's equity portfolio. But almost all the eighteen stocks Mehta reportedly invested in sustained their blue-chip status from the time of his investment in the late 1980s and early 1990s to 2024. The ₹36,575 crore market value as of 31 August 2021 was more than twice the ₹16,045 crore liabilities estimated by the custodian in January 2016.

The government's handling of investments in crisis situations has been inconsistent. After the Ketan Parekh scam erupted in 2001, the government was astute enough to split the investments of UTI's Unit Scheme 1964 (US-1964) into two separate corpuses when it came under severe redemption pressure. While the stressed assets were hived off to one corpus, the healthy assets were actively managed in a second corpus. As most of Mehta's investments in the eighteen stocks were blue chips even in 1992 and with effective oversight could have offset his liabilities, why did the government choose to sell these shares at their market prices and settle for a relatively paltry ₹4,041 crore? Astute handling, as in UTI's case, would have worked better.

As per the list of Mehta's equity investments reported by his family and media reports, there are at least two stocks he and RJ purchased—ACC and Tata Tea. Like RJ's listed equities portfolio, Mehta's eighteen stock portfolio outperformed the market over a long period of time. The difference in the two investors' capital raising methods was stark, though. RJ traded in stocks, currencies and commodities, and borrowed money to invest. These activities comply with the law in letter and spirit. Mehta diverted the monies banks transferred to his account for the purchase of government securities to buy shares. He also engaged in pump and dump schemes. The illegalities in fund raising cut short Mehta's career but the legal action that followed did not deter others from emulating him.

The 1992 securities scam is a landmark event in India's history. It paved the way for stronger and stricter market regulation. Though SEBI was incorporated in 1988, it lacked teeth. In the aftermath of the 1992 securities scam, SEBI was given statutory powers. The SEBI Act was passed in the same year, making the market regulator the apex authority for India's capital markets and ending the hegemony of independent stock exchanges owned and operated by brokers.[28] But these changes did not thwart yet another scam engineered by Mehta's apprentice, Ketan Parekh, who concocted a market meltdown barely a decade later.

5

Pentafour Bull

THE 1966-BORN KETAN PAREKH AND HARSHAD MEHTA, WHO WAS twelve years older, were as different as chalk and cheese. While Mehta was born to a modest family in Raipur, Parekh was the scion of Narbheram Harakchand Parekh, a large institutional broker that was subsequently renamed NH Securities. Mehta barely managed to scrape through his exams to secure a B.Com degree; Parekh was a chartered accountant. Mehta was brash and flamboyant whereas Parekh was quiet and discreet.

Dalal observes, 'Shy and serious, he hung around the fringes of Harshad's high-spirited group of flashy bull operators, and that itself may have saved him except for the one single case in which he was Accused No. 10 – it was case 3 of 1996, CBI v/s Canbank Mutual Fund which is being heard by the Special Court to try scam related offences.'[1]

But both men were determined to stride Dalal Street like a colossus. Parekh culled out a strategy, which was essentially a subset of Mehta's. He purchased shares at heavily discounted prices from promoters. He then engaged in circular trading through entities he controlled. This drove up share prices and attracted the attention of retail investors (mostly), who also traded and invested in these stocks, fuelling the escalation of prices to dizzying heights, and boosted trading volumes. The artificially boosted trading volumes satisfied one of the fund managers' criteria for stock selection—liquidity. Parekh would then sell these shares to mutual funds. This arrangement was attractive to promoters as they were able to borrow more by pledging their stakes, whose value had appreciated considerably. The losers were retail and mutual fund investors as prices of stocks dropped.

Yet another of Parekh's service offerings was investing in soon-to-be listed companies. *India Today* reported in a February 2001 column, 'If the stock market is one of the movers of the new Indian economy, Parekh was one of the prime movers of that market … legend has it that IPOs are filed with Parekh before they hit the market.'[2]

Parekh was in the right place at the right time and was assisted by Mehta's brother, Ashwin. The effect of the global dot-com boom, which prevailed from 1995 to 2000, rubbed off on India. Sensex, which was battered by both the 1992 securities scam and the March 1993 Bombay blasts, started climbing from March 1999 onwards. As in the case of the West, telecom, media and technology (TMT) stocks were the flavour of the day. Sensex touched 5,000 for the first time on 8 October 1999 and 6,000 four months later on 11 February 2000. But it was not just market factors that fuelled the index's impressive rise.

One of Parekh's earliest successful investments was Pentafour, a software company whose price–earnings (P/E) ratio was abysmal at about 2.0 when he purchased it. Pentafour's price and trading volumes rose dramatically courtesy Parekh's circular trading. Government-controlled mutual funds and retail investors lapped up Parekh's holdings, thereby facilitating his enormously profitable exits.

Dus Ka Ek Aur Ek Ka Dus

Parekh purchased stakes in high-profile listed entities, mostly software firms, and engineered their price rise by ten to twenty times. These stocks came to be known as the K-10 stocks and comprised Global Telesystems, Zee Telefilms, Himachal Futuristic Communications Limited (HFCL), Silverline, Satyam Computers, Aftek Infosys, DSQ Software, Ranbaxy, Pentamedia Graphics and Visual Soft. Sometimes, Digital Global and SSI were also included in K-10 stocks.[3]

Zee's price was rigged up to ₹1,500, which translated to a P/E ratio of 250. The stock's ludicrous valuation is evident when juxtaposed with Sensex's P/E ratios of 12.86 in FY1999 and 19.76 in FY2000.[4] The global dot-com boom and Parekh's pump and dump schemes had both contributed to the 54% jump in Sensex's valuation in a single year. Parekh's comrades endorsed certain stocks with the slogan '*dus ka ek aur ek ka dus*'. This implied that a ₹10 face value share would be split into ten shares of ₹1 each, and each of these ₹1 shares would zoom up to ₹10,000. The share price of Global Telesystems, a little-known manufacturer of fax machines, grew 4,338% in three years from ₹80 in March 1997 to ₹3,550 in March 2000! Parekh convinced the market that Global Telesystems was a new economy company. After propelling DSQ Software's share price ten-fold from ₹250 to ₹2,500 in three months, Parekh stopped trading the stock. Dalal and Basu opine DSQ Software's 'promoter Dinesh Dalmia's penchant for large-scale speculation on his own account probably outran Ketan's appetite for manipulation'.[5] Parekh also acquired a stake in the Hyderabad-based Global Trust Bank, ostensibly to diversify.

In January 2000, Parekh rather uncharacteristically threw a 'Millenium Bash' at Mandwa, an island off the coast of Bombay where he owned a seaside bungalow. His guests included emerging software czars, fund managers and a few Bollywood stars. The guests assembled at Taj Mahal Hotel's Sea Lounge for a champagne reception before being ferried in high-security catamarans to Mandwa. The millenium bash was unequivocal proof of the sea change in Parekh's personality. He bought a Cadillac and a Lexus, a car Mehta favoured. His inner circle now included HFCL's promoter Vinay Maloo, Australian media moghul Kerry Packer and his son James, politician Amar Singh and actor Amitabh Bachchan. A year and three months later, on 30 March 2000, the CBI arrested Parekh.

What caused the Pentafour Bull's downfall? The environment and Parekh's own actions.

If Mehta had diverted monies from the money market to purchase shares, how did Parekh finance his pump and dump schemes? After all, he needed money to purchase shares from promoters, albeit at discounted prices. Parekh had three key sources of funding. He availed a ₹200 crore line of credit from a small Ahmedabad-based entity, Madhavpura Co-operative Bank, by pledging shares whose market value exceeded ₹300 crore. Needless to mention, the collateral primarily comprised the overvalued K-10 stocks, whose share prices Parekh had rigged. Madhavpura issued pay orders to various Parekh-promoted entities, including Classic Share & Stockbrokers, Panther Investrade and Panther Fincap. These entities would in turn present the pay orders to BoI, which would discount them.

Parekh had not just acquired a stake in Global Trust Bank (GTB). The bank also financed Parekh, his associates and issuers of K-10 stocks such as Zee Telefilms and HFCL, in violation of regulatory norms. Though GTB's exposure to entities associated with Parekh was over ₹250 crore, the bank's chairman Ramesh Gelli 'has been on record to say that under the RBI norms his lending to Parekh cannot exceed ₹100 crore'.[6]

Parekh's pump and dump schemes, by which he sold stocks to mutual funds at inflated prices, was the third source of funding.

Black Friday

The dot-com boom started running out of steam, which was one of the two contributory factors for Sensex heading south after scaling 6,000 in February 2000. Sensex declined by 30% in the next year to end February 2001 at 4,247 points. On 28 February and 1 March, while Sensex rose in response to Yashwant Sinha's union budget, the share prices of bellwether software stocks, including Infosys and HCL, declined. Rumours of Parekh's payment problems started making the rounds. On 2 March 2001, a day that would come to be known as Black Friday, the bears swung into action on BSE, hammering down share prices, especially those of the K-10 stocks. In the week ending 2 March, the value of short sold stocks rose by a significant ₹64 crore. Sensex shed 228 points on 2 March. The bear cartel, which included Radhakishan Damani, did not believe that the fundamentals of stocks like HFCL and Global Tele warranted the dizzying rise in their share prices during the year gone by. They had started building short positions since early 2001. RJ informed journalist Shekhar Gupta in 2021 that he too had bet that the prices of stocks Parekh had invested in would decline. The eternal optimist remarked that he had earned '95% wealth in capital markets as a bull. Few occasions in life, it is profitable to be a bear'.[7] I wonder whether RJ had invoked his inner George Soros when he shorted the Harshad Mehta and Ketan Parekh stocks.

The bear attack, which began on 2 March, continued on Monday, 5 March. The mutual funds to whom Parekh had sold stocks at inflated prices witnessed their portfolio depreciate in value during the last year. They sold their holdings at lower prices when the bear attack was underway to cut their losses. Sensex lost close to 76 points on 5 March. Rumours of a payment crisis started doing rounds in BSE on 2 and 5 March. SEBI raising the margin requirements, denying a payment crisis and affirming that

BSE held a sizable ₹2,400 crore as capital and margins did not quell the rumours.

On 8 March, SEBI banned short sales. However, a payment crisis erupted at the Calcutta Stock Exchange (CSE), an entity that had gained notoriety for bonafide and grey market deals being concluded side by side at the bourse's premises. Three brokers who operated for Parekh on the CSE defaulted: Dinesh Singhania, Ashok Poddar and Harish Biyani.

Coincidentally, on 8 and 9 March, Parekh-controlled entities presented ₹137 crore worth pay orders issued by Madhavpura to BoI for discounting. As 10 and 11 March (Saturday and Sunday) were holidays, BoI discounted the pay orders and released ₹65 crore credit to Parekh-backed entities on Monday, 11 March. By 11 p.m. on 12 March, RBI declared Madhavpura a defaulter and instructed that BoI return the pay orders unpaid on 13 March. However, BoI had already released the funds to Parekh-backed entities. The government-owned bank summoned Parekh for several meetings and demanded the repayment of loans. The broker expressed his inability to repay the entire outstanding due to the ongoing income tax raids and repaid just ₹7 crore. BoI filed a criminal complaint against Parekh with the CBI, which arrested the broker on 30 March.

Image credit: GCMMF

Ripple Effects

Madhavpura admitted that it had had lent ₹200 crore to Parekh, whereas as per RBI regulations, it was not supposed to lend over ₹15 crore to a single entity. In reality, its lending to the Pentafour Bull was four times higher. RBI formulated a reconstruction scheme for Madhavpura in 2001 as the deposits of the urban co-operative banks in Gujarat with the scam-tainted lender amounted to ₹800 crore. A decade later, Madhavpura continued to be a loss-making entity, its net worth was negative and non-performing assets constituted 99.99% of its total advances! In June 2012, RBI cancelled Madhavpura's licence.[8]

GTB's chairman Gelli stepped down in April 2001, barely a week after Black Friday. The Government of India vide a notification dated 13 August 2004 amalgamated GTB with public sector lender, Oriental Bank of Commerce (OBC). In April 2020, OBC and Union Bank of India merged with Punjab National Bank.

On 12 November 2007, SEBI debarred Parekh from capital markets for fourteen years for engaging in market manipulation in nine stocks—HFCL, Zee Telefilms, Adani Exports, Global Tele, Ranbaxy, Sri Adhikari Brothers, Shonkh Technologies, Padmini Technologies and Aftek Technologies. Adani Exports was subsequently renamed as Adani Enterprises, and as of 2024, is a constituent of Nifty50 and BSE100.

Parekh's first conviction was not for engineering the 2001 stock market scam. The Bombay Court had sentenced Parekh, Hiten Dalal and five others to one-year rigorous imprisonment in the 1992 Canfina scam case.[9] A special CBI court convicted him again in March 2014 for cheating and sentenced him to two years rigorous imprisonment.[10]

India Today reported in a July 2012 column,

> KP may have been implicated in the 2001 securities scam and serving a 14-years SEBI ban, but the market knows that he has

Figure 5.1: SEBI's Press Release on Debarring Parekh from Capital Markets

भारतीय प्रतिभूति और विनिमय बोर्ड
Securities and Exchange Board of India

प्रेस विज्ञप्ति
PRESS RELEASE

संपर्क प्रभाग, सेबी भवन, बांद्रा कुर्ला कॉम्प्लेक्स, बांद्रा (पूर्व), मुंबई - 400 051
Communications Division, SEBI Bhavan, Bandra Kurla Complex, Bandra (E), Mumbai – 400 051
दूरभाष / Tel: +91-22-26449000 ईमेल / email:press@sebi.gov.in वेबसाइट /website: www.sebi.gov.in

' 12, 2007 PR No.: 295/2007

Order against Shri Ketan V. Parekh and his associated entities

3I conducted investigations into the buying, selling and dealings in the scrips of Himachal Futuristic Communications Limited, Zee Telefilms Limited, Adani Exports Limited, bal Tele-Systems Limited, Ranbaxy Laboratories Limited, Shri Adhikari Brothers Television Network Limited, Shonkh Technologies International Limited, Padmini Technologies ited and Aftek Infosys Limited during the period October 1999 to March 2001.

investigations revealed that Shri Ketan V. Parekh and 17 other entities who were directly/indirectly related/associated to him were involved in market manipulation in the esaid scrips in violation of SEBI (Prohibition of Fraudulent and Unfair Trade Practices Relating to Securities Market) Regulations, 1995 and/or SEBI (Substantial Acquisition of res and Takeovers) Regulations, 1997. The modus operandi adopted by all the above mentioned entities in manipulating various scrips was, by and large, the same and Shri an V. Parekh was found to be the master mind behind all the acts of omission or commissions by these entities.

iew of the above, Dr. T.C. Nair, Whole Time Member, SEBI, has passed an order dated November 12, 2007:

lestraining Shri Ketan V. Parekh and his 10 associates namely Shri Kartik K. Parekh, Classic Credit Ltd., Panther Fincap and Management Services Ltd., Luminant Investment 'vt. Ltd., Chitrakut Computers Pvt. Ltd., Saimangal Investrade Ltd., Classic Infin Ltd., Panther Investrade Ltd., Goldfish Computers Pvt. Ltd., and Nakashtra Software Pvt. Ltd. om accessing the securities market and also prohibiting them from buying, selling or otherwise dealing or associating with the securities market in any manner whatsoever, vhether directly or indirectly, for a period of fourteen years.

lestraining Shri Navinchandra N. Parekh, Shri Kirtikumar N. Parekh, Shri Jayant N. Parekh and Shri Vipul D. Parekh, from accessing the securities market and also prohibiting iem from buying, selling or otherwise dealing or associating with the securities market in any manner whatsoever, whether directly or indirectly, for a period of one year.

lestraining Triumph International Finance India Ltd., Triumph Securities Ltd., and NH Securities Ltd. from accessing the securities market and also prohibiting them from buying, elling or otherwise dealing or associating with the securities market in any manner whatsoever, whether directly or indirectly, for a period of five years.

egard to the entities namely, Shri Ketan V. Parekh, Shri Kartik K. Parekh, Classic Credit Ltd., Panther Fincap and Management Services Ltd., Luminant Investment Pvt. Ltd., rakut Computers Pvt. Ltd., Saimangal Investrade Ltd., Classic Infin Ltd. and Panther Investrade Ltd., which were covered under SEBI order dated December 12, 2003 barring them from securities market), this order shall run concurrently and shall be deemed to be effective from December 12, 2003.

egards the remaining entities, the order shall come into effect from the date of the order.

full text of the order is available on the website: www.sebi.gov.in

nbai
ember 12, 2007

been active. Crooked promoters approach him with money bags and profit-sharing arrangements to 'chalao' their stocks for multiple benefits. Because he is banned from trading, it is very difficult to establish his involvement. Brokers often talk about KP's partnership with a hot-shot politician's son – a partnership which has enabled KP to make enough money in 2006–07 to pay off ₹400 crore of his liabilities to Madhavpura Mercantile Co-operative Bank. He still owes ₹400 crore to the depositors of this bank which was liquidated after the scam.[11]

India Today's assertion that Parekh was still active in the market was correct. SEBI, in an ex-parte interim order-cum-show cause notice dated 2 January 2025, alleged that Parekh, a Singapore national named Rohit Salgaocar and twenty others had engaged in front-running and thus generated ₹65.77 crore unlawful gains. SEBI's interim order stated that Parekh and Salgaocar had colluded with a foreign portfolio investor, whom the regulator's interim order refers to as 'Big Client', to rig share prices. The interim order further stated that the duo had availed the services of traditional money carriers who operate outside the formal banking system called Angadias, Kolkata-based brokers, and a trader each from Motilal Oswal Financial Services and Nuvama Wealth Management to carry out their front-running trades.

SEBI's investigation uncovered two trading patterns the front-runners deployed: 'Buy-Buy-Sell' and 'Sell-Sell-Buy'. In a 'Buy-Buy-Sell' pattern, the front-runners would first buy shares, then the Big Client would place their buy orders, causing the prices to rise. The front-runners would then sell the shares for a profit. Similarly, in a 'Sell-Sell-Buy' pattern, the front-runners would short-sell shares before the Big Client placed their sell orders, only to buy the shares back later at a lower price.[12]

SEBI's interim order includes illustrations of five stocks with which Parekh and Salgaocar had executed front-running trades—Titan, HDFC Limited, PB Fintech (Policy Bazar), Cholamandalam Investment and Finance Company and Tube Investments. NDTV Profit reported that Tiger Global Management was the 'Big Client' SEBI alluded to, a charge denied by the US-based investment firm.[13] SEBI's interim order recommended that Parekh, Salgaocar and their twenty associates be debarred from the securities market for 'an appropriate period' and associating with any registered intermediary. Parekh, Salgaocar and their associates have been given twenty-one days' time to file their replies with SEBI.[14]

Narrating the career trajectories of Mehta and Parekh is necessary to provide a context to RJ's career. RJ was born in July 1960, which is the mid-point of Mehta's (July 1954) and Parekh's (December 1966) years of birth. Their paths crossed at Dalal Street. Yet their careers were very different. A comparison of Mehta's, Parekh's and RJ's capital raising and investing strategies will explain the longevity of their careers and the quality of their franchise. RJ's investment career spanned thirty-seven years while Mehta and RJ were tainted by scandal within a decade. An understanding of RJ the man is necessary to understand the longevity of his career in a high stakes industry.

6

The Ascent

RJ'S PASSION FOR INVESTING, EXPOSURE TO EQUITIES SINCE childhood, his knowledge of finance and accounting (yes, they are allied but different) gained through the chartered accountancy course, a desire to learn continuously and his network propelled his meteoric rise.

Business Model

While RJ is renowned for his investments in listed equities, what many retail investors may be unaware of is that he was a versatile investor who conducted several types of investment transactions. Utpal Sheth, who became CEO of RaRe Enterprises and transitioned to being an advisor to the firm since 1 January 2025, says, 'We [RaRe Enterprises] were active both in public markets and in private equity. We worked on multiple transaction structures including initial public offerings (IPOs), preferential allotments, pre-IPOs, distressed transactions, structured deals, mergers and acquisitions, warrants etc. You name it. We have done every possible kind of transaction.'[1]

Atul Suri, a former employee of RaRe Enterprises and CEO of Marathon Trends, a wealth management firm, shared a snippet in a September 2022 interview with *The Economic Times*. Suri observed,

> 'I think that he [RJ] had 3X our brain power. He could be sitting with you, looking at the screen, probably giving orders and yet talking about investments so he could trade, a trader's mindset; he could be an investor, investor's mindset and yet he could get a phone call from a private equity investor and handle something. So he excelled in three areas. He proudly said he was a trader because he made his capital through trading. How did he fund his investment? Through trading. He was a very successful investor that is what people know about but the fact is that the wealth that he has created in the last few years has been actually monetising his PE plays. In the secondary market, he did not have any of those 100X kind of plays in the last few years. In fact, it was monetising the PE plays which really gave him the 100X. I think that is the reason for his wealth creation.'[2]

What did Suri mean when he opined that RJ's PE plays were far more profitable than his listed equity investments? RJ first invested in Star Health and Allied Insurance in May 2019. As he purchased shares both from Star Health and other investors ahead of its listing, the average price at which he purchased the insurer's share is not known. But it is likely that his investment at least trebled at the time of Star Health's December 2021 listing, which occurred slightly over two-and-a-half years after his first investment. In contrast, the market value of RaRe Enterprises' listed equity holdings doubled between June 2019 and December 2021; capital markets were recovering from the COVID-19-induced crash during the latter half of this period. However, PE is a riskier venture than investing in listed equities, and even RJ wasn't immune to losses—he lost money backing certain firms, such as A2Z.

RJ revealed some of his key medium- to long-term equity investments made since the 1990s in a July 2020 interview with

ET Now. Bharat Electronics (BEL), a PSU that manufactures defence equipment, was a constituent of RJ's portfolio for nine years (1998–2007), during which time the stock price rose ninety times. Two investments RJ made in the 1990s appreciated hundred-fold. The first was the footwear brand Bata, in which he was invested up to 2019 for around twenty-three years. The second was Apollo Hospitals, which was in RJ's portfolio for seventeen years (1998–2015). He was not only happy with Apollo's stock performance but also impressed with its founder, Dr P.C. Reddy. In a 2012 address to the students of Flame University, RJ observed, 'Dr Reddy of Apollo has one-and-a-half drinks daily in his eighties. He is active. Everything done in moderation is good.'[3] Moderation was a trait RJ admired and unfortunately did not emulate.

RJ invested in two more PSUs in the 2000s. Shipping Corporation of India was in RJ's portfolio from 2000 to 2007, during which time its price appreciated by 1200%! Yet another defence PSU, BEML (formerly Bharat Earth Movers Limited), appreciated hundred-fold when RJ was invested in it from 2001 to 2007. RJ revealed that his PSU investments were immensely profitable, notwithstanding which people used to refer to him as '*gadha*' (donkey) and '*bondhu*' (dimwit). PSUs have not captured Indian investors' imagination despite the advantages of government backing, the transparency listed entities afford and a higher dividend yield. Even as of July 2024, the BSE PSU index's dividend yield of 2.20% is almost twice Sensex's 1.15%. Moreover, the PSU index's PE ratio of 12.53 is almost half Sensex's 24.17 and price-book multiple of 2.23 is just 57% of Sensex's 1.15.[4]

The jewel in RJ's crown—the watch and jewellery maker from the Tata stable, Titan Company Limited—was added to his portfolio sometime during 2002 at ₹35 a share.[5] The value of RJ's stake in Titan for the quarter ended 30 June 2022—the last complete quarter RJ oversaw RaRe Enterprises before his demise in August 2022—was ₹10,549 crore; the share price had skyrocketed to ₹2,352. Titan accounted for a third of the market value of stocks in which RaRe Enterprises owned more than 1% stake.

Other multi-bagger investments RJ added to his portfolio during the 2000s are the credit rating agency CRISIL, the pharma company Lupin, the industrial products company PRAJ Industries, and the pesticide and agrochemicals manufacturer and a constituent of the Tata group, Rallis. Remunerative investments RJ made in the 2010s were the tractor manufacturer Escorts Kubota and Tata Communications.[6] These are a subset of the listed equity investments that are the most transparent constituent of RJ's $5.8 billion (₹47,183 crore) net worth.

RJ also profited by shorting the shares of the multinational mining company Vedanta and Videocon Industries during the Ketan Parekh years (late 1998 to 2001).[7] Videocon is a conglomerate, which, as of 2024, is under the Corporate Insolvency Resolution Process, and its founder Venugopal Dhoot, along with ICICI Bank's former CEO Chanda Kochhar, is accused of defrauding the lender.

Even RJ was not immune to losses. He mentions that in 1997 he lost money investing in software stocks and ₹20 crore in private equity, but acknowledges that he learnt from these losses. RJ often quoted George Soros, an investor whom he looked up to, to describe his views on profits and losses: it's not whether you're right or wrong, but how much money you make when you're right and how much you lose when you're wrong.

George Soros became the target of the BJP government's ire when he stated in a February 2023 speech ahead of the Munich Security Conference that Prime Minister Narendra Modi was 'no democrat' but the Adani 'affair' could 'open the door to a democratic revival' in India.[8] Soros, also known as the man who broke the Bank of England, shot to fame by leading a speculative attack on the pound in 1992 and earning $1 billion in the process. The UK had joined the European Exchange Rate Mechanism

(ERM) in 1990 and was committed to keeping the British pound within a set band against the Deutschemark. Central banks support currencies by hiking interest rates. The Bank of England (BoE) was unable to do so as the UK's benchmark rate was already high at 10% and so was unemployment at over three million. On 16 September 1992, a date which came to be known as Black Wednesday, Soros correctly bet that the pound would be devalued. Though BoE announced that it would hike the benchmark rate to 15%, it did not do so, and suspended the UK's membership from the ERM. Soros earned the $1 billion profit by squaring his short positions on the pound.[9] *Forbes* estimated the 1930-born Soros' net worth in 2017 to be $25.2 billion, which was more than four times RJ's net worth as of August 2022. In 2018, Soros transferred $18 billion from his family office to Open Society Foundations, a grant-making organisation he founded with the mandate of supporting civil society groups engaged in advancing justice, education, public health and independent media. Soros' net worth declined after this transfer to $6.7 billion as of July 2024 [10]

RJ observed, 'I learnt optimism and (the importance of) business models from (Warren) Buffett. I learnt guts and timing from Soros. [He correctly anticipated] that the EMU [European Economic and Monetary Union] between the Deutschemark and British pound will not last … But do not get pressurised by Buffett, Soros etc. Read about them, observe, and respect them.'[11]

While RJ stated that he learnt the importance of being gutsy from Soros, I believe he was inherently courageous. Utpal Sheth recalled an astonishing incident from the 1990s. 'One day a man came to the office and put a gun to Bhaiya's head. But the way he responded was amazing. All he said was, "These are market hours. Let me earn money. I can pay you only if I earn money; I can't if I don't. So, in your own interest, please go away. Come back later. Don't worry, I'm here. I'm not going away." And the man did go away.'[12]

Panchsheel

It would not be incorrect to conclude that RJ adopted an industry-agnostic approach while investing in listed equities, covering a wide range of industries. He eschewed information technology stocks as he admitted he did not understand technology and also burnt his fingers investing in software stocks in 1997. This is an interesting similarity he shares with Warren Buffett, who also claimed not to understand technology until he made a major investment in Apple only in 2016.[13] The two legendary investors were unimpressed by cryptocurrencies too. Whereas Buffett called Bitcoin a 'mirage', RJ described trading and investing in bitcoin as 'speculation of the highest order'.[14]

RJ used five metrics to decide whether or not to invest in a stock—people, patience, technology, frugality and governance. The quality of the founding team, the perseverance of the management team in building a sound business, using technology as a differentiator and a competitive advantage, being cost-effective and having sound corporate governance were, according to him, prerequisites that determined an entity's success and created multi-baggers.[15]

Sheth highlighted this point: 'We are not big on very, very detailed financial models. But we would make our projections, which are linked to our assumptions, no matter what companies would give. But at the end of the day, the decision was not made only on numbers. The qualitative factors are as important, if not more important, than the quantitative factors.'[16]

RJ considered IndiGo and DMart to be amongst the greatest Indian companies. DMart, founded by Radhakishan Damani, operates a chain of supermarkets and hypermarkets. IndiGo is India's largest airline by fleet size. Despite operating in vastly different industries, both companies share a similarity—they are cost leaders. Rakesh Bhatia and Rahul Gangwal founded IndiGo as a low-cost airline in 2006. Three factors resulted in several airlines reporting losses and ultimately failing in India—a price-sensitive market, expensive aviation turbine fuel (ATF) and regulation that at times worked to the detriment of airlines. The duo demonstrated that it was possible for an airline to be consistently profitable in India by offering a no-frills, punctual service coupled with a 'sale and lease back' financing strategy. RJ pointed out that Bhatia and Gangwal did not divert the proceeds from selling IndiGo aircraft to lessors to their personal investment vehicles but invested them instead in their airline. This move demonstrated the founders' integrity and resulted in IndiGo's low indebtedness. RJ believed that IndiGo and DMart were the greatest and most frugal Indian companies in 2016, when both businesses had a consistent track record of profitability and low financial leverage.[17] It is no wonder that IndiGo and DMart share prices rose by 170% and 228% over the five years spanning July 2019 to 2024, outperforming Sensex, which appreciated by 101%.

Amit Goela, a partner at RaRe Enterprises, mentions that RJ invested in SpiceJet and IndiGo, but these investments were only moderately profitable and hence, sold.[18] Trendlyne data indicates RJ purchased 7.5 million SpiceJet shares sometime between 1 April and 1 July 2018, upped his stake to 10 million in the quarter ended 30 June 2019, and sold his entire stake in the quarter ended 31 December 2019. Trendlyne, which reports the listed equity holdings of at least 1% of investors on a quarterly basis since 31 December 2015, does not capture RJ's investment in IndiGo, which listed on 10 November 2015.

The Boss

Considerable information is available in the public domain about RJ's listed equity holdings and certain private equity investments. But how did RJ assemble his team? How did they collaborate?

Utpal Sheth reveals, 'RaRe Enterprises is a partnership firm that was formed much before I joined. Rakeshji was a one-man army assisted by a back office. I was the first professional to join RaRe Enterprises on the investing side. I joined in 2003. We built an investment team of ten. To date, we remain a team of ten people. Mr Amit Goela is another early member of the team. My sister, Ushma, is also with RaRe Enterprises. She joined in 2008.'

Goela met RJ in 1994 when he was living in Kolkata. The two men met at the wedding of a common friend, Amitabh Sonthalia. Goela recollected, 'We hit it off instantly and met when either Rakeshji visited Calcutta or I travelled to Mumbai. I was working at ITC Classic Finance and had nothing to do with broking. I had a little bit of interest in the markets but not at the level Rakeshji was operating. I moved to Bombay in 1996. I was a merchant banker those days and helped him in securing a couple of company introductions. I also arranged a few management meetings for him.

'In 1997, I started working for Alchemy. It was then a brokerage firm Rakeshji founded in partnership with Hiren Ved, Lashit Sanghvi and Ashwin Kedia. It subsequently evolved into a portfolio management firm, Alchemy Capital. I used to help RJ with research when I was at Alchemy. I joined RaRe Enterprises in 2007.'[19]

RJ recruited Rajiv Agarwal, an alumnus of Benares Hindu University, in 2006. Rajiv recalled, 'My grandfather and Rakeshji were friends. So, the two of us had heard of each other. In the early 2000s, the private equity (PE) investments made by RaRe Enterprises turned out to be duds. I was working at Accenture then. Rakeshji invited me to join RaRe Enterprises, specifically to oversee its PE business.'[20]

RJ's nephew, Vishal Gupta, is yet another member of the RaRe Enterprises investment team. Gupta recounted, 'Though I grew up in Hyderabad, I spent a lot of time with Mama (RJ) in Mumbai during my holidays. I'd sit with him in the office and learn about investing. I found it interesting but I wanted to be a lawyer. In fact, after finishing college, I arrived in Mumbai to study at Government Law College. But the day before I was to pay my fees, he took me to Geoffrey's and, over a three-hour conversation, changed my mind about law and convinced me to become a chartered accountant. That conversation changed my life, and made Mama an integral part of my professional as well as personal life. Once I was done with my accountancy, I came back to Mumbai and started working with Rare. He asked me to submit my CA certificate to Utpalbhai, and I started in the back office, next to the toilets. "Don't think you will get special privileges as the boss' nephew," he said. He yelled at me a lot those first few years, both at work and at home. This made things challenging for me. I hero-worshipped Mama, given his story and the fact that he had made it without a godfather or government access, things they say you can't do without. Besides, I'd been top of the class all my student life. I had cleared my chartered accountancy on my first try, and worked at EY. So, it was tough for me to accept that the uncle I loved and admired treated me like an idiot. My parents tried to reassure me, saying he praised me to them. But he never did it to my face, till the end. I lived and worked with him for three-and-a-half years. It was intense, and the breadth of work we did was amazing. When I went away to do my MBA, he hugged me with tears in his eyes and said, "Promise me you will come back to work with me." I promised, and I did return, just one week before we admitted him to the hospital.'[21]

RJ's recruitment and investment processes share a striking similarity. He invested in and bet on people. He looked beyond the CV and track record, and had an understanding of the humans he recruited. This resulted in the creation of a very loyal team that steered RaRe Enterprises through several business cycles.

Yet another distinguishing feature about his team was that unlike other institutional investors, the members of RaRe Enterprises' investment team did not track specific industries like financials, telecom, media and technology, infrastructure, etc. They are generalists. The investment team members are conversant in tracking and investing in multiple industries. But they do focus on one of the two verticals—listed equities and PE. Agarwal mostly worked on PE deals, while listed equities were Goela's mainstay. Ushma worked on listed equities too, though the PE investment in Baazar Style Retail was her brainchild. Sheth and Gupta straddled both verticals. Gupta quipped, 'I covered listed equities from 9 a.m. to 3.30 p.m. and PE from 4 p.m. onwards.'[22]

An investment team member at RaRe Enterprises began the day by tracking the news. Goela observed, 'We begin the day by keeping abreast of the occurrences in India and overseas and the impact of these events on our trading and investment portfolios. Pre-2000, whatever news we got was only from the newspapers. From around 1997, foreign institutional brokers started publishing research on Indian stocks, which started impacting share prices. We had to be aware of their buy, sell and hold recommendations. Bloomberg's entry in India marked another source of information. Post the global financial crisis (2007–2008), everyone started watching the global markets. In 1999–2000, people would watch CNBC and figure out what was happening in NASDAQ. Tech stocks were booming in India then. The first half of the day was devoted to tracking markets and companies.

'Then, we discuss specific stocks. Some days are busy but no major decisions were taken. The days when investment decisions are taken are hectic. On the days RaRe Enterprises traded aggressively, everyone was on red alert. Several people met Rakeshji during the course of the day. He would call us and say "Idar aa jaa" (come here) and include us in the meetings.'

Sheth recounted, 'There was never a dull moment working with Rakeshji. It was actually almost a 24x7 situation. He would call me in the middle of the night. Sometimes we would have meetings that would begin at 7 p.m. and go on till 2 a.m. There have been transactions that we have closed same day we first met the company. There have been deals that have dragged for more than a year. So, it was exhilarating. He empowered us a lot.

'It was difficult to match his pace. You would eventually see how he thought. You may not see it when he conceptualised an idea. Rakeshji would have very strong views about everything. If you disagreed, he would not like it. But he would listen, iterate that in his mind and then come back. He would not dismiss anything out of hand. He really cared. He was a man with a golden heart. He may lose his temper and use very colourful language with you; the next day he would say sorry. That was his greatness. He really valued relationships.'[23]

Stewardship

RaRe Enterprises was purely a financial investor in most of the companies it held stakes in. But RJ was also the chairman of Aptech and Hungama Media, and was on the board of directors of Viceroy Hotels, Concord Biotech, Provogue India and Geojit Financial Services, thereby sharing his expertise with these companies. Of these, Hungama and Provogue are unlisted entities as of 2024 and Aptech, Concord and Geojit are listed firms in which RaRe Enterprises holds stakes. RJ owned a 13.35% stake in Viceroy Hotels in 2012; he sold the stock in the quarter ended 31 March 2018.

RJ did not restrict himself to reading the board papers prepared by companies and sharing his views with the senior management of investees. He and his team at RaRe Enterprises did a deep dive analysis of entities and shared their findings and recommendation with the management. For example, in 2012, RJ deputed two analysts to visit Titan's headquarters in Bangalore. The duo interacted with the watch and jewellery maker's senior management for two days and returned to Mumbai excited. When they shared the deck on Titan's prospects with RJ, the optimist quipped, '*Peeta mein hoon, chadti tere ko hai* (I drink and you get high).' Titan proved both the analysts and RJ wrong by outperforming the projections in five years.

One of the two analysts was Utpal Sheth, whom RJ first met in 1997 while the two men were waiting at the ASK Financials office to meet its founder, Asit Kotecha. Sheth heard RJ discussing liquor stocks and interjected with the advice of remaining invested. Sheth opined that the valuation of liquor stocks was cheap and that they were poised for long-term growth and sustained profits. RJ acquiesced and also recruited the 1971-born Sheth, who was then working at Enam Financial's investment banking division, to work at RaRe Enterprises. Sheth would become CEO of Rare Enterprises. [24]

Bhaskar Bhat, Titan's former managing director, revealed the impact of these presentations on the management, 'Rakesh helped the Titan management. He would come, do a two-day deep dive and inspire the management. When someone talks like this to the management, you don't need ESOPs (employee stock option plans).'

Metro Brands chairman Rafique Malik, Escorts Kubota's CMD Nikhil Nanda and Kotak Mahindra Bank's founder Uday Kotak echo this sentiment. Malik acknowledged, 'He encouraged and counselled to use every crisis as an opportunity.' RJ invested in Metro when it was still an unlisted entity in 2002 and did not sell his stake during its 2021 IPO. The footwear brand accounted for close to 7% of RaRe Enterprises' listed equities market value as of June 2024. Despite not being a shareholder in Kotak Mahindra Bank, RJ had a one-hour session with the bank's board at the behest of his friend, Uday Kotak, to 'infuse optimism'.[25]

RJ's sense of fiduciary responsibility was not restricted to India Inc; he was a philanthropist like his role model, the Tata group. 'I treat charity as my fourth child and will divide my wealth equally among all my children,' promised the stock magnate, who pledged to donate a quarter of his wealth to the causes he supported. RJ was a trustee of Agastya International Foundation, a nonprofit that attempts to bring education to India's underdeveloped regions.[26] Non-government organisations RJ assisted included Friends of Tribal Society and IIMPact—an outfit that educates 60,000 girls living in villages. RJ's support to the Healthcare Technology Innovation Centre at IIT Madras enabled fifty research scholars to pursue MS and PhD programmes. SEARCH (Society for Education, Action and Research in Community Health) was able to provide healthcare to 40,000 tribal and rural people living in Gadchiroli, a less developed district in Maharashtra. RJ collaborated with Dr R.V. Ramani of Sankara Eye Foundation to build a hundred-bed, super-specialty eye hospital in Panvel, Maharashtra. The hospital works on an 80-20 model, with 20% of the patients paying for the treatment of the other 80%.[27] Ashoka University, in recognition of the significant support received over the years, launched the Rakesh Jhunjhunwala School of Economics and Finance in February 2023.[28] The EdelGive Hurun India Philanthropy List 2021 designated RJ 'the most generous new entrant'; he had donated ₹50 crore to charitable causes that year.[29]

The Buffett Benchmark

RJ's meteoric rise and success in investing in multi-baggers resulted in him being christened 'India's Warren Buffett'. During an interview with Reuters, RJ observed, 'It's not a fitting comparison … In terms of wealth and success and maturity, he's far, far ahead. I'm Rakesh Jhunjhunwala. I've lived the world on my own terms. I do what I enjoy. I enjoy what I do.'[30]

Forbes values the 1930-born Warren Buffett's net worth as of July 2024 at $128.30 billion, which is twenty-two times RJ's net worth at the time of his demise.[31] The comparison is not appropriate for two reasons. First, RJ broke into the ranks of the global wealthy and became a billionaire in dollar terms while focusing on entities operating in India, whose currency has always been weak vis-à-vis the dollar. Second, RJ's investment career spanned thirty-seven years (1985–2022). Buffett created an eponymous partnership, which acquired Berkshire Hathaway (BH) in 1956. BH was then a textile company and subsequently evolved into his flagship investment vehicle. As of 2024, Buffett's has spent sixty-eight years in investing through BH and is still going strong. 'Compounding is the eighth wonder of the world. He who understands it, earns it. He who doesn't, pays it' is a quote often attributed to Albert Einstein. The longer the holding period of sound investments, the greater will be the wealth accumulation. Compounding has clearly worked in Buffett's favour.

The two experts do share similarities, however. First, RJ and Buffett are renowned for picking stocks with tremendous upside potential.

Second, their equity investments are the most transparent but not the sole constituent of their businesses. BH's equity investments accounted for a third of its $1.07 trillion assets as of 31 December 2023. Insurance constitutes 43% of BH's assets. Railroad, utilities and energy account for the balance 24%.[32] In short, Buffett's investment vehicle BH is a conglomerate. RJ not only invested in stocks but also traded in them, and was a private equity investor. He generated capital for investing through trading.

Third, while both of them invested in the stocks of several entities, their ten largest holdings accounted for a bulk of their listed equities portfolio. BH's and RaRe Enterprises' listed equities portfolio as of 30 June 2024 are in Appendices 1 and 2, respectively. There have been few significant changes in RaRe Enterprises' listed equities portfolio between the time of RJ's demise and 30 June 2024. Hence, this comparison is apposite. BH's listed equities portfolio consisted of thirty-nine stocks, of which the ten largest holding accounted for 92% of the market value. RaRe Enterprises' listed equities portfolio comprised twenty-six stocks with the ten largest holdings contributing to 83% of the market value. BH's largest holding, Apple, accounted for close to 47% of the listed equities market value. RaRe Enterprises' holding in Titan was 38% of the market value of its listed equities.

Fourth, financial services stocks comprising shares issued by banks, insurers and non-banking finance companies (NBFCs) accounted for 29% of BH's listed equities and 20% of RaRe Enterprises'. With the listing of Star Health and Allied Insurance in December 2021, financial service stocks accounted for 30% of RaRe Enterprises' listed equities. Star Health's share price has been declining since listing, resulting in a decline in the share of financial service stocks in the RaRe Enterprises portfolio to 18% by June 2024. I believe the significant exposure to financial services stocks is by design. The performance of financial institutions (FIs) is closely correlated with that of the economy. If these FIs are multinationals, then their performance is correlated to that of the countries in which they operate. By holding stakes in US-centric (Capital One and Nu Holdings) and multinational (Bank of America, Citigroup, Chubb, Mastercard, Visa, Moody's) FIs, Buffett is benefitting from the global macroeconomy. India's improving banking and insurance penetration underpins the growth prospects of its financial services industry. This in turn is likely to result in a significant appreciation of RJ's investments in financial services stocks.

Fifth, Buffett and RJ were at the right place at the right time. Buffett admits, 'You don't know whether you're going to be born black or white. You don't know whether you're going to be born male or female. You don't know whether you're going to be born infirm or able-bodied. You don't know whether you're going to be born in the United States or Afghanistan.' The ovarian lottery is 'the most important event in which you'll ever participate … It's going to determine way more than what school you go to, how hard you work, all kinds of things … The womb from which you emerge determines your fate to an enormous degree for most of the seven billion people in the world … Just in my own case: I was born in 1930, I had two sisters that have every bit the intelligence that I had, have every bit the drive, but they didn't have the same opportunities ... if I had been a female, my life would have been entirely different.'[33]

RJ too was born with several advantages. He was born in a community that encouraged entrepreneurship and is legendary for its business acumen, the Marwaris. His father's interest in equity investing exposed him early to stock markets. Living in Mumbai enabled the young RJ to visit Dalal Street with the comfort of returning home every day and thus master the tangible and soft skills required to become a suave investor. He began his career in 1985, six years before the Indian economy was liberalised in 1991, and thus had the opportunity to participate in an extraordinary bull run. Sensex, which was trading at around 270 at the dawn of 1985, skyrocketed by 21,899% to 59,537 at the time of RJ's demise in August 2022. Yet another stroke of luck was that India's long-term capital gains tax (LTCG) was zero from 2000 to 2017, an eighteen-year period that coincided with half of RJ's thirty-seven-year investment career. This meant investors did not have to pay LTCG on stocks they owned for at least a year. The reinvestment of profits earned from the sale of stocks RJ owned for at least a year enabled him to grow his investment portfolio exponentially. India raised its LTCG tax to 10% in 2018. Most importantly, RJ never tired of acknowledging, 'I am born lucky ... best of parents, best of siblings, best of wife, best of friends ... what else can a man want?'[34]

7

The Legend, The Myth, The Man

RJ HELD HIS PARENTS IN HIGH REGARD. IN SEVERAL INTERVIEWS, he said that it was he who lived with them, and not the other way around. His appreciation of his mother's cooking was evident when he quipped, 'Though Rekha has observed my mother for years, she cannot replicate my mother's dal. Trading and cooking cannot be taught; they have to be learnt.' RJ was mostly vegetarian and preferred spicy, home-cooked food. He liked Chinese and Italian cuisine too. Balki, who shared RJ's dabba at his office, states that the investor was not a big eater. Geoffrey's at Mumbai's Nariman Point was his favourite watering hole. RJ's fondness for whisky and cigarettes proved to be his undoing.

The intimacy RJ and his brother Rajesh shared was evident with the latter supplementing his pocket money and also helping him raise capital to invest. RJ observed, 'I have a very special relationship with my elder sister Sudha and her in-laws. I lived in their house. Ashokji [Sudha's husband] is a very, very close friend of mine. He helped me during my tough times, which I will never forget.' Ashok Gupta revealed that RJ 'argued a lot with his father and brother. ... [They] agreed to disagree.'

Rekha and RJ's daughter, Nishtha, was born in June 2004 and their twin sons, Aryaman and Aryavir, in March 2009. Balki observes that the siblings are grounded, which reflects Rekha's upbringing.[1]

Vishal Gupta quipped, 'Every evening, he would pull out a transparent Hello Kitty pouch containing pencils, erasers and sharpener from his Montblanc bag. He'd sharpen the pencils carefully before turning to her books. When I questioned the use of the Hello Kitty pouch, he'd snap, "I like it. Don't touch it!"'

Nishtha confessed, 'No matter how horrible my grades were or how unhealthy my food was, my dad only cared about my happiness. He said, "As long as you're happy, you can do anything." There was a day when my dad tried to teach me mathematics. Let's just say, I will always struggle with this subject because my dad always did the calculations for me in his head and on the calculator. Even though we didn't have the same opinion on my career choice and I was quite clueless about my future, my dad was always unbelievably supportive. I loved the arts and he was a stock market genius. Complete opposites, but this difference never interfered with his unconditional love and support for me. My dad was, is and always will be my rock. He will stay with me and support me, wherever I am and whatever I am doing.'[2] As of 2025, Nisha is pursuing an undergraduate degree in media and communications at Regent's College, London. Aryaman and Aryavir are enrolled in the International Baccalaureate programme at Hillspring International School at Tardeo, Mumbai.[3]

The Jhunjhunwala family moved their residence to the upscale Il Palazzo at Little Gibbs Road, Malabar Hill, Mumbai. *Moneycontrol* reported that an apartment in Il Palazzo, where RPG group chairman Harsh Goenka lives, was valued at ₹20 crore in March 2022. RJ wanted to upgrade to a standalone home for his family. He set his sights on Ridgeway Apartments, which was just 500 metres away from Il Palazzo and comprised twelve residential units that HSBC and Standard Chartered had bought to house their senior management. RJ spent ₹371 crore buying Ridgeway; he purchased six apartments each in 2013 and 2017 for ₹176 crore and ₹195 crore, respectively. He demolished the building and began building a 70,000 square foot home spread across fourteen storeys.[4] The fourth floor has a banquet hall; a spa and a gym are located on the eighth floor; a large family room and four spacious guest bedrooms are on the tenth floor; and the sea-facing terrace includes a gazebo, a six-seater dining table, a bar, outdoor seating areas and a lawn dotted with trees.[5] RJ used to call Balki from the construction site of his new home to show him the progress.[6] Sadly, he did not live to move into his new home.

The Human

RJ's fiftieth and sixtieth birthday bashes attracted extensive media coverage. For his fiftieth birthday in July 2010, he flew with family and friends in a chartered plane to Mauritius. Guests included Bhaskar Bhat, Kishore Biyani, Tina Ambani and cricketer Ajit Agarkar. Bhaskar Bhat insisted on buying tickets for himself and his wife in a commercial aircraft so that there was no conflict of interest. RJ grudgingly accepted the decision.[7] Exotic dancers greeted the guests at the airport and hotel. Rahat Fateh Ali Khan and Roop Kumar and Sunali Rathod performed for the guests. There were themed parties, including a casino night. The family put up a skit titled 'Pachas Ke Sholay' (Fiery Fifty). Champagne, malt and cigars were available in abundance. Rajesh flew the paanwala chacha (the uncle who made paan) to Mauritus to make the famous Breach Candy paan for the guests.[8]

Even COVID-19 couldn't dampen the irrepressible investor's sprits. He organised a grand online Godfather-themed bash.

Dressed up as Marlon Brando—tuxedo, rose et al.—he sent out invites that read, 'An offer you can't refuse. You have no choice. No choice at all, my friend. Capisce?' The guests also dressed up, danced and made commemorative speeches. Shankar Mahadevan and Kavita Krishnamurti performed live. So did a DJ set.[9]

RJ was outspoken and, by his own admission, short-tempered, both at home and outside. He admitted that he had lost his temper several times with Rekha, while she may have done so probably twice. Balki once told Rekha, 'You deserve a Bharat Ratna for putting up with Rakesh.'[10] Investor Madhusudan Kela, a self-confessed acolyte of RJ, disclosed, 'In the competitive world of stock markets, no one wants to share. We used to call him "Bhaiyya" [brother]. I am a beneficiary of Rakesh Jhunjhunwala's wisdom. He treated us like his brothers. Bhaiyya was unwell when my mother passed away. He was the first to come and last to go. When I protested, he shot back, "Is it possible that I do not come when your mother passes away?" He allotted Akasa Air shares to me saying, "This is going to be very big. Consider this my gift to you." He used to scold but he made his point and ensured we did it [what he asked us to do]. He would call later and apologise. People who were close to him never minded his anger.'

Balki agrees, 'People did not mind Rakesh's temper not because he was rich but because they knew he did not mean a lot of things he said. He would calm down in fifteen to twenty minutes.' Kela goes to the extent of saying, 'My life may be divided into two phases—before meeting Rakesh bhaiyya and after meeting him.'[11]

Nikunj Dalmia, managing editor of *ET Now*, describes RJ as 'the original folk hero of Indian stock markets'. Dalmia observed, 'He is an extraordinary human being. His word is his bond. When I was thinking of migrating from Delhi to Bombay, Rakesh Jhunjhunwala told me three things. Learn to take risks. Think big. You will always have a home in Bombay.'[12]

Integrity was an attribute RJ valued both in the entities he invested in and in people. RJ invested significantly in multiple

Tata Group companies, including Titan, Tata Motors, Tata Communications, Rallis and Indian Hotels. The share of Tata Group stocks in his core listed equities portfolio has ranged from 40% to 61% since December 2015. It was not just the earning potential of these stocks that attracted RJ. He asserted, 'Tatas are blessed by God. They are my role models in life.'

RJ's reaction to the uncharacteristically public ouster in 2016 of the Tata Group's chairman, Cyrus Mistry, reflected his loyalty to the conglomerate. Udayan Mukherjee, *Business Today*'s global business editor, observed that RJ was enraged when the Tatas and Mistry locked horns. 'So you know there was this Cyrus Mistry versus Ratan Tata—a spat going on at that point in its full bloom—and I walked in to find Rakesh talking about Cyrus and the kind of adjectives he was using ... He was so angry that if Cyrus had walked into that room, then I feared to think what may have happened. He was so angry,' Mukherjee quipped.[13]

The motto of RaRe Enterprises, 'Insight, Intellect, Integrity', echoes RJ's beliefs and overlaps with the group's core values: integrity, responsibility, excellence, pioneering, unity.[14]

The Department of Income Tax has raided RJ's premises at least a couple of times, and he and Rekha paid SEBI a combined ₹21.70 crore to settle charges of alleged insider trading of Aptech shares in July 2021. Bhaskar Bhat called RJ after a raid. RJ brushed aside Bhat's concerns, remarking, 'I'm a diamond in a sack of coals.' Sumit Agarwal, a lawyer and founder of Regstreet Law Advisors, represented RJ in the Aptech case. Agarwal reminisced, 'He never withheld his words or tone. I distinctly remember an anecdote when he and I were going to SEBI for a meeting. It was related to a matter where SEBI's way of looking at certain transactions was different than his. After debating with me for long and understanding the pros and cons of certain options, he suddenly said that the regulators are like your spouse. Right or wrong, you should always defer to them to keep harmony. Life is all about perspectives. Let's settle it and move on.'[15]

RJ often remarked, 'When you invest in a small company, you are backing an individual. I don't mind losing money when an individual fails. [It] Emotionally hits me if a person's character is not good.' He believed he had misjudged the quality and character of the entrepreneurs of the engineering, procurement and construction (EPC) firm A2Z Maintenance and Engineering Services (subsequently renamed as A2Z Infra Engineering Limited) and the medical packaging company, Bilcare. RJ confessed, 'I had blind faith in both the companies but I have learned from my mistakes.'[16]

Misplaced trust neither dented RJ's faith in humans nor slowed his lightning quick decision-making. Amit Goela revealed that he had decided to invest in Akasa Air within forty-eight hours.[17] Ramesh Damani elucidated RJ's thought process, 'He ran a large business from his briefcase and head. He had figured out most companies in India mentally. So, when an opportunity presents itself, he had already figured the company out and could act quickly.'[18] It took even less time, a few hours, for RJ to foray into film production.

Bollywood Beckons

Balki, who met RJ at the ICICI Bank event, returned to his day job at Lintas Lowe and films. Three months later, Balki was looking for backers to bankroll his spouse filmmaker Gauri Shinde's debut film and Sridevi's return to the silver screen—*English Vinglish*. Balki reached out to various producers and assured them that he would be fully accountable for *English Vinglish* as it was Shinde's first film as a director. Though the producers were enthused by the project, they wanted to make the film at half the budget. This was unfeasible as the film was being shot in the US. Even the production costs would not have been covered at half the budget, despite the couple offering to work pro bono.

One afternoon, as Balki's assistant was sorting his business cards, a friend visited him. The friend's attention was drawn to RJ's business card.

The friend asked Balki, 'How do you know Rakesh?'

'I don't know Rakesh,' the filmmaker replied.

When the friend held up RJ's business card, Balki recollected meeting him at the ICICI Bank event. It was as this juncture that his friend enlightened him to the fact that RJ was the rockstar of Indian capital markets.

Balki thought, 'He (RJ) seemed like a nice guy. I want this film to be made. Let me give him a call.'

When Balki called RJ and introduced himself, the latter suggested that they meet for a drink. The filmmaker replied that all he needed was some time to brief RJ about Shinde's film.

RJ shot back, 'Why don't you come now?'

Balki responded, 'I'm at Lintas. I'm in Express Towers.'

RJ quipped, 'Just look out of your window. I'm two buildings away.'

Balki reached RJ's office and gave him a one-liner about *English Vinglish*. RJ didn't seem to care and remarked, 'OK. Let's go. What is the budget?'

Balki shared the budget with RJ. Pat came the next question, 'What are the tranches in which the payments need to be made?' Balki provided the details and walked back to his office.

The making of *English Vinglish* in Balki's own words follows.

'I don't know how he managed it. When I returned to my office, I found a cheque signed by Rakesh to meet the first tranche of expenses waiting for me. We had not signed any papers. We had not formed a company. All that was done later for accounting purposes ... At every date I needed money, the funds were in before I asked for it. There were no questions asked. Rakesh also roped in R.K. Damani to finance *English Vinglish*.

'At one point of time, when we were shooting the dollar shot up (vis-à-vis the rupee) by 20–25%. I couldn't ask him for money.

So, I put in my own money and completed shooting. After the film got over, Rakesh asked me, "What is the budget of this film?" When I told him what transpired, Rakesh remonstrated, "You didn't take this much from me. Why did you put in your own money?" He cursed me.

'Though he did not earn much from the film, he recovered every penny. But he was so proud of the film and insisted, "Whatever you do henceforth, you do it with me."

Rakesh screened *English Vinglish* multiple times for his family and friends.'

RJ financed four of the five films Balki directed after *English Vinglish* was released: *Shamitabh* (released in February 2015), *Ki & Ka* (April 2016), *Chup!* (September 2022) and *Ghoomer*, which hit the screens a year after RJ's demise in August 2023. *Pad Man*, which was released in February 2018, was jointly produced by the leading man Akshay Kumar's wife Twinkle Khanna and Prerna Arora. R.K. Damani was RJ's co-financier for *Shamitabh* and *Ki & Ka*. Except for *Shamitabh*, which was made at a budget of ₹49 crore, all other films had budgets ranging from ₹20 to ₹30 crore. The recoveries from box office and other avenues exceeded the budgets for all films except *Shamitabh* and *Ghoomer*. RJ did not read the scripts of the five films he financed, nor did he ask Balki for accounts. As in the case of investing, RJ's success rate was high, with three of the five films recovering costs. However, the profits he made from film financing pale in comparison to his investment earnings. Producing films was a passion and not a vocation for RJ. In a July 2020 interview with *ET Now*, RJ declared, 'I made all films with Balki. I trust Balki.'[19]

As RJ's health deteriorated, he set up an overdraft facility to ensure Balki had adequate funds to make films. This is despite Balki informing RJ that he preferred not to produce his own films so that he could focus on the creative aspect. Balki's decision did not dampen RJ's ebullience; he suggested to Balki, 'Let's do something big! Let's form a studio.'

RJ, characteristically, felt a sense of kinship towards Balki. He insisted that Utpal Sheth manage the filmmaker's investments. Balki observes, 'It was a relationship without logic; an inexplicable friendship. We did not talk much, but it was a divine relationship. I was sad when he stopped drinking for health reasons. Nevertheless, watching me drink after he had quit made Rakesh happy. We share a wonderful relationship with Rekha and the kids. Even while investing he would focus on the people behind the venture. Lots of people find him unpleasant because he wears his heart on his sleeve. You can love him or hate him. You can never be indifferent to Rakesh. He was a sharp man. His mind worked faster than his speech and sometime words came out garbled.'[20]

The Seer

The rockstar investor's predilection for inherently risky ventures was evident in his choice of vocation and hobbies—share trading, investing, PE ventures, film financing and horse racing. Yes, RJ was interested in horse racing too. He owned a herd of seventeen horses, some of which he jointly purchased with Ashok Gupta and one with Berjis Desai, a lawyer and former managing director of J. Sagar Associates. These horses had interesting names like Mahatezi Nifty, and Always Bullish. The horse RJ bought with Desai was named Sensex; it did not perform too well at the races.[21] RJ's horses raced at the top locations in India and won many races.

'When his (RJ's) horse qualified for the Derby, he was very excited. We showed up at the grounds the evening before the race. That's when the placements are given and the odds are placed. Everybody around us was all la-di-da and there were the two of us, in our office clothes. But he didn't care about any of that. He was just there to enjoy himself. When he discovered that horse owners go and sit in the stables in the evening and chat, he got very excited. For one–two months, he went to the stables every day after work. But then the phase passed. However much he loved horse racing, Rakeshbhai would never stake too much on any race. He never forgot that his primary profession was the capital markets. He enjoyed the races, but he never got distracted by them,' Goela reminisced.[22]

Ramesh Damani too vouches for RJ's extraordinary focus. He recalled an incident when he, RJ and a few other friends were at their favourite watering hole, Geoffrey's. 'Rakesh stumbled. For the next five minutes, we tried to get him a chair to sit, water, towel, etc., and call a doctor. By the time we got him home, he was talking on his mobile to his broker ... Even when he travelled overseas and partied till late in the night, he was up in the morning.'[23]

But RJ was no gambler. That he had the requisite qualifications for share trading, investing and PE ventures was evident, as well as the fact that he was extremely skilled at these. In film financing and horse racing, he deployed the money he could do without. In several interactions with the media, RJ spoke eloquently about the rise of India. He unequivocally believed that the country's rise to become a superpower was inevitable given its abundant natural resources, skilled population, democracy and the independence of institutions, and the prevalence of the rule of the law. In fact, when they first met, RJ and R.K. Damani bonded over their optimism about India's growth prospects and the efficiency gains the country's capital markets would achieve. This was years before Dr Singh presented the epochal budget in 1991, when BSE was a traders' cabal and NSE was not even incorporated. R.K. Damani describes RJ as the man who 'saw the future of India'.[24]

It is these twin traits that differentiate the two other Big Bulls, Harshad Mehta and Ketan Parekh, from RJ. To RJ, wealth was a by-product of the vocation he was passionate about—investing. When a journalist from NDTV asked, 'What will you be if not an investor?' RJ replied, 'I cannot do anything but invest. Markets are my passion.' RJ confessed in that February 2019 interview, 'Wealth is not happiness. Wealth is comfort and independence. The quest to earn wealth has subsided.'[25]

The global financial crisis of 2007–2008 overshadowed a landmark occurrence. In 2008, forty-seven-year-old first-generation investor, RJ, debuted on the *Forbes* Billionaires List. He was ranked 1,062nd, with a reported net worth of $1 billion (₹4,350 crore). He was not the first Indian to feature on the list. The Birla family with a net worth of $2.1 billion, Lakshmi Mittal ($1.5 billion) and the then undivided Ambani family ($1.1 billion) had featured in *Forbes*' inaugural list of 1996.

RJ refused to recommend stocks during his interactions with the media. Not only is this practice illegal but there is also unlikely to be a 'one size fits all' stock. Shares that cater to investors seeking recurring income through dividends may be very different from equities that facilitate wealth accumulation through capital gains. But he waxed eloquent about the earning potential of listed Indian corporates and financial institutions and India's robust growth prospects. RJ never tired of emphasising the importance of integrity among investors and the impeccable corporate governance standards India Inc. must uphold.

In October 2021, RJ had made a presentation to Prime Minister Modi on the Indian economy and its prospects. Rekha accompanied him to New Delhi. He reportedly announced during the presentation, '*India ka time aa gaya*' (India's time has come) and that the country's economic fortunes were set to change beyond imagination. He predicted India's per capital income would exceed $6,000 by 2030.[26] The country's per capita income was $2,250 in 2021 and $2,485 in 2023.[27] RJ made mistakes which he divulged without hesitation. He acknowledged that he lost money in trading, investing and his PE ventures. The veteran investor underscored the importance of learning from mistakes and moving on. But the one mistake he made on a sustained basis and that he was unable to rectify was ignoring his health. Over the years, he had contracted chronic kidney affliction, diabetes and ischemic heart disease, which is a deficiency in the supply of blood to the heart.[28] His fondness for smoking and drinking complicated matters. The sixty-two-year-old spent much time in hospitals during the four to six months preceding his demise on 14 August 2022 at Breach Candy Hospital, Mumbai. Social media was inundated with pictures of a wheelchair-bound RJ launching Akasa Air a week before his demise on 7 August.

Amit Goela, Berjis Desai and Bhaskar Bhat were unanimous in their view that RJ ought to have taken better care of his health. Goela lamented that RJ 'ignored health out of hubris. He got all that he wanted—career, wealth, kids though late. Meeting (Narendra) Modi was the high point of his life. He felt his views were respected.' Ramesh Damani, who described RJ's career as an 'improbable journey through Dalal Street' reiterated, 'It was the first time in thirty years that someone in Dalal Street was recognised in New Delhi.'[29]

In 2008, Warren Buffett was ranked as the world's richest man with a $62 billion net worth. RJ's ascent was at least as impressive, if not more so, than that of his illustrious predecessor, Buffett, and other legendary investors, including George Soros, Jim Simons, Stanley Druckenmiller and Bill Ackman. The reasons are three-fold. First, his investment vehicle, RaRe Enterprises, is unlisted. The Buffett-helmed and listed Berkshire Hathaway (BH), for instance, raised a modest (by BH standards) $784 million through an issue of Class B shares in 1996. While listed entitles like BH and hedge funds helmed by the aforesaid rockstar investors raise money from institutional and high-net-worth investors to grow their assets, RJ reportedly did not. While RaRe Enterprises does borrow, it has not issued equity to third parties. Second, the above-mentioned investors employed hundreds of analysts and PhDs to conduct research and write algorithms; these formed the basis of their investments. RaRe Enterprises, on the other hand, employs less than fifty people comprising ten investment professionals and back-office staff. Third, despite investing almost entirely in India, where asset values tend to be lower than in developed economies like the US and UK, and the currency is weaker, RJ catapulted to the global big league.

Rakesh Jhunjhunwala had several nicknames—'Big Bull', 'Bhaiyya', 'Rocky' and 'RJ'. However, given his faith in and aspirations for his country of birth, I believe that the most apposite epithet for the legendary investor who emphasised wealth accumulation with honesty would be 'Mr India'.

Part 2

Listed Equities

8

Lies, Damned Lies and Statistics

VETERAN JOURNALIST DEBASHIS BASU, WHO CO-AUTHORED *The Scam* and *Absolute Power* with his wife and journalist Sucheta Dalal, observed that 'Rakesh Jhunjhunwala is known to have started his investing journey in 1985 with ₹5,000. He was worth ₹50,000 crore when he passed away two weeks ago. That is a compound annual return of 65% over 37 years. If these numbers are correct, Rakesh is one of the world's most successful investors. Just ahead of him is James Simons of Renaissance Technologies who wrapped up a return of 66% between 1988 and 2018, the year for which his last data is available. The returns of legendary investors like Warren Buffett, George Soros and Stanley Drucker-Miller ... are in the high-20s or low-30s. Many top investors barely manage 20% over a long period of time.'[1]

RJ had earned ₹5,000 by running a small business of crown caps before he embarked on a career as an investor. This ₹5,000 was RJ's seed capital as he began his investing journey.[2] His brother's clients lent him a not insignificant ₹7.55 lakh or $61,035 at the average 1985 exchange rate of ₹12.37 per US dollar, which is a considerable sum even in 2025. *Forbes* estimated RJ's net worth at the time of his demise in August 2022 to be $5.8 billion or ₹47,183 crore at the average 2022 exchange rate of ₹81.35 per dollar. The difference in exchange rates used to convert dollar to rupee could account for the difference between my estimate of ₹47,183 crore and Basu's ₹50,000 crore, or Basu may have rounded off RJ's net worth. There are several types of exchange rates, including bid rate, ask rate, mid-rate, and the averages of daily, weekly, monthly, calendar and financial years.

Forbes estimates billionaires' net worth as the sum of the market value of the listed equities and a variety of other assets, including private companies, real estate and art minus borrowings. The publication states, 'We don't pretend to know each billionaire's private balance sheet (though some provide it). When documentation isn't supplied or available, we discount fortunes.'[3]

RJ's wealth consisted of listed equities, unlisted or private equity investments, RaRe Enterprises' trading book, and some real estate. Utpal Sheth observed, 'Rakeshji was very versatile. He traded commodities, currencies and equities. Like the Chinese who eat anything that moves, he traded in anything that moved.'[4] Amit Goela observed, 'Rakeshji traded in all assets which were liquid and whose prices fluctuated.'[5]

The financial data provider, Trendlyne, reports on a quarterly basis billionaires' listed equity holdings (number of shares) in companies in which they hold at least a 1% stake. In other words, Trendlyne reporting does not cover the listed equity holdings of investors, should their stakes in companies be less than 1%. It reports this data for Indian investors from 31 December 2015 onwards. The data provider's estimate of the aggregate market value of RJ's (including his wife Rekha's) holdings in listed equities as of 30 June 2022, which is seven weeks before his demise on 22 August, was ₹30,752 crore.

Trendlyne also reports market values of the individual stocks for the most recent quarter. The market values of individual stocks since 31 December 2015 is not published. I calculated the aggregate value of RJ's holdings of listed equities as of 30 June 2022 using NSE's share price data as ₹30,752 crore, whereas Trendlyne's estimate is ₹25,398 crore. The difference between Trendlyne's and my estimates may be due to different share prices used to value RJ's holdings in listed equities. As in the case of exchange rates, there are different types of share prices, including daily opening price, closing price, bid price, ask price, and the average of share prices for the day, week, month, and year.

So, we now have two estimates each for RJ's net worth—₹47,183 crore and ₹50,000 crore—and listed equities' market value: ₹25,398 crore and ₹30,752 crore. This gives us four data points for the share of listed equities in RJ's net worth. As of 30 June 2022, this share is estimated to range from 51% (the ratio of ₹25,398 crore to ₹50,000 crore) to 64% (the ratio of ₹30,752 crore to ₹47,183 crore). RJ stated in an interview to NDTV in October 2016 that 97% his wealth was in equities; this included his investments in companies in which he held less than 1% stake and private equity investments.[6]

So why did I provide this data-intensive and mind-numbing explanation instead of just saying, 'Listed equities may have constituted at least half of RJ's net worth at the time of his demise'? The reasons are threefold. First, to acclimatise you, dear readers, to the rest of this chapter, which is in the same vein. Second, to impress upon you that in the chimerical world of finance, even numbers do not offer the comfort of accuracy. The third reason, a corollary to the second, is that data and number crunching are just two of the several inputs an investor ought to employ in decision-making. A non-exhaustive list of other inputs includes a sound understanding of the businesses an investor wishes to invest in, domestic and global capital markets, macroeconomy and politics, investors' sentiments, and intuition. These are the attributes that differentiate rockstar investors like RJ, Buffett and R.K. Damani from the chaff.

Given that listed equities are the single largest asset class in RaRe Enterprises' portfolio, understanding the stocks RJ invested in and their performance is essential to decoding his wealth creation strategy. Trendlyne also reports the 'net worth' of affluent Indian investors (whom the website labels as superstars) on a quarterly basis.

I calculated the market value of RaRe Enterprises' core equity portfolio (CEP)—investments in listed entities in which it had at least a 1% stake—using Trendlyne's reporting of number of shares and the quarter-end share prices for thirty-seven quarters spanning December 2015 and December 2024. My calculation of the aggregate market value of RaRe Enterprises' CEP ranged from 95% to 105% of Trendlyne's net worth for twenty-three of the thirty-seven quarters, with both estimates being equal for five quarters. Net worth is the difference between an individual's or a company's assets and liabilities. As my estimates are mostly in line with Trendlyne's, I suspect that Trendlyne defines net worth as the aggregate market value of listed equities. In other words, it has not deducted liabilities from the aggregate market value of listed equities.

There are two reasons for my computation of the market value of RaRe Enterprises' listed equities not being identical to Trendlyne's estimates. First, as explained earlier in this chapter, there are different types of share prices. Second, Trendlyne has not reported RJ's holdings in certain entities for one or more quarters. (Trendlyne did not respond to my emails and tweets requesting an explanation.) I have made certain assumptions regarding RJ's shareholdings in the quarters for which Trendlyne has not reported the data. The data gaps and my assumptions are delineated in Appendix 5. RJ's quarterly holdings in listed equities and 'net worth' as reported by Trendlyne and my estimates of their market value and dividend income are also in Appendix 5.

Of the thirty-seven quarters of RaRe Enterprises' shareholdings reported by Trendlyne—31 December 2015 to 31 December 2024—RJ actively managed the portfolio for twenty-seven complete quarters, or 6.75 years, spanning 1 October 2015 and 30 June 2022 (referred to as reference period in this chapter). During this period, RJ oversaw a total of fifty-nine stocks, of which it is not possible to estimate the return of one stock—Adinath Exim Resources. This is because RJ owned Adinath for just one quarter since Trendlyne started reporting his portfolio composition; the stock was sold during the quarter ended 31 March 2016. I was unable to ascertain when, and at what cost, RJ purchased Adinath.

Dear reader, a final note before we dive in—please remember that when I mention Titan accounted for 36% of RaRe Enterprises' core equity portfolio or CEP, the actual share of Titan in the company's entire listed equities portfolio is lower. This is because the list of entities in which RJ's stake was/is less than 1% is not available in the public domain.

Battles and Wars

The market value of RaRe Enterprises' CEP quadrupled from ₹7,742 crore on 31 December 2015 to ₹30,752 crore on 30 June 2022 at a CAGR of 24%. But this meteoric rise in market value has neither been unidirectional nor smooth. The market value of RJ's CEP dipped in eight of the thirty-seven-quarter reference period. The maximum and minimum quarterly depreciation were 28.26% (which occurred in the quarter ended March 2020) and 2.59% (December 2016) and the average quarterly drop in portfolio value was 10.7%. The maximum and minimum appreciation in the eighteen profitable quarters were 1.61% (September 2016) and 45.37% (December 2021), with an average quarterly gain of 14.15%.

However, these statistics are misleading, as RaRe Enterprises' CEP comprises the plain vanilla stocks and the investments

RJ had made in unlisted entities that were subsequently listed through IPOs, also known as private equity (PE) investments. Six PE investments made by RJ listed through IPOs since 1 January 2021. Three PE investments listed in 2021—Metro Brands, Nazara Technologies, and Star Health and Allied Insurance. The fourth PE investment, Concord Biotech, listed a year after RJ's demise in August 2023. Baazar Style Retail and Inventurus Knowledge Solutions listed in 2024. These PE investments have to be excluded from the growth in CEP's market value as their purchase is not accounted for. The performance of RJ's PE investments is narrated in two chapters: 'Jackpot!' and 'Janus Stock'.

If the PE investments are deducted from RJ's CEP, the portfolio's market value growth during the reference period moderates to a still impressive 275% at a 16% CAGR. The number of quarters in which the portfolio value appreciated and depreciated remained unchanged at eight and eighteen, respectively. The average quarterly depreciation inched up to 11.18% when PE investments are excluded vis-à-vis 10.70% for the CEP. The average portfolio appreciation during the eighteen profitable quarters was 11.65%, which is markedly lower than the 14.15% delivered by RJ's CEP.

Nevertheless, RaRe Enterprises' eighteen profitable quarters during the reference period were more than double its eight loss-making quarters. Even after excluding the listing of PE investments, the 11.65% average gain in the eighteen profitable quarters was higher than the 11.18% loss in the eight loss-making quarters. Sceptics may point out that the 11.65% average return for the profitable quarters was an unimpressive 47 basis points (one basis point is 0.01% or one-hundredth of a percentage point) higher than the 11.18% average portfolio depreciation during the loss-making quarters. However, the 209.7% aggregate return (11.65% multiplied by eighteen quarters) of the profitable quarters is more than double the 89.44% aggregate loss (product of 11.18% and eight quarters).

These statistics underscore a statement RJ used to often repeat, 'One must lose several battles to win a war.' What he meant was that volatility is an inalienable characteristic of stock markets; hence, enduring periods of portfolio depreciation is essential for long-term wealth accumulation. RJ also implied that investors ought to remain invested long enough to earn meaningful returns.

Deducting the six PE investments and Adinath Resources from the sixty-one stocks in RaRe Enterprises' CEP narrows the firm's exposure to fifty-four stocks during the period spanning 31 December 2015 and 30 June 2022. The term 'exposure' denotes that RJ was invested in fifty-four stocks for the whole, or part of, the reference period.

RJ had purchased seventeen of the twenty-nine stocks he remained invested in as of 30 June 2022 on or before 31 December 2015, translating to a holding period of at least six-and-a-half years for close to 59% of the number of stocks. These stocks more than trebled in value from ₹4,802 crore on 31 December 2015 to ₹14,910 crore on 30 June 2022 (Table 8.1). The share of these seventeen stocks in the market value of RaRe Enterprises' CEP net of PE investments rose from 62% on 31 December 2015 to 73% on 30 June 2022. If the PE investments are included, the share of the seventeen stocks in the market value of RaRe Enterprises' CEP moderates to 48% as of 30 June 2022.

This holding period and return data offers important insights for investors. Prudent stock selection coupled with long holding periods in excess of five years are likely to result in handsome returns. Just as a rolling stone gathers no moss, frequent stock churns may not accumulate wealth.

RaRe Enterprises' holdings of listed equities fluctuated quarter on quarter. This is because 'quite incredibly, he (RJ) held a trading book and investment book for the same stock and built a Chinese wall between the two'.[7] RJ's ability to trade and invest in the same stock may have resulted in RaRe Enterprises booking profits even on stocks whose prices declined. Passive investors, who cloned

RaRe Enterprises' CEP but did not replicate RJ's trades, would have earned lower returns.

Triple L Portfolio

Table 8.1 not only highlights the robust return of RJ's CEP but also the contribution of its single largest constituent, the watch and jewellery maker from Tata group's stable, Titan Company Limited. The share of Titan in the market value of RaRe Enterprises' CEP rose from 36% on 31 December 2015 to a peak of 58.6% on 30 September 2019, then gradually moderated to 34.3% on 30 June 2022. The decline in the share of Titan in RaRe Enterprises' CEP occurred both on account of share sales and the listing of RJ's erstwhile PE investment, Star Health, that resulted in a 45% spike in market value in the December 2021 quarter. Data supports the admiration RJ professed for the Tata group in numerous forums. The share of Tata group stocks—Titan, Tata Motors, Indian Hotels, Rallis India and Tata Communications—rose from 46% on 31 December 2015 to a peak of 61% on 30 September 2019, before declining to 44.5% on 30 June 2022. Conspicuous by its absence in RaRe Enterprises' CEP was the jewel in Tata group's crown, Tata Consultancy Services, and other technology stocks.

Star Health and Allied Insurance, which became a constituent of RJ's listed equities' portfolio after its IPO, accounted for 22.7% of his CEP in December 2021 and 24.5% by 30 June 2022. RJ's holding in credit rating agency, CRISIL, which is a subsidiary of S&P (Standard & Poor's), was 9.5% of his CEP on 31 December 2015, though it progressively declined to 4.1% to 30 June 2022. The market value of RJ's investments in bank stocks rose from less than 1% of his CEP to close to 6% during the reference period.

Several professional investors, including RJ, manage lumpy portfolios, which are portfolios where a few stocks account for a large proportion of market value. The Bill Ackman-helmed

Table 8.1: The 17 Mainstays of RJ's Core Equity Portfolio (CEP)

	31 December 2015			**30 June 2022**		
	Shares (Million)	***Price (₹)***	***MV (₹ Crore)***	***Shares (Million)***	***Price (₹)***	***MV (₹ Crore)***
Agro Tech Foods Ltd	1.88	486.80	91	2.00	788.35	158
Anant Raj Ltd	9.50	15.94	15	10.00	113.75	114
Aptech Ltd	16.81	44.82	75	18.11	172.93	313
Autoline Industries Ltd	1.25	46.75	6	1.75	75.75	13
Bilcare Ltd	2.00	60.00	12	2.00	63.05	13
CRISIL Ltd	4.00	1,839.20	736	4.00	3,127.35	1,251
Valor Estate (formerly D B Realty Ltd.)	5.00	50.65	25	5.00	63.35	32
Edelweiss Financial Services Ltd	10.00	28.16	28	15.13	31.46	48
Escorts Kubota Ltd	12.48	135.15	169	1.83	1,733.00	317
Fortis Healthcare Ltd	5.00	178.50	89	31.95	278.45	890
Geojit Financial Services Ltd	22.54	37.10	84	18.04	50.50	91
Karur Vysya Bank Ltd	4.24	75.93	32	35.98	58.75	211
Man Infraconstruction Ltd	3.00	23.73	7	4.50	85.05	38
NCC Ltd	45.23	64.40	291	78.33	58.60	459

	31 December 2015			30 June 2022		
	Shares (Million)	*Price (₹)*	*MV (₹ Crore)*	*Shares (Million)*	*Price (₹)*	*MV (₹ Crore)*
Prozone Realty Ltd.	3.15	29.05	9	3.15	24.85	8
Rallis India Ltd	20.01	165.20	330	19.07	212.50	405
Titan Co Ltd	77.02	363.70	2,801	44.85	2,352.05	10,549
Total			**4,802**			**14,910**

Note: MV - Market value
Source: Trendlyne & Bloomberg

Pershing Square Capital Management's $16.7 billion assets are invested in just twelve stocks.[8] Professional investors like RJ and Ackman are better equipped to manage lumpy portfolios as they have the requisite skills, knowledge and network. Besides, investing is their day job.

However, the concentration risk arising from lumpy portfolios adversely impacts retail investors, who usually have a day job and little time to monitor their portfolios in at least three ways. First, should the share prices of the entities in which investors have disproportionately large holdings decline steeply, the portfolio value would depreciate. Second, which is relevant for investors who borrow against shares, is that they would face margin calls. Investors may be contractually obliged to replenish their margin accounts with additional securities and cash at a time they are strapped for liquidity. Third, should dividend payouts decline, investors would have lower income to meet their living expenses and to invest in other securities or businesses.

The second aspect of RaRe Enterprises' CEP is its low dividend yield (dividends expressed as a percentage of the market value of shares). Though dividends from the CEP more than trebled from an estimated ₹55 crore in 2016 to ₹174 crore in 2022, the dividend yield has been consistently and significantly lower than 1%. In fact, the dividend yield of RJ's CEP ranged from 41% to 61% of that of MSCI India, which itself is lower than those of the MSCI stock indices of developed and developing nations, including the US, Australia, China and Brazil. Hence, investors who need the recurring cash flows may choose to invest in high dividend-paying stocks like Titan and CRISIL, but cloning his portfolio will not serve their purpose.

Two factors explain the low dividend yield of RJ's CEP. First, the dividend yield was not a metric RJ focused on during the stock selection process. Twenty-two of the fifty-four stocks RJ had an exposure to during the reference period paid no dividends. Second, dividend yield became a casualty to the skyrocketing

Table 8.2: Listed Equities' Dividend Yields Underperform the Indexes

	2016	**2017**	**2018**	**2019**	**2020**	**2021**	**2022**
Dividend Receipts (₹ Crore)	55.32	70.63	78.09	95.03	76.31	140.07	174.23
Dividend Yield							
Listed Equities	0.61%	0.62%	0.64%	0.76%	0.66%	0.60%	0.54%
Listed Equities excl PE						0.68%	0.74%
MSCI India	1.47%	1.30%	1.51%	1.26%	1.09%	1.00%	1.18%

Source: Author calculations, Trendlyne & https://en.macromicro.me/collections/5738/msci-index-dividend-yield/48221/msci-dividend-yield

market value of RJ's CEP. The quadrupling of market value of CEP added an estimated ₹23,010 crore to RaRe Enterprises' portfolio between December 2015 and June 2022. This outstripped the trebling of dividends and depressed the dividend yield.

Sheth observed, 'Dividend was not a consideration for RaRe Enterprises while making an investment decision. Having made the decision, we would push our investee companies to improve their payouts. We think increasing dividend payout improved investees' valuation and inculcated better cash flow discipline. But more importantly, Rakeshji met his personal expenses, supported charitable causes and paid interest for the leverage on RaRe Enterprises' balance sheet with the dividend income.'[9]

A third characteristic of RJ's CEP was the dominance of large-cap stocks. These constituted at least three-fourths of RJ's CEP during most quarters between December 2015 and June 2022. The share of mid-cap stocks declined from 17% in December 2015 to 8% in June 2022, while the share of small caps ranged from 3% to 6%. The trading volumes of large-cap stocks tend to be high and they are typically more liquid that mid- and small-cap stocks, as in, they can be bought / sold or used as collateral to borrow more easily. According to Kotak Securities, the market cap of large-cap stocks exceeds ₹20,000 crore. Mid-cap stocks' market cap ranges from ₹5,000 to ₹20,000 crore, while that of small-cap stocks is lower than ₹5,000 crore.[10]

Mark Twain is supposed to have quipped, 'There are three kinds of lies: lies, damned lies and statistics.' Investors, in my view, ought to be most wary of statistics. A single metric like PE ratio or dividend yield seems to convince thousands, if not millions, of non-professional investors to buy securities whose risk–return profiles they barely understand. The data regarding the size of RJ's CEP and its impressive growth does not reveal its lumpy and low dividend-yielding but liquid nature. Nor does it disclose that the portfolio growth is not entirely organic. The listing of RJ's PE investments, particularly Star Health and Allied Insurance in December 2021, resulted in the portfolio's market value more than doubling that year. Similarly, the trebling of dividends belies the portfolio's low dividend yield. In investments, as in the case of politics and law, the devil can cite Scripture for his purpose.

This is not to suggest that investors eschew statistics in decision-making but use multiple metrics and incorporate global and national macroeconomic developments, industry- and company-specific events, views of the larger investor community, and their own expectations in decision-making. Past performance is no guarantee of future success. Investment is both an art and a science, and is more of a forward-looking exercise than a post-mortem. The following chapters demonstrate RJ's mastery over the quantitative and qualitative and the rational and irrational nature of investing, which propelled his meteoric rise.

9

Bombay House

IN JUNE 1920, THE BOMBAY MUNICIPALITY SOLD TWO PLOTS OF land on Homi Modi Street located in the city's Fort area. The buyer commissioned George Wittet—a reputed architect who also designed Gateway of India, the Prince of Wales Museum (now called Chhatrapati Shivaji Maharaj Vastu Sangrahalaya) and other iconic buildings—to conceptualise a building plan. The result was a four-storey structure with a distinctive Edwardian neoclassical façade. This building was renovated by architect and urban conservationist Brinda Somaya, of Somaya and Kalappa Consultants, who retained and refurbished the façade. In March 2014, it became the first heritage structure in India to get a gold rating as a green, environmentally friendly building, awarded by the Indian Green Building Council (IGBC), the domestic chapter of the US Green Building Council. The ground floor of the building, as of 2024, includes a shared space with an in-house coffee lounge, informal breakout places, a digital museum and a kennel for stray canines. The buyer of the plot was Sir Dorabji Tata, the second chairman of the eponymous group. The building is Bombay House, the headquarters of the Tata group.[1]

From inception, profits were not the sole motivator for the Tatas. In addition to kickstarting India's first steel plant and hydroelectric project, the group's founder, Jamsetji Nusserwanjee Tata, conceived of a university of science, 'the like of which England did not have at that time'—the Bengaluru-based Indian Institute of Science. Jamsetji set up a provident fund scheme for his employees, a first in India, as well as an accident compensation fund.[2] Yet the Tata group's rise to the very top of India Inc. has been far from smooth.

In 1907, when Sir Frederick Upcott, chief commissioner for railways in India, heard that the Tatas were going to set up a steel plant, he quipped, 'Do you mean to say that Tatas propose to make steel rails to British specifications? Why, I will undertake to eat every pound of steel rail they succeed in making.' In the next decade, the Tatas supplied the British government 2,414 kilometres of steel rails, which enabled India's erstwhile coloniser to transport troops and war materials in Mesopotamia. Sir Dorabji, Jamsetji's son, observed after the delivery of the aforesaid consignment, 'He [Upcott] would have had some slight indigestion.'[3]

In 1982, the Tatas were looking to foray into watch manufacturing. Before liberalisation, government policies stipulated that only PSUs and small-scale industries may engage in watch manufacturing. Minoo Mody, the then CEO of Tata Sons, the group's holding company, met the secretary of the Ministry of Commerce and Industry to put forth the Tatas' case. The secretary pre-empted a discussion by declaring, 'Take it from me, Mr Mody, the Tatas will never make watches.' The meeting lasted all of two minutes.[4] The next chapter, 'The Watch Project', narrates how the bosses at Bombay House surmounted this obstacle to create a market leader.

In 1998, Tata Motors launched India's first indigenously developed passenger car—Tata Indica. The response was lukewarm. So, in 1999, a team from Tata Motors led by Ratan Tata, who had succeeded his uncle J.R.D. Tata as the chairman of the Tata group, met officials of the Ford Motor Company in Detroit in a bid to sell their passenger car business. *Financial Express* reported, 'Ford apparently told Tata they would be "doing them a favour" by buying the car business. This incident didn't go down well with Ratan Tata and he called off the sale ...' Tata Motors then focused on turning around its passenger car business. Ford experienced severe financial stress amidst the 2007–2008 global financial crisis (GFC). One of its UK brands, Jaguar, reported $700 million losses during the GFC and had accumulated $10 billion losses during the nineteen-year period Ford owned it. Ford had paid $5.5 billion to purchase two British brands, Jaguar and Land Rover, between 1989 and 2000. In 2008, Tata Motors purchased both Jaguar and Land Rover for less than a third of the price Ford had paid—$1.7 billion.[5] In 2024, Tata Motors was the nineteenth-largest automobile company globally by revenue ($41.90 billion). Ford was the fifth-largest car manufacturer with $158.10 billion revenues.[6]

As of 2024, the Tata group continues to be India's largest conglomerate by a wide margin. The aggregate full float market cap of its at least twenty listed companies was ₹35.68 lakh crore or trillion as of end-August 2024, which is equivalent to 11.57% of India's GDP. The market cap of Reliance Industries (RIL) and Jio Financial Services combined is ₹22.48 trillion or 7.29% of the GDP. The market cap of Adani group's ten listed entities—Adani Enterprises, Adani Ports & Special Economic Zone, Adani Green Energy, Adani Power, Ambuja Cements, Adani Energy Solutions, Adani Total Gas, Adani Wilmar, ACC and NDTV—was ₹16.56 trillion or 5.37% of the GDP.

It is indeed interesting that RJ chose to invest in multiple Tata group companies, but there are no media reports of him investing in RIL and Adani. This is despite these stocks outperforming Sensex, which rose by 204% during the decade ending August

2024. The share prices of RIL and the Adani group's flagship entity—Adani Enterprises—appreciated by 540% and 4,598%, respectively, during this period. RJ did invest in ACC though at the beginning of his career, decades before Adani acquired the cement manufacturer in 2022.

What distinguishes the Tata group from RIL and Adani is their long track record, philanthropic trusts being the majority shareholders of the group's holding company, Tata Sons, and the conglomerate's core values—integrity, responsibility, excellence, pioneering and unity. The founding families of RIL and Adani continue to hold majority stakes in their listed entities. While dividends were not the primary consideration for RJ to invest, the dividend yields of RIL and Adani's listed entities are very low. As of 14 April 2024, the dividend yields of RIL and the flagship company of the Adani group, Adani Enterprises, were 0.41% and 0.06%, respectively.

The Tata group's holding company is Tata Sons, which holds 25% to 75% stakes in its listed companies valued at ₹18.91 trillion as of end-August 2024. The unlisted companies of the Tata group include Tata Capital, with assets of ₹1.77 trillion, Tata International (₹10,481 crore) and Tata Teleservices (₹4,810 crore). Philanthropic trusts that support education, health, livelihood generation and art and culture together hold a 66% stake in Tata Sons.

On a standalone basis, that is, excluding subsidiaries, notably Tata Consultancy Services, joint ventures and associates, Tata Sons is a large and immensely profitable entity. Its FY2024 PAT was ₹34,564 crore or a mouth-watering 79% of its ₹43,893 crore revenues. In September 2023, RBI had designated fifteen entities, including Tata Sons, as non-banking finance companies—upper layer (NBFC – UL).[7] The central bank mandated that the entities designated as NBFC – UL list within three years.[8] Tata Sons repaid close to ₹21,808 crore of its borrowing by 31 March 2024, leaving just ₹363 crore of non-convertible debentures and preference shares on its balance sheet. Following the debt reduction, Tata Sons was no longer obliged to list. That the holding company sold ₹21,907 crore investments within six months demonstrates its financial clout.[9] Tata Sons also paid its shareholders ₹707 crore dividends in FY2024 (FY2023: ₹404 crore), of which the various Tata trusts received an estimated ₹467 crore, enabling them to support various philanthropic causes. Tata Sons is a behemoth if the performance of its subsidiaries, joint ventures and associates were included. Its ₹49,001 crore consolidated PAT in FY2024 is just over 10% of its ₹4.77 trillion revenues.

During the period spanning 31 December 2015 and 30 June 2022 (that is, two months before his demise), the market value of RJ's investments in Tata group stocks rose from 45% of his CEP to a peak of 61% in September 2019 and moderated to 42% in June 2022. In rupee terms, RJ's holdings in Tata group stocks grew more than fourfold from ₹4,178 crore in end-December 2015 to ₹16,746 crore in June 2022.

RJ held more than 1% stakes in five Tata stocks between 31 December 2015 and 30 June 2022: Tata Communications, Rallis India, Indian Hotels, Tata Motors and Titan. While the next chapter discusses Titan in detail, we shall examine the others here.

Tata Communications

Prior to the opening up of India's telecom sector, two PSU-monopolies controlled India's telephony. Bharat Sanchar Nigam Limited (BSNL) and Videsh Sanchar Nigam Limited (VSNL) provided domestic and international telephony services, respectively. VSNL was also an internet service provider (ISP) and was an immensely profitable, zero-debt entity whose ₹1,779 crore PAT was a robust 22% of ₹7,966 crore revenues in FY2001. India's international telephony monopoly had accumulated ₹4,840 crore cash that exceeded its ₹3,481 crore liabilities.[10]

VSNL also owned 773.1-acre vacant lands in Pune, Kolkata, New Delhi and Chennai.[11] However, storm clouds were looming on the horizon.

In September 2000, the government announced that private players may offer international telephone services from April 2002 and decided to exit the sector. Competition implied that the profits of incumbents would come under pressure. Arun Shourie, India's union disinvestment minister from 1999 to 2004, remarked, 'VSNL is just a chungi [an octroi post] ... once you abolish the chungi and have free movement, it has no value.'[12] Despite being aware of the imminent weakening of VSNL's business and financial profiles, the Tatas bid for and were awarded the mandate to buy VSNL. The Tata group purchased a 25% stake in VSNL for ₹1,439 crore, while the government retained a 26% shareholding. In May 2002, the Tatas launched an open offer to purchase another 20% stake from the public at ₹202 per share. The public offer was oversubscribed by 20%, and the Tatas paid ₹1,151.40 crore to the selling shareholders. Thus, the Tata group had acquired a 46% stake in VSNL for about ₹2,590 crore. The government transferred VSNL's ₹2,250 crore cash to its coffers while selling a 25% stake to the Tatas. VSNL's vacant lands were transferred to another listed entity—Hemisphere Properties—in which the government continues to hold around 51% stake as of June 2024.

Competition and the slashing of tariffs resulted in VSNL's financial profile weakening. Competition had led to tariffs halving from ₹48 per minute to ₹24, which the rise in call volumes were inadequate to offset. VSNL's revenues and PAT had more than halved since FY2001 to ₹3,411 crore and ₹756 crore, respectively, in FY2005. VSNL was renamed Tata Communications Limited (TCL) in FY2008. The company altered its business model as well; it cut its reliance on the voice-tariff business and made a slew of acquisitions.

According to CRISIL, by 2024,

> TCL owns the world's largest submarine fibre network—more than 500,000 kilometre (km) of subsea fibre—and more than 210,000 km of terrestrial fibre. Over 70% of the world's telecommunication (telecom) companies use the networks of TCL to bring their mobile services to customers. Around 80% cloud giants are connected to their businesses through TCL and over 25% of the global internet routes are on the networks of the company. The operations of TCL are diversified across the data business, and include cloud, digital collaboration and security services, apart from the core connectivity services. TCL, being an integrated solutions provider and with its strategic shift to a platform-based service provider, is believed to have no direct end-to-end competitor in India or overseas. TCL has an established network, which still has unutilised data traffic carrying capacity, which will help the company face any competitive pressures as demand for the cables is expected to increase.[13]

RJ purchased slightly over 6.40 million shares of TCL during the quarter ended 31 December 2020, when the telecom company's share price ranged from ₹933 to ₹1,006. TCL's financial performance was then lacklustre; revenues had barely doubled since FY2001 to ₹17,138 crore in FY2020 and the company had reported a ₹85 crore loss.[14] Years of losses had eroded TCL's net worth, resulting in a heightened liabilities-to-net worth ratio of 147.43 times. TCL's performance improved with the company reporting in excess of ₹1,000 crore annual profits in FY2021 and FY2022, resulting in the liabilities-to-net worth ratio moderating to a still elevated 19.57 times by FY2022.[15] RJ pared his holding in TCL slightly to around 6.15 million shares by 30 June 2022. The market value of RJ's holding in TCL remained flat at around ₹643 crore between December 2020 and June 2022. TCL accounted for just 1% of RJ's CEP on 30 June 2022.

Rallis India

Another Tata group company that constituted 1.30% of RJ's CEP (market value: ₹515 crore) on 30 June 2022 was Rallis India. Rallis was one of the seventeen stocks that RJ had purchased before 31 December 2015 and remained invested in till his demise. Rallis, a Tata Chemicals subsidiary, is a pesticides and agrochemicals company. It has a strong presence in all three segments of the pesticide industry—insecticides, fungicides and herbicides—and also sells hybrid seeds, plant growth nutrients and organic compost. The company sells its products in India and overseas.

Rallis' financial profile is stable—it is a consistently profit-making company whose liabilities-to-net worth ratio has been moderate at below 0.70 times between FY2016 and FY2022. However, its revenue growth during this seven-year period is sluggish at a CAGR of 7%. Rallis' PAT margin of 6.24% in FY2022 was 271 basis points lower than the 8.96% in FY2016. Its share price appreciation has also been unimpressive: it rose from ₹165.20 in end-December 2015 to ₹212.50 in end-June 2022 at a CAGR of 3.95%. A fixed deposit in a bank would have generated a higher return. It is this mediocre share price performance that resulted in the share of Rallis stock in RJ's CEP declining from 3.60% in end-December 2015 to 1.30% in end-June 2022. The company has a consistent track record of paying dividends, though.

Indian Hotels

In 1899, Jamsetji Tata incorporated Indian Hotels Company Limited (IHCL), which inaugurated its first hotel, the Taj Mahal Palace, in Mumbai in 1903. Raosaheb Sitaram Khanderao Vaidya drew up Taj Mahal Palace's original plans. English architect W.A. Chambers enlarged the size of the hotel's central dome when he took over the hotel's construction after Raosaheb's demise.

According to *Vogue*, 'When it opened, the hotel boasted a series of firsts: American fans, German elevators, Turkish baths and English butlers. The building was also the first in Bombay to be lit by electricity. Eventually it also ended up having the city's first licensed bar, India's first all-day dining restaurant, and the country's first international discotheque, Blow Up.'[16] Taj Mahal Palace transformed the city's skyline and was dubbed the best hotel east of the Suez.[17] One-and-a-quarter century later, in 2024, IHCL is a multinational hospitality chain that employs over 40,000 people to operate 335 hotels in over 150 locations across twelve countries.

However, even such a seasoned hotel chain is not immune to black swan events. When COVID-19 struck, IHCL's revenues crashed by 62% from ₹4,596 crore in FY2020 to ₹1,740 crore in FY2021. The company reported ₹796 crore losses in FY2021 vis-à-vis ₹364 crore PAT the previous year. RJ purchased 12.50 million shares of IHCL in the quarter ended June 2020 when its share price ranged from ₹74 to ₹78, which is half its peak share price in 2020, ₹151. IHCL was trading at ₹272 on 12 August 2022—two days before his demise on Sunday, 14 August.

Hotel chains have high fixed costs even when the occupancy rates of their rooms decline and restaurants don't operate. Hence, IHCL raised ₹1,982 crore in November 2021 through a 1:9 rights issue that is, shareholders were given the right to purchase one share for every nine shares they owned at ₹150 per share.[18] To ensure that the rights issue was fully subscribed to, IHCL priced its shares within the range at which they traded between 1 January and 15 November 2021—₹93.75 to ₹237.40. RJ's holding more than trebled to 37.5 million shares in the quarter ended 31 December 2021; he is likely to have subscribed to the rights issue and purchased more shares from the market. The rights issue was followed by a second round of equity issuance to institutions through a ₹2,000-crore qualified institutional placement (QIP) in March 2022, which was also fully subscribed. IHCL issued shares at a price of ₹201 per share during the QIP.[19] The QIP was priced within the range at which the IHCL stock traded in between 1 July 2021 and 15 March 2022—₹133.05–237.40.

IHCL used the equity raised to repay borrowing, and finance capital expenditure and operating expenses. The lifting of COVID-19 related restrictions resulted in the resumption of travel and occupancy rates in hotels improving. IHCL's revenues rose to ₹3,211 crore in FY2022, while losses moderated to ₹265 crore in FY2022. By FY2023, revenues and profits exceeded pre-COVID-19 levels. IHCL's liabilities-to-net worth ratio had more than halved to 0.58 in FY2023 from 1.69 in FY2021.

RJ gradually upped his holding to slightly over 44.3 million shares by end-June 2022, in tandem with the improvement in the hotel chain's operating and financial performance. IHCL's share price had more than trebled to ₹262.85 by end-June 2022. RJ's holding by end-June 2022 was ₹1,165 crore, or 2.90% of his CEP. It had grown more than twelve-fold from ₹93 crore in end-June 2020, underpinned by share purchases and rising share price.

Tata Motors

The Indian automobile industry comprises four segments—passenger vehicles (PVs), commercial vehicles (CVs), two-wheelers and three-wheelers. Tata Motors is the largest player in the CV segment with a market share of 35.49% in April 2024. It is also the third largest company in the PV segment with a market share of 13.71%. Maruti Suzuki with a market share of almost 41% and Hyundai (14.84%) are the largest and second largest PV manufacturers in India.[20]

Tata Motors, which was previously known as Tata Engineering and Locomotive Company (TELCO), is the second largest listed entity of the Tata group by full-float market cap, after TCS. Tata Sons and other Tata group entities together held a 46.36% stake in Tata Motors as of end-June 2024. The company began manufacturing locomotives and other engineering products in 1945. The first commercial vehicle, the TMB 312 truck, was launched in 1954. Tata Motors started manufacturing heavy CVs in 1983 and light CVs in 1986. It forayed into the PV segment with the launch of Indica in 1998.[21]

RJ invested in two different types of Tata Motors stocks, common shares and DVRs, during two distinct time periods. DVRs are shares with differential voting rights that is, investors in DVR shares may have higher or lower voting rights than common shareholders. Tata Motors DVR holders had lower voting rights than common shareholders; hence the price of DVRs were lower than those of the common shares. RJ invested in Tata Motors DVRs before December 2015. According to Trendlyne, he owned 16.43 million DVRs by end-December 2015. The DVRs were trading at ₹265.45, which translated to a market value of ₹436 crore and constituted 4.70% of his CEP. RJ upped his stake in Tata Motors DVRs to 17.43 million shares during the quarter ended 30 June 2016, a move that coincided with these instruments' price rising. He maintained his shareholding for three quarters up to 31 December 2016. During this period, the DVRs' price peaked to ₹348.70 on 30 September 2016, and so did their share in RJ's CEP to 5.40%. RJ sold his entire holding of Tata Motors DVRs between 1 January and 30 June 2017, by which time their price had declined to ₹263.30.

RJ invested in Tata Motors again three years later; it was the second Tata group stock RJ invested in during COVID-19. However, the automobile manufacturer was struggling even before the outbreak of the pandemic. Its consolidated PAT in FY2017 and FY2018 were lower than in FY2016. It reported a whopping ₹28,724 crore consolidated loss in FY2019. Tata Motors chairman, N. Chandrasekaran, observed, 'From an operational performance perspective, the last twelve months have been challenging for JLR. These have resulted in the business reporting a revenue decline this year and an operating loss. Our sales from

China declined by 34.1% this year compared to the previous year. The company faced headwinds from external factors, including slowdown of sales in China and Europe along with internal factors of high fixed cost structures, dealer network profitability and high investment leading to cash outflows. JLR is taking steps to cut costs while taking a calibrated approach towards future investment in the product portfolio ...'[22]

The aforesaid initiatives took time to implement. Tata Motors' losses declined, though the company remained in the red till FY2022. Tata Motors returned to profitability only in FY2023. RJ purchased 40 million common shares during the quarter ended 30 September 2020, when the automobile manufacturer's share price ranged from ₹105 to ₹133. RJ upped his stake to 42.75 million shares in the quarter ended 31 March 2021. He then reduced his stake to 36.25 million shares by end-June 2022, gradually but not unilaterally. RJ was buying and selling Tata Motors shares even as its share price more than trebled from ₹133 on 30 September 2020 to ₹450 on 30 June 2022. What was the rationale? Sensex rose by close to 40% between September 2020 and June 2022, reflecting the recovery of India and the rest of the world from COVID-19. Tata Motors stock clearly outperformed the index. When RJ sold Tata Motors stock even as its share price was rising sharply, he probably needed the funds for other investments. He also realised some capital gains in the process. The share of Tata Motors common shares rose from 3.6% of RJ's CEP as of September 2020 to a peak of 6.4% the very next quarter and moderated to 4.1% in June 2022. RJ sold 3.75 million Tata Motors shares between end-September 2020 and end-June 2022, notwithstanding which the market value of his holding more than trebled from ₹531 crore to ₹1,630 crore over a twenty-one-month period.

At the time of RJ's demise, the four Tata stocks—Tata Communications, Rallis, Indian Hotels and Tata Motors—accounted for 7% of his CEP or ₹3,953 crore and had paid over ₹65 crore dividends between 31 December 2015 and 30 June

2022. But RJ's holding in a fifth Tata company accounted for a third of his CEP, or ₹12,793 crore, and paid an estimated ₹150 crore dividends during the six years and nine months ending 30 June 2022. This jewel in RJ's crown, Titan, is the protagonist of the following chapter.

10

The Watch Project

IN JUNE 2010, THE GOVERNMENT OF INDIA AUCTIONED A PART OF its telecom spectrum. There were not many takers, as the incumbent telecom companies did not find the bandwidth particularly attractive. An inconspicuous internet service provider registered at Ambavadi in Ahmedabad, Gujarat, Infotel Broadband Services Private Limited (IBSPL), won the auction by placing the winning bid of ₹12,847.77 crore. Hours after the auction, Reliance Industries Limited (RIL) acquired a 95% stake in IBSPL for ₹4,800 crore. An executive from an incumbent telco admitted, 'We would have entered the bidding if we had known Mukesh (Ambani) was going to end up owning this bandwidth ... (By emerging from) behind this unknown company, he managed to get the spectrum at a far cheaper price.'[1]

This was not the first time India Inc. had to resort to stratagem to achieve its ends. Before the epochal budget of 1991 ushered in India's liberalisation, even a consumer electronics industry like watches was subject to stringent government control. Regulations stipulated that only PSUs and small enterprises may manufacture watches. The Bengaluru-headquartered Hindustan Machine Tools (HMT), a central PSU, was the market leader.

The Tata Group and Tamil Nadu Industrial Development Corporation (TIDCO), a PSU tasked with strengthening the state's manufacturing capabilities, were both interested in foraying into watch manufacturing. TIDCO had contacted a potential technical collaborator, France Ebauches SA, and invited Tata Press to be a joint venture partner. A Tamil Nadu cadre IAS officer, Iravatham Mahadevan, then posted at TIDCO, was previously a joint secretary in the Ministry of Industrial Development in New Delhi. He had met Xerxes Desai and Anil Manchanda, who were working with Tata Press and were scouting for new industries for the group to diversify. In March 1982, TIDCO and Tata Industries submitted an application to the government to manufacture two million watches. While the government approved TIDCO's venture, it rejected Tata Industries' involvement as a joint venture partner.

Six months after the secretary of the Ministry of Commerce and Industry perfunctorily declined to even discuss Tata Sons setting up a watch manufacturing facility with its CEO Minoo Mody, a new company—Questar Investments—was set up in March 1983 explicitly for 'The Watch Project'. Mody, Desai and Manchanda were the promoters. In February 1984, TIDCO signed a technical collaboration agreement with France Ebauches and a joint venture agreement with Questar to set up a watch manufacturing company, Titan Watches Ltd. Titan is an acronym for Tata Industries (TI) and Tamil Nadu (TAN). The senior management of TIDCO was aware that Questar was effectively controlled by the Tata group. The government approved the application TIDCO and Questar jointly submitted to incorporate a watch manufacturing company. Tata Sons later acquired Questar through a rights issue.[2]

Supplanting the Timekeeper to the Nation

Between 1984 and 1985, Titan zeroed in on Hosur, an industrial town in Tamil Nadu 41 kilometres away from Bangalore, so that it could tap into the overstaffed HMT's talent pool. The new entrant purchased a fifteen-acre plot of land from State Industries Promotion Corporation of Tamil Nadu (SIPCOT), yet another state PSU, and began the construction of its plant. In July 1985, Titan recruited I.K. Amitha, retired executive director of HMT, as its senior vice president of operations.

The twin prerequisites for assembling watches are dexterity with hands and the ability to engage in repetitive work. Titan, like the Japanese, used a psychodiagnostic test (PDT) to assess the latter attribute. Titan was looking for employees over sixteen years of age who had passed tenth grade. Desai observed, '... we wanted fresh minds. We sent teams of people to small towns; young boys and girls were given attitude and aptitude tests. If one hundred applied, around three got selected.'[3] Hence the company's forty-strong recruitment team scoured and employed shop floor employees from Hosur and other small towns. This provided the much-needed boost to employment and economic growth in Tamil Nadu's and Karnataka's small towns.

In March 1987, Titan launched its first set of watches, which were promoted by a memorable advertisement campaign created by Ogilvy & Mather. The advertisement campaign was characterised by an absence of celebrity endorsement; it focused on the watches. Customers would visit Titan showrooms with a copy of the print advertisement to show the salesperson the model they wished to buy. The television advertisement incorporated Mozart's twenty-fifth symphony, which Desai found uplifting, and is amongst the longest running advertising features in India.[4]

Figure 10.1: Titan's First Print Advertisement

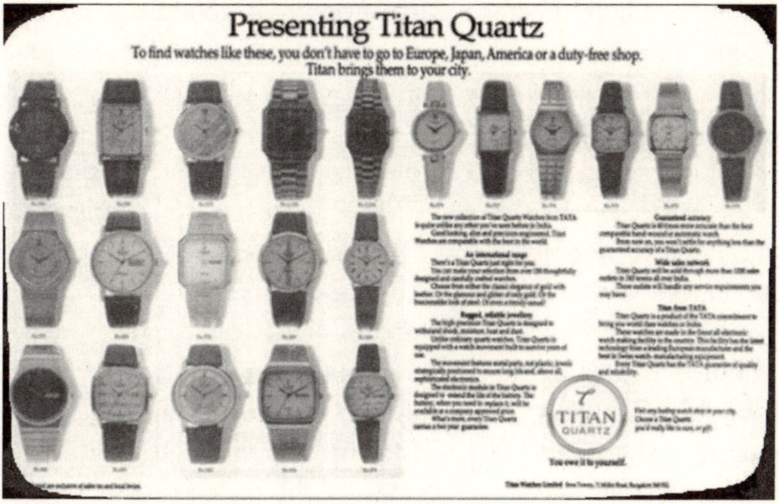

Source: https://www.titancompany.in/our-heritage

In the financial year ending 30 June 1987, during which time Titan sold watches for not more than four months, the company reported ₹2.89 crore revenues and a marginal loss of ₹5 lakh. The watchmaker reported ₹26 lakh PAT the very next year that was generated from an almost seven-fold growth in revenues to ₹19 crore.[5] In December 1987, Titan inaugurated its first showroom at Bangalore's Safina Plaza on Infantry Road. The air-conditioned, well-appointed, customer-centric outlet was striking in comparison to HMT's spare showrooms.

Titan's second key innovation was that it chose to bypass distributors and tie up with local entrepreneurs in India's big cities to set up showrooms. This was because appointing distributors, who had been selling HMT watches for decades, would have been difficult. An advantage of eliminating distributors was that both Titan and the local entrepreneurs earned higher margins. Titan trained the showroom owners in the art and science of selling consumer electronics, which enhanced customer service quality. It departed from market practice by requiring their showroom owners to buy watches up front for cash rather than selling watches in bulk on credit. Titan benefitted from receiving cash from showroom owners upfront and reducing its working capital cycle. The showroom owners, who paid cash upfront to Titan, were more committed.

Titan initially started manufacturing both mechanical and quartz watches, while HMT's product suite consisted of mechanical watches only. Mechanical watches, both hand-wound and automatic, had more components and required greater maintenance than quartz watches. However, quartz watches entailed higher investment. With the assassination of Indira Gandhi in October 1984 and Rajiv Gandhi becoming the prime minister, the extent of government micromanaging businesses declined somewhat. For watchmakers, this meant that they could independently decide the product mix. Titan chose to assemble quartz watches only.

Attractive watches that required less maintenance promoted by effective advertisement campaigns and sold by well-trained salespersons in plush showrooms contributed to brisk sales. By 10 April 1989, barely two years since Titan had commenced operations, the company had sold a million watches. The timekeeper to the nation, HMT, was selling six million watches annually. By April 1992, Titan started the construction of a township for its employees at Hosur. It was designed by Charles Correa, an architect and urban planner who also designed Navi Mumbai and several iconic monuments.

19 = 22

Meanwhile, in March 1994, Titan inaugurated a new state-of-the-art jewellery-making facility at Hosur and started selling and started selling 18-karat gold watches studded with precious stones under the brand name 'Tanishq'. Desai coined the brand name by combining the words 'tan' and 'nishq', which mean 'body' and 'jewellery', respectively. Indian consumers preferred 22-karat jewellery, on account of which Tanishq jewellery was not initially well received. Tanishq acted upon consumer feedback and started manufacturing 22-karat jewellery as well.

To win customer confidence and differentiate itself in India's fragmented jewellery market, Tanishq installed Karatmeters—devices that assessed the purity of gold in real time—in its showrooms in February 1998. Tanishq then announced that consumers may check the gold content of jewellery purchased elsewhere free of cost at its showrooms. People thronged Tanishq showrooms. Several women wailed when they realised that their jewellery was not made of 22-karat as they had believed, and a few jewellers stormed into Tanishq showrooms accusing the brand of ruining their business. Tanishq had to call the police. While Tanishq became a household name, its sales did not improve.

So, Tanishq launched the 'Impure to Pure' scheme. Customers could test the jewellery they had purchased elsewhere on Tanishq's Karatmeter. If the gold content was higher than 19-karat but lower than 22-karat, customers could exchange their old jewellery for Tanishq's 22-karat jewellery by paying only the manufacturing charges; Tanishq undertook to foot the price of gold. The jeweller's sales soared.

However, not all of Titan's ventures were successful.

The European Mishap

When the P.V. Narasimha Rao-helmed minority Congress party formed the Union Cabinet in June 1991, India's foreign exchange reserves were precariously low. The government asked corporates to source the foreign exchange required for their businesses of their own accord. Previously, corporates would apply for foreign exchange to their banks. So, Titan decided to foray into Europe with the launch of watches and jewellery in the United Kingdom in April 1993. This diversification was Desai's brainchild and one that

Manchanda did not agree with. Manchanda resigned from Titan in June 1993, a decision that Desai accepted with a heavy heart.

Manchanda was right. 'The lower end of the market was dominated by local brands, the middle by the Japanese while the upper end belonged to the Swiss brands.'[6] Titan's jewellery did not have many takers in Europe either. Titan tried to sell watches through independent retailers. However, Swiss watchmakers threatened to stop supplying their watches to those retailers who sold Titan products. Titan struggled to pay salaries and some of the employees it had hired in its European offices turned out to be untrustworthy. Its European operations were unable to turn profitable even in 2002, nine years after the company had launched its watches and jewellery.

Yet another venture of Titan's was its collaboration with Timex, the US' largest watch brand. In November 1992, Titan tied up with Timex to make and sell mass market brands. The joint venture was not a success. By December 1997, Titan and Timex ended their marketing alliance, with the latter taking over the marketing, design, sale and service of its products. The failure of Titan's predominantly urban network to boost sales in rural areas, which was Timex's target market, resulted in a 'fall in volumes, rise in input costs and an inventory pile-up'.[7] Titan launched its own mass market brand, Sonata, in April 1997.

Change of Guard

On 31 March 2002, eighteen years after Titan was incorporated, Desai retired. His legacy was awe-inspiring. He had created education and employment opportunities for youth in small towns, overseen the development of a township at Hosur, spearheaded the creation of two market leaders in India—Titan and Tanishq—and was instrumental in crafting one of India's longest-running advertisement campaigns. On 1 April, Bhaskar Bhat succeeded Desai as Titan's second managing director.

Bhat had his task cut out for him. Desai had nurtured the evolution of the watchmaker from a start-up to a titan that generated ₹727 crore in revenue in FY2002 and one that was consistently profitable from the second year of operations that is, FY1988. However, the profit margin (PAT divided by revenues), which had peaked at 8.84% in FY1995, declined year on year thereafter and was barely 1.80% in FY2002—the last year Desai was Titan's managing director.[8]

The sizable investments Titan made in its European division without commensurate increase in revenues and profits resulted in its liabilities-to-net worth ratio more than doubling from 1.83 times in FY1987—the first year of the watchmaker's operations—to a precarious 3.73 times in FY2002. The decline in Titan's profit margins and accumulation of liabilities should not be interpreted as Desai's inability to run a business profitably and restrict its indebtedness to sustainable levels. As a professional manager, he made four decisions—focusing on quartz watches, diversifying into the jewellery business, expanding to Europe and collaborating with Timex. While the first two decisions resulted in Titan and Tanishq becoming market leaders, the third and fourth did not achieve the desired outcomes. The weakening of Titan's financial profile was collateral damage, which Bhat had to set right.

Titan's financial performance further deteriorated in FY2003, Bhat's first year as managing director. While revenues grew to ₹761 crore, PAT margin touched an all-time low of 1.51% and the liabilities-to-net worth ratio was an unsustainable 5.89 times![9] Titan continued innovating and simultaneously focused on improving its financial performance. The world's slimmest watch, Titan Edge, was launched in May 2002. Titan's website describes Edge's positioning as follows: 'In a room full of men and women wearing complex gadget-like devices, the slimmest watch does what these gadget-like timepieces are never able to do, that is, to stand out effortlessly.'[10]

In April 2003, Tanishq launched the Gold Harvest scheme. Akin to banks' recurring deposit schemes, this required customers to pay eleven monthly instalments to Tanishq. The jeweller would pay the twelfth instalment, and customers could buy jewellery with the money equivalent to twelve instalments. Customers found the scheme attractive, as buying jewellery became more affordable. Tanishq benefitted from enhanced customer loyalty and higher recurring cash inflows that reduced borrowing and interest costs. The Gold Harvest was not a Titan innovation; several regional jewellers offered similar schemes. However, a market leader from the trustworthy Tata stable launching the scheme resulted in its resounding success.

In June 2004, Titan launched its precision engineering business. Renamed as Titan Engineering & Automation Limited, the company's full-fledged machine building, automation and component manufacturing businesses cater to global markets.[11] Titan Raga—a line of watches for women that drew inspiration from art, culture, nature and contemporary fashion trends to create watches that were trendy and timeless—was relaunched in September 2006.[12] By December 2006, Titan wound up its European businesses, which had accumulated losses of ₹110 crore since its inception in the early 1990s. The watchmaker provided for these losses in its financial statements during the four-year period spanning FY2003 to FY2007. In February 2007, Titan partnered with the makers of the historical film *Jodhaa Akbar* and made the jewellery used in the movie. In March 2007, eyewear was launched under the 'Titan Eyeplus' brand.

Titan's financial performance reflected the impact of the new business and product launches since FY2003 and the closure of the European business. The company's liabilities-to-networth ratio started declining from FY2004. In FY2005, revenues surpassed ₹1,000 crore. In two years, that by FY2007, revenues had almost doubled to ₹2,097 crore, PAT margin improved to 4.76% and, most importantly, the liabilities-to-networth ratio was well entrenched in the safe territory at a minimal 0.39 times![13]

However, Titan did not rest on its laurels. In September 2013, the perfume line 'Skinn' was launched, and in January 2016, Titan Juxt, a hybrid smartwatch, was introduced in collaboration with Hewlett-Packard. On 6 January 2016, the Cabinet committee on economic affairs announced the closure of the erstwhile market leader, HMT. A Press Information Bureau note stated, 'With a cash assistance of ₹427.48 crore, the three loss-making subsidiaries of HMT Ltd, namely HMT Watches Ltd, HMT Chinar Watches Ltd, HMT Bearings Ltd, will attain closure after separation of about 1,000 employees through attractive VRS/VSS (voluntary retirement scheme/voluntary separation scheme) and settlement of their dues.'[14]

In February 2017, Titan launched its sari brand—Taneira. By FY2024, Titan's revenues and PAT had grown to ₹51,617 and ₹3,496 crore, respectively, translating to a PAT margin of 6.77%. The liabilities-to-net worth ratio was 1.76 times; but if liquid assets—cash, bank balances and mutual fund investments—were deducted from liabilities, the ratio moderated to 1.42 times. Interestingly, Titan's largest business as of FY2024 is jewellery, contributing to 89% of its consolidated revenues and 93% of its profits. Its legacy business, watches, is a distant second, accounting for 8% of revenues and profits. The eyewear line, which is profitable, and other small businesses brings up the rear.[15]

Has Titan's share price moved in line with its meteoric rise? Before analysing its share price performance, we need to take a step back and look at how the company raised equity.

The Age of Innocence

According to Titan's FY1987 annual report, the Tata group and TIDCO subscribed to 3.55 million shares priced at ₹10 each in FY1986, thereby investing equity of ₹3.55 crore. The duo invested another ₹20.41-crore equity between FY1987 and FY1989, which resulted in Titan's paid-up share capital increasing to ₹23.95 crore by end-March 1989. Titan's shares were priced at ₹10 each up to end-March 1989.[16]

In FY1990, Titan raised ₹14.22 crore by floating convertible debentures cum rights issue. These debentures paid 12.5% interest and were oversubscribed 2.58 times. Titan's FY1990 annual report states, 'Convertible debentures of ₹100 each, amounting to ₹284.46 lakhs, was converted into 10 equity shares of ₹10 each, at par, on 31 March 1990.' Titan had turned profitable in its second year of operations, FY1988, and had reinvested all its profits in the business. In other words, the watchmaker did not pay dividends in FY1988 and FY1989. The book value of a Titan share as of end-March 1989 was ₹10.59. The company had offered the debenture holders a discount of ₹0.59 per share! Titan also paid its maiden dividend in FY1990. The watchmaker declared a maiden dividend of 15% or ₹1.50 per share, which was subject to tax, and amounted to ₹3.60 crore or 83% of its ₹4.33-crore PAT that year.[17]

Compare Titan's maiden equity raise with One97 Communications' (Paytm) ₹18,300-crore IPO in November 2021. Paytm, which is India's second largest listing as of 2024, priced its shares at ₹2,150. This share price included a ₹2,149 premium over the ₹1 par value of Paytm's share. Paytm had reported losses of ₹42,256 crore in FY2019, ₹29,424 crore in FY2020 and ₹17,010 crore in FY2021. Its PE ratio was negative. Notwithstanding this dismal performance, Paytm's IPO price of ₹2,150 was almost twenty-one times its pre-listing book value per share of ₹104.[18] The fintech's robust prospects supposedly justified its IPO price. Unsurprisingly, Paytm's share price crashed by 27% on the listing day to around ₹1,560.[19] The company, which continues to be loss-making, reported losses of ₹14,224 crore in FY2024.[20] Its share price as of end-June 2024 was 81% lower than the IPO price at ₹402.20.

Data on Titan's share price is available on the NSE website from 1 January 1996 onwards. The share price had appreciated eleven-fold to ₹116 by 1 January 1996. Between 1 January 1996 and 31 December 2002, Sensex rose by a lacklustre 8.58%—a reflection of the dot-com bubble bust and the unravelling of Ketan Parekh's pump-and-dump schemes. Titan's share price declined by a third during this seven-year period in tandem with declining profits and accumulating liabilities.

RJ made his first investment in Titan during the last two years of this seven-year period, when the watchmaker's share price touched lows of ₹27 in 2001 and ₹34 in 2002.[21] RJ explained in an interview, 'I didn't know zilch about Titan. One day I was sitting, I was very bullish, a broker called Daaki called me. He said five lakh shares of Titan, which were trading at ₹34, were available to him at ₹32. I called my friend Lashit, he said not to buy it as Morgan Stanley was expected to sell 90 lakh shares and that I will get it cheaper. But I didn't listen to him and bought those 5 lakh shares and slowly accumulated 12.5 lakh shares. I thought not to leave the shares despite Lashit's view.'[22]

RJ met Titan's managing director, Bhaskar Bhat, when its share price had risen to ₹44. The investor confessed that he had visited several Tata offices and found Titan different—the employees were young and the environment vibrant. Bhat was scheduled to meet RJ at 6 p.m. but was delayed in an employee union meeting. He assured RJ that their meeting would begin at 6.30 p.m. The meeting began at 6.45 p.m. and lasted four hours, during which RJ had Bhat's undivided attention. It was only after Bhat's wife called him six times that he answered her call. Between the time RJ invested in Titan's stock and his meeting with Bhat, he had researched the watchmaker and mastered its business model, financial profile, stock performance and prospects. RJ shared his insights with Bhat, who stated that Titan faced an uphill task but the company would achieve it.[23] However, Titan's operating, financial and share price performance exceeded RJ's and Utpal Sheth's optimistic estimates.

Titan raised its second round of equity when it floated a ₹126.83-crore rights issue between 25 March and 24 April 2006. The rights issue gave Titan's existing shareholders the option to buy 21.14 million partly convertible debentures (PCDs) of ₹600 each in the ratio of one PCD for twenty equity shares owned. The convertible component of the PCD was priced at ₹350 and the non-convertible portion at ₹250.[24] Each convertible component of a PCD was swapped for one share of ₹10 par value at a premium of ₹340. Titan paid an interest of 6.75% on the non-convertible component of the PCDs and listed them on the stock exchanges.[25] Titan's share price ranged from ₹744 to ₹871.25 during the period of the rights issue, which indicates that the shareholders received more than a 50% discount on the share price. This issue was oversubscribed by 20%. It is not known if RJ subscribed to these PCDs. In June 2011, Titan announced a 1:1 bonus issue and a 1:1 stock split, which resulted in a quadrupling of the holdings of shareholders without them having to purchase shares.

Titan did leave considerable value on the table for its shareholders both during its 1990 and 2006 equity raises. The largest beneficiaries were TIDCO and the Tata group, which together held a 52.89% stake in the watchmaker as of 31 March 2006. The stakes of TIDCO and the Tata group through Tata Sons Private Limited, Tata Investment Corporation, Tata Chemicals, Ewart Investments and Piem Hotels remained unchanged at 27.88% and 25.02%, respectively, as of 30 June 2024.

Titan is by far TIDCO's most successful joint venture to date with its holding of 247.48 million shares as of 30 June 2024 valued at a whopping ₹84,293 crore. TIDCO's second most valuable investment is its 26.02% stake or 2.60 million shares in the erstwhile Aditya Birla group company TANFAC Industries, whose market value as of end-June 2024 was ₹559 crore.[26] Surat-based Anupam Rasayan India Limited purchased the Aditya Birla group's stake in TANFAC, which is one of India's largest suppliers of fluorine chemicals, in March 2022.

RJ initially purchased 5,00,000 Titan shares and subsequently upped his stake to 1.25 million shares sometime between 2001 and 2002 and at prices ranging from ₹32 to ₹125. He did not pare down his stake in Titan even in 2011, when its share price, after adjusting for the bonus and rights issues, had crashed by 81%. The European debt crisis and concerns about India's slowing economic growth and declining profits of corporates on account of rising interest rates and input costs resulted in Sensex shedding a quarter of its value.

The conviction in Titan and its long-term prospects was so immense that RJ made an incredible move. He exited from Bharat Electronics Ltd (BEL) and Bharat Earth Movers Limited (BEML), which by then were significant multibaggers, and switched to Titan. The purchase price in Titan at the time of the switch was almost thirty times RJ's initial Titan purchase price. It is what Ramesh Damani calls 'RJ's ability to back up the truck'. Ironically, when RJ started to invest in Titan, the balance sheet was not investable. He studied the jewellery, gold and retail business, and the fact that the management possessed the ability to deliver. RJ realised that the culture at Titan was different. The Titan management, led by the redoubtable Bhaskar Bhat, possessed high credibility powered by the reputation of the Tatas. The opportunity in the jewellery business, combined with the fact that Indians would trust the Tatas in gold purchases more than anyone else, was a prime driver. Titan's franchisee model and the value creation abilities of the company's management team were critical components of RJ's conviction. Titan was a multibagger of gargantuan proportions. Over a span of twenty years, the stock multiplied 2,000 times from its initial acquisition price.[27]

RaRe Enterprises had accumulated 93.81 million Titan shares by 31 December 2015 but pared down its stake to 54.39 million shares at the time of RJ's demise to moderate the concentration risk of its portfolio. Titan's share in RaRe Enterprises' CEP consequently declined from 37% in end-December 2015 to 32% in end-June 2022, which was the last complete quarter RJ helmed the company. Notwithstanding the sale of shares, the market value of RJ's Titan stake more than trebled from ₹3,412 crore in December 2015 to ₹12,793 crore in June 2022. The watchmaker's share price had risen almost 309 times since RJ's first investment and, after adjusting for the bonus issue and share splits, to ₹2,471.95 on the day of his demise. RaRe Enterprises also earned close to ₹150 crore dividends from Titan shares between December 2015 and June 2022.

11

Banking on Banks

THE FIRST TIME AN INDIAN BANK BROKE INTO THE RANKS OF the world's largest was in July 2023, following the reverse merger of the country's then largest mortgage lender, HDFC Limited, with the subsidiary it founded, HDFC Bank. This transaction catapulted HDFC Bank into the global big league; it became the world's seventh largest bank by market cap. JP Morgan was then and continues to be, as of October 2024, the world's largest bank by market cap.[1] But market cap is a volatile metric. A host of factors, including changes in share price, equity issues and buybacks, and mergers and spinoffs, can result in market cap changing drastically overnight.

Assets are a more stable and apposite metric to assess a bank's size. India's largest bank, the State Bank of India (SBI) with consolidated assets of ₹67.34 trillion as of March 2024, is the forty-seventh largest bank in the world. With consolidated assets of ₹40.30 trillion, HDFC Bank is ranked seventy-fourth.[2] So, why is SBI's market cap lower than HDFC Bank's despite its assets being 67% higher? HDFC Bank's 19.44 times PE ratio and ₹1,682 share price on 4 October 2024 is higher than SBI's 11.61 times and ₹794.

It is indeed striking that the largest bank domiciled in India, the country with the third highest purchasing power parity (PPP) adjusted GDP in the world, is ranked forty-seventh in terms of assets. In contrast, four banks domiciled in China and two in the US—countries ranked first and second in terms of PPP-adjusted GDP—feature among the ten largest banks by assets.[3] Decades of draconian government control, political interference in lending decisions, loan waivers, poor appraisal in some instances and fraud have impeded the emergence of a world-class bank in terms of scale and quality. HDFC Bank, whose assets are not among the ten largest banks globally, is an exception. In November 2020, *The Economist* published a column titled 'Who is the World's Best Banker?' in which it credited Aditya Puri, HDFC Bank's first managing director, for building a world-class institution.[4]

Robust business and financial profiles are essential prerequisites to achieve financial inclusion in a large and populous country like India. The country's suboptimal financial inclusion is evident in its corporate and household debt-to-GDP ratios, which lag the metrics of the other large economies. Banks subscribing to government securities to comply with the high CRR and SLR norms and small corporate bond markets have resulted in lower credit access for corporates and households. Improved regulation, appraisal and sale of defaulted loans to asset reconstruction companies have resulted in the ratio of India's non-performing loans (NPL) to total bank loans declining from 10% in 2017 to 4.8% in 2022.[5] Nevertheless, India's NPL ratio is higher than that of other large economies. India's insurance density (insurance premium per capita) and penetration (the ratio of insurance premium to GDP) also lag the metrics of other large economies (Table 11.1).

While the current situation is not ideal, the growth prospects for Indian banks and insurance companies are immense. This is

Table 11.1: Financial Inclusion and Insurance Density and Penetration of the Five Largest Economies

	PPP Adjusted GDP, $ Billion	***Government Debt/GDP, %***	***Non-FI Debt/ GDP, %, [2]***	***Household Debt/GDP, %***	***Bank NPLs/ Total loans, %***	***Insurance Premium***	
						Per Capita, $	***% of GDP***
	2023	**2023**	**2023**	**2023**	**2022**	**2023**	**2023**
China	32,931	46.90	283.50	62.10	1.66	508	3.9
USA	27,358	122.30	256.30	72.90	0.72	9,640	11.9
India	13,342	84.30	181.20	42.30	4.81	95	3.7
Japan	6,507	156.10	400.10	65.20	1.23	2,938	8.9
Germany	5,544	63.60	69.10	51.30	1.20	2,910	5.5

Source: World Bank, Asian Development Bank, Bank for International Settlements & Swiss-Re

what incentivised RJ to invest in financial service stocks, the market value of which rose from 12% in December 2015 to 33% of his CEP in June 2022. Star Health and Allied Insurance was one of RJ's private equity investments. Its listing in December 2021 resulted in the market value of financial services stocks trebling from 10% in September 2021 to 30% in RJ's portfolio. The market values of RJ's holdings in four financial services firms—Edelweiss Financial Services, Geojit Financial Services, Indiabulls Housing Finance and Multi Commodity Exchange—progressively declined from 3% in December 2015 to less than 1% in June 2022. The share of RJ's investments in banks rose from less than 1% in December 2015 to 5% in June 2022. This chapter describes RJ's rationale for investing in three banks—Federal Bank, Karur Vysya Bank and Canara Bank.

Federal Bank

The Travancore Federal Bank was incorporated on 24 April 1931 with an authorised share capital of ₹5,000 at Nedumpuram in Kerala. The bank mobilised the savings in the region and lent the same to farmers and industries. It was initially successful but, by 1944, was on the brink of liquidation. This was when Kulangara Paulo Hormis, aided by his family and friends, acquired a controlling stake in the bank. Hormis was born in an agrarian family. He had just started his career as an advocate when he embarked on the entrepreneurial journey to acquire and turn around this ailing bank. Hormis helmed the bank for thirty-six years, during which time he oversaw its revival and expansion from a single branch lender to a nationwide institution comprising 285 branches. The lender was renamed Federal Bank in 1947.

The polymath Hormis was elected as an MLA to the Travancore Cochin Assembly as an Indian National Congress candidate in 1954. In March 1979, he retired from Federal Bank as its chairman but continued as a director on its board for two more years. Hormis, who had developed a mechanism to effectively finance agriculture and the economically weaker sections of society long before microfinance became a buzzword, passed away in 1988 on India's Republic Day, 26 January.[6]

In 1994, Federal Bank's shares listed on the stock exchanges through an IPO, which was oversubscribed by about sixty times.[7] Federal Bank's FY1997 annual report is the earliest available in the public domain. According to this document, the bank had around 350 branches and generated ₹45.19 crore post-tax profits on assets of ₹4,367 crore in FY1996. In the next twenty years, that is, by FY2016, the number of Federal Bank's branches would more than treble to 1,252, its PAT and assets would skyrocket by ten and twenty-one times to ₹486 crore and ₹91,554 crore, respectively.[8]

By FY2016, Federal Bank's asset base was barely 3% of India's largest bank, SBI's ₹916 billion. But its financial metrics were stronger. Federal Bank's FY2016 return on assets was 0.57% vis-à-vis SBI's 0.46%, capital adequacy ratio (CAR) was 13.93% (SBI: 12.40%), and net non-performing asset (NPA) ratio, at 1.64%, was less than half of SBI's 3.81%.[9] According to Trendlyne, RJ purchased 27.07 million Federal Bank shares between January and March 2016, which must have entailed an investment of approximately ₹125 crore.[10]

A year later, along with Federal Bank's chairman and managing director Shyam Srinivasan (SS), RJ addressed the media. His rationale for investment is evident from his statement: 'First of all, like a true businessman, I must say I am invested in Federal Bank. It has been an extremely profitable investment. But I think the best is yet to come. And that the best is coming is apparent on the horizon. It is great to know that Federal Bank is one of the earliest appliers of technology to banking. In the last three, four, five years, it has grown out of the avatar of being a local, regional bank to being a national bank. I am very glad to know that they represent 1% of lending in India. It's a bank with fierce loyalty from its customers.'[11]

Between March 2016 and 2018, Federal Bank's share price more than doubled from ₹45.85 to ₹98.30, while its return on assets had improved from 0.57% to 0.75%. However, its NPA ratios, though low, had inched up. The gross NPA ratio rose from 2.84% in FY2016 to 3% in FY2018, and the net NPA ratio correspondingly crept up from 1.64% to 1.69%. This development caught RJ's eye. The investor's knowledge, attention to detail and hands-on approach to investing is evident in his conversation with SS after Federal Bank announced its FY2018 results.[12]

> *RJ*: I don't understand the ₹65–70 crore credit cost because ₹2,800 crore is your gross NPA and ₹1,550 crore is your net NPAs. You say you recognise ₹1,300 crore next year.
>
> *SS*: ₹1,100–1,200 crore, yes.
>
> *RJ*: So, your gross NPAs will become around ₹4,000 crore.
>
> *SS*: ₹1,100–1,200 crore will be slippages for next year. Recoveries roughly in a quarter, if you've seen, are ₹222 crore in Q3 [of FY2018] and ₹239 crore in Q4.
>
> *RJ*: Fresh slippages will be much lower then, at around ₹500–600 crore.
>
> *SS*: No, fresh slippages will be around ₹1,100–1,200 crore. You have to net off the recoveries and upgrades.
>
> *RJ*: Right. So, if ₹200 crore is upgrade, gross NPAs should not be more than ₹3,000–3,200 crore.
>
> *SS*: Increase in gross NPAs should not be more than ₹400 crore.

Retail investors should pause to think if they are knowledgeable and have the time to engage in stock picking or are better off investing in mutual funds.

Federal Bank delivered a solid performance between FY2016 and FY2022—a period characterised by robust growth, stable financial performance and diversification of business profile. The bank's consolidated assets more than doubled to ₹2.26 trillion, return on assets increased to 0.94%, CAR rose to 15.77% and net NPA ratio declined (improved) to 0.96%. That the lender bettered its financial performance while growing its corporate lending portfolio is indeed impressive.

Corporate lending is a business in which larger banks like SBI, HDFC and ICICI have three distinct advantages—a lower cost of funding that enables them to lend at competitive rates, longer track record and entrenched relationships. Notwithstanding the offerings of larger competitors, Federal Bank's corporate loans increased from 27.9% of consolidated assets in FY2016 to 35.6% in FY2022. The bank's legacy business, retail loans, also rose from 38% to 42.7%, while treasury investments declined from 34.1% to 21.7%. Federal Bank's treasury book did not shrink between FY2016 and FY2022; it grew at a CAGR of 8% during the six-year period. However, the CAGRs of the retail and corporate loans were much higher at 18.5% and 21%, respectively.

Federal Bank's share price appreciation mirrored its performance—it more than doubled from ₹45.85 in end-March 2016 to ₹106.65 in end-March 2022. RJ, who owned 27.07 million Federal Bank shares as of March 2016, kept upping his stake during the next six years. He did trim his stake in certain quarters, though. By end-March 2022, RJ's stake in Federal Bank more than trebled to 96.72 million shares. The market value of his holding in Federal Bank shares rose more than sixfold, from ₹124 crore or 1.3% of his CEP in March 2016 to ₹1,032 crore (2.6%). RJ also earned approximately ₹39 crore dividends between FY2016 and FY2022 from his Federal Bank shares.

Karur Vysya Bank

Yet another over eighty-year-old bank RJ invested in was Karur Vysya Bank (KVB), which was founded by Venkatarama Chettiar and Athi Krishna Chettiar on 22 June 1916. Historian V. Sriram observes, 'The terms Chettiar, Chetty, Shroff, Seth, and Sethia are all derived from the Sanskrit term—Sreshtin—which means they were the best in the community to be entrusted with one's wealth.'[13] The Chettiars are a trading community renowned for their business acumen and whose presence and business interests spread across Tamil Nadu, Andhra Pradesh, Sri Lanka and Southeast Asia for centuries. KVB is headquartered in Karur, a town located in the Chettinad region of southern Tamil Nadu. KVB floated its first rights issue in 1954, which implies that its shares were listed even earlier.[14]

KVB's FY1998 assets and PAT, as per its FY1999 annual report, the earliest available in the public domain, were ₹2,524 crore and ₹43.54 crore, respectively. By FY2016, PAT and assets had grown eleven and twenty-three times to ₹486 crore and ₹58,985 crore, respectively. A cursory observer of KVB's share price trend will be taken aback that RJ invested in the bank despite its share price more than halving from ₹176 on 1 January 1996 to ₹75.93 on 31 December 2015. But this puzzling trend was due to the measures KVB had adopted to improve its capitalisation and cultivate shareholder loyalty.

KVB floated three rights issues between 2002 and 2011. In the October 2002 rights issue, KVB gave shareholders the option to buy one share for every share they held at a price of ₹60, which was 61% lower than the minimum price at which the bank's share had traded in the previous year. In the December 2006 equity raise, shareholders could buy one KVB share for every two shares they owned at a price that was 72% lower than the preceding one year's minimum traded price: ₹70. Investors had the opportunity in February 2011 to buy two KVB shares for every five they owned for ₹150 apiece, which represented a 60% discount to the last one year's lowest share price. KVB's paid-up share capital skyrocketed from ₹5.99 crore in March 2002 to ₹94.49 crore in March 2011 following the three fully subscribed rights issues.

Additionally, KVB's September 2010 bonus issue awarded investors two shares for every five they owned. While bonus issues do not impact an entity's capital structure, they are a mechanism to reward shareholders. An investor who owned 100 KVB shares in March 2002 and subscribed to the three rights issues would have owned 588 shares by March 2011. The investor would have been allotted 120 of the incremental 488 shares free of cost as part of the bonus issue and would have purchased the remaining 368 shares at a discount of at least 60% to the minimum price in the preceding year. The market value of the investor's holding would have also grown sixfold, from ₹38,455 in March 2002 to ₹2.35 lakh in March 2011. We do not know when RJ invested in KVB, but we do know he owned 4.24 million shares, the market value of which constituted 0.3% of his CEP, by end-December 2015.

KVB sustained its investor-friendly policies. The bank declared a stock split in November 2016 by which every share was divided into five shares. The holdings of all shareholders rose fivefold. RJ owned 21.06 million KVB shares by December 2016. This was followed by a rights issue in October 2017 that allowed shareholders to buy one KVB share for every six they owned at a price of ₹99. The discount during this rights issue was lower than the previous three rights issues but nevertheless meaningful at 5%. RJ trimmed his holding in KVB by 9% during the quarter ended December 2017. So, we don't know whether he subscribed to the issue. KVB also announced a bonus issue in August 2018 through which shareholders were awarded one share for every ten they owned. RJ's stake in KVB shares in the quarter ended September 2018 rose by 8% to 33.23 million shares. KVB's share in RJ's CEP peaked at 2.1% during this quarter.

KVB was consistently profitable. Along with the multiple rights issues, this enabled the bank to remain well-capitalised. The bank's Achilles' heel was, however, its asset quality. Its gross NPA ratio almost trebled from 1.30% in FY2016 to 3.58% in FY2017, and further deteriorated to 8.79% in FY2019. KVB adopted the diametrically opposite strategy to Federal Bank's to improve its asset quality and executed it successfully. The bank focused on retail lending and simultaneously trimmed its corporate lending. Retail loan ticket sizes are much lower than corporate loans, and the number of borrowers is much higher. Banks with robust appraisal and risk management systems tend to build retail loan portfolios of sound asset quality.

Between FY2016 and FY2022, KVB's retail and treasury assets grew at CAGRs of 8.5% and 4%, respectively, while the corporate loan book shrunk by 0.2%. This strategy bore fruit once the Indian economy started recovering from COVID-19. KVB's gross NPA ratio improved from 7.94% in FY2021—the period which coincided with the pandemic—to 6.03% in FY2022 and further to 1.40% by FY2024.

Rising NPAs and COVID-19 resulted in KVB's share price more than halving from ₹101.21 in end-March 2017 to ₹48.85 in end-March 2022. RJ bought 2.4 million KVB shares in the quarter ended 30 June 2020, when the bank's share price ranged from ₹29.25 to ₹34.55 apiece. RJ's shareholding in KVB grew more than eightfold from 4.24 million shares in December 2015 to 35.98 million in June 2022. The market value of his holding appreciated more than six times, from ₹32 crore to ₹211 crore, during this period. Dividend income from KVB shares between December 2015 and June 2022 was approximately ₹12 crore.

Canara Bank

The final three listed equity investments RJ made during the year preceding his demise were in public sector stocks. He purchased 57.5 million Steel Authority of India Limited (SAIL) shares in the quarter ended 31 March 2021, 29.1 million Canara Bank shares and 25 million National Aluminium Company Limited (NALCO) shares in the following quarter. SAIL and NALCO were his largest and smallest investments of the three, whose market values were ₹817 crore in end-June 2021 and ₹242 crore in end-September 2021. But RJ remained invested in SAIL and NALCO for just three full quarters. He sold SAIL in the quarter ended 31 March 2022 and NALCO in the following quarter.

Banking as we know it was introduced in the Madras Presidency in the 1640s. The British dominated this business for centuries. By the end of the 1860s, there were at least three banks in Madras (which was renamed Chennai in 1996)—the Bank of Madras, the Chartered Bank and Mercantile Bank. The large commercial firms of Arthunbot's, Binny's and Parry's also provided banking services. Indians entered formal banking at the dawn of the twentieth century. They set up six banks in the early twentieth century—the Thanjavur Permanent Fund that morphed into Thanjavur Bank in 1901; South Indian Bank (1903); Kumbakonam City Union Bank (1904); Madras City Union Co-operative Bank (1905); the Canara Banking Corporation, Udupi (now the Corporation Bank); and the Canara Hindu Permanent Fund, Mangalore (now Canara Bank) both in 1906. Thus, the third banking investment that RJ owned at the time of his demise was also in an institution that was established more than eighty years ago—Canara Bank.[15]

Canara Bank was among the fourteen banks that were nationalised on 19 July 1969. Another six banks were nationalised on 16 April 1980. The government over the years merged these banks, on account of which there are twelve listed public sector banks in India as of 2024. Canara Bank is the fourth largest bank in India by assets. Its growth over the decades has been fuelled by organic business expansion and mergers with other banks. The government-mandated mergers of the ailing Lakshmi Commercial Bank in 1985 and Syndicate Bank in 2020 were the most recent. Canara Bank has been no stranger to controversy as well. The Janakiraman Committee identified Canbank Financial Services, the bank's merchant banking subsidiary, as one of the entities that issued fraudulent bank receipts (BR) and accepted fake BRs from the Bank of Karad when Harshad Mehta was active in Dalal Street.[16] In June 2018, the UK's Financial Conduct Authority (FCA) slapped a £890,000 ($1.2 million) fine and debarred Canara Bank from accepting deposits for five months for systematic anti-money laundering failures.[17]

Canara Bank's strengths include its status as a public sector bank—the Government of India holds a 62.93% stake as of June 2024—strong market position with its assets accounting for 5.68% of the Indian banking sector's assets, and its large scale, as is evident from a customer base of 1.14 million and an extensive network of 9,627 branches.[18] The lender's weakness is its financial profile. Canara Bank's gross NPA ratio ranged from 8.21% to 11.84% and was higher than the average for all Indian banks in five years of the six-year period between FY2016 and FY2021. This resulted in the bank reporting losses in three of the six years. Its CAR, though higher than the regulatory minimum, was also lower than the average for the banking industry.

In February 2017, Canara Bank floated a ₹1,124-crore rights issue that gave shareholders the option to buy one share for every ten they owned at a price of ₹207. The rights issue price was almost 33% higher than the bank share's minimum traded price the preceding one year. With close to 98% of the shareholders subscribing to the rights issue, Canara Bank raised ₹1,098.31 crore.[19] The government injected an aggregate ₹5,442.29 crore equity in FY2018 and FY2019 in the lender.[20] The government directive to merge Syndicate Bank with Canara Bank was accompanied by a ₹6,571-crore equity infusion in FY2020.[21] Canara Bank raised another ₹4,500-crore equity through two QIPs in December 2020 and August 2021.[22]

By March 2022, the bank had reported profits for two consecutive years. The gross NPA ratio, though high, had improved to 7.51%, and CAR had touched a seven-year peak of 14.95%. RJ, after buying 29.1 million Canara Bank shares in the quarter ended 30 September 2021, purchased another 6.5 million shares between January and March 2022. Canara Bank shares accounted for 2.6% of RJ's CEP in end-June 2022. The bank also paid dividends for the first time in five years in June 2022, which translated to a ₹23-crore income for RJ.

Investment Thesis

It is interesting to observe RJ invested in two well-managed, mid-sized, private-sector banks (Federal Bank and KVB) and one large public-sector bank that was not out of the woods yet (Canara Bank). RJ's logic for investing in the three banks may be understood by juxtaposing their performance and valuation with those of the BSE Bankex, an index comprising ten bank stocks. While Federal and Canara Banks are constituents of Bankex, KVB is not.

Federal Bank's and KVB's five-year share price increase outperformed the Bankex, while the two banks' ten-year share price appreciation underperformed the index (Table 11.2). When RJ first invested in KVB before December 2015 and Federal Bank in 2016, he may have deduced that the stocks of these fundamentally sound banks were undervalued and hence had the potential to appreciate. His intuition was vindicated. With Federal Bank evolving to be a bank with country-wide presence and KVB improving its asset quality, their stocks outperformed the Bankex between October 2019 and 2024. Even after this outperformance, the PE and price-to-book-value (PB) ratios of Federal Bank and KVB are lower than those of the Bankex as of October 2024. This is an example of value investing, which is an investment strategy that involves picking stocks that appear to be trading for less than their intrinsic value.[23]

RJ engaged in 'bottom fishing' when he purchased the Canara Bank stock during the quarter ended September 2021. Canara Bank's PB ratio ranged from 0.22 to 0.57 times between March 2019 and September 2021. A going concern's PB trading at less than 1.0 time implies that the book value of the firm's assets is

Table 11.2: Valuation Metrics and Share Price Performance of Federal Bank, KVB & Canara Bank

As of 4 October 2024	**Price Earnings Ratio**	**Price-to-Book-Value Ratio**	***5-Year Capital Gains***		***10-Year Capital Gains***	
			₹	%	₹	%
Canara Bank	6.54	1.12	71.64	198.94	38.85	56.47
Federal Bank	12.23	1.63	107.9	125.76	131.97	213.79
Karur Vysya Bank	9.79	1.66	149.9	255.58	118.67	132.03
BSE Bankex	14.39	2.50		86.54		232.95

Source: www.bseindia.com

higher than its market cap; hence the stock is trading at a bargain price. With Canara Bank returning to profitability in FY2021 and demonstrating an improvement in asset quality, RJ may have believed that the stock's upside potential was high. Even as of October 2024, Canara Bank's PE and PB ratios are trading at steep discounts to Bankex's. The chapter titled 'Legacy' analyses whether RJ's view on Canara Bank was justified.

Canara Bank, Federal Bank and KVB share two interesting similarities. First, all three banks were founded more than eighty years ago and have a track record of conducting business through several business cycles. Second, they were all headquartered in South India. Sriram Veeraraghavan, partner, Sammati Consulting and Analytics LLP, observes, 'In India, there are five categories of scheduled banks—a government bank, public sector banks, institution-promoted private sector banks, private sector banks and small finance banks. SBI is a category unto itself; though listed, it is an arm of the government that performs the role of RBI wherever the central bank is not present. SBI's loans, deposits and assets account for a quarter of the Indian banking system as of 2024. The government has majority stakes in public sector banks, whose operations are spread across India and in certain instances overseas. Banks promoted by institutions like HDFC Bank, ICICI Bank and Axis Bank (formerly UTI Bank) are headquartered in Mumbai and have a pan-Indian presence too. HDFC Bank and ICICI Bank are the second- and third-largest lenders in the country. There are around ten banks, both public and private sector, headquartered in South India, most of which are fundamentally strong. This is a reflection of the higher literacy rates and better credit culture—a reflection of the superior socio-economic development of the states they are headquartered in.'[24]

While Canara Bank, Federal Bank and KVB accounted for 5% of RJ's CEP in June 2022, a single financial services stock accounted for another 5% of his portfolio. This stock was the second-highest dividend earner for RJ, generating an estimated

₹105 crore between January 2016 and June 2022. Titan was the highest dividend paying stock in RJ's portfolio, generating ₹150 crore for the investor. The following chapter is about RJ's second most valuable investment—CRISIL.

12

The Cash Machine

IN WILLIAM SHAKESPEARE'S *HAMLET*, ACT 1 SCENE 3, POLONIUS, King Claudius' chief minister gives this succinct advice on the dangers of debt to his son, Laertes:

'Neither a borrower nor a lender be,
For loan oft loses both itself and friend,
And borrowing dulls the edge of husbandry.'

Yet, governments, businesses and individuals borrow and lend. Financial institutions (FIs) like banks and non-banking finance companies (NBFCs) are a distinct business that borrow at a lower interest, lend at a higher rate and earn a spread or net interest margin in the process. Debt is not necessarily a dangerous phenomenon when cautious lenders loan monies at viable interest rates to responsible borrowers, who in turn deploy the funds in income-generating activities and assets and repay the advance.

Lenders expect eligible borrowers to possess five attributes or 'Cs'. Borrowers ought to be of good character. They must also have the capacity to borrow. In other words, borrowers ought not to be heavily indebted. Lenders track borrowers' debt-to-income ratios to assess their capacity. Debtors must possess capital and collateral. A collateral is an asset that a debtor pledges with a creditor to enable the latter to sell the property and recover the loan in case of non-payment. Creditors charge higher interest rates on unsecured debt or loans without collateral, such as personal loans and credit card loans, than on secured debt like housing and vehicle loans. The borrower's condition is the fifth attribute; it refers to the track record, professional and/or business and financial profiles, and prospects of individual debtors and businesses as well as the terms and conditions associated with debt—tenure, interest rate and collateral.

Two pivotal stakeholders in the debt ecosystem are credit information companies (CICs) and credit rating agencies (CRAs). CICs like India's TransUnion CIBIL, Experian and Equifax assess the creditworthiness of individuals and small businesses. CRAs, of which there are seven in India as of 2024, assess the probability of default of governments, FIs and corporates. CRISIL, CareEdge (previously known as CARE Ratings) and ICRA are India's three largest CRAs with a combined market share of 85%. These three CRAs are listed on BSE and NSE. While CRISIL and ICRA are subsidiaries of S&P and Moody's, respectively, India Ratings and Research is the wholly-owned arm of Fitch. Hence, the big three international CRAs have a significant presence in India through their subsidiaries.

The Trailblazer

In January 1987, ICICI Limited, Unit Trust of India and a group of public-sector insurance companies and banks founded CRISIL. The CRA was the brainchild of Narayanan Vaghul, the then chairman and managing director of ICICI Limited, and Pradip Shah, who had assisted in the incorporation of HDFC Limited in 1977.[1] Vaghul and Shah were CRISIL's founding chairman and managing director, respectively. The Industrial Finance

Corporation of India (IFCI) set up ICRA in 1991, while Industrial Development Bank of India (IDBI) incorporated CARE in 1993.

By 1992, CRISIL had not only established its franchise within India but also overseas. The CRA offered technical assistance and training to set up Rating Agency Malaysia Berhad and MAALOT, the Israeli securities rating company. CRISIL floated an IPO in November 1993, through which it raised ₹10 crore by selling 2 million shares at ₹50 apiece. The IPO was oversubscribed by 2.47 times. According to CRISIL's FY1997 annual report, the CRA earned ₹7.57 crore post-tax profits from ₹21.68-crore revenues in FY1996.

In February 1996, CRISIL and S&P entered into a strategic business alliance to strengthen the former's skills and processes. S&P acquired a 9.68% stake in CRISIL in May 1997, when the CRA's share price ranged from ₹248 to ₹309.75. In March 2000, CRISIL acquired INFAC—a research provider to India's financial sector—for ₹7 crore.[2]

Between FY1996 and FY2003, CRISIL's revenues had more than quadrupled to ₹76.25 crore and PAT had more than doubled to ₹16.67 crore. The CRA's shares were trading between ₹239 and ₹551 apiece in 2003, when RJ first purchased 10,000 shares.[3] In December 2003, CRISIL acquired the London-based Economatters (later the Gas Strategies Group) for £1.5 million (approximately ₹11.41 crore). Economatters provided natural gas-related consulting, information and training, and conference-organising services.[4] In 2004, the CRA acquired a 9% stake in the Caribbean Information and Credit Rating Agency Limited, to which it was already providing technical assistance, for $300,000 (approximately ₹1.36 crore).

Liar's Poker

As of March 2005, CRISIL's promoter group comprising ICICI Bank (with a 10.75% stake), UTI (7.56%), United India

Insurance, LIC, SBI, Canara Bank, and Central Bank of India held a 32.49% stake in the CRA. The shareholding of institutional investors and S&P was 29.63% and 9.43%, respectively. Retail investors, private corporate bodies, CRISIL's directors and their relatives together held 14.19%. RJ and Rekha were the largest shareholders; the couple owned 9,08,091 shares equivalent to a 14.26% stake.

A milestone in CRISIL's evolution was S&P's conditional open offer to acquire an incremental stake of over 41.67% at a price of ₹775 per share in April 2005. S&P's offer to purchase a 41.67% stake was contingent upon existing shareholders tendering adequate shares. S&P, which held a 9.43% stake, wished to purchase another 41.67% so that it could own a majority stake of slightly over 51% in CRISIL. S&P had appointed Kotak Mahindra Capital Company as its financial advisor and manager.

Uday Kotak reminisced, 'Rakesh and I did not speak to each other during the period of the open offer. I was representing S&P and it would have been a conflict of interest. He initially held out because he realised that CRISIL's share price would appreciate if the conditional offer was successful. Rakesh was in touch with my team to assess how many shares other investors were tendering. My team was tight-lipped and reminded him that should the offer not go through, S&P may rethink its 9.43% stake. Both Rakesh and I believed that S&P acquiring a majority stake in CRISIL was important. So, he sold a part of his stake during the open offer, without which S&P may not have succeeded. It was important for a ratings company to have S&P as a partner.'[5]

RJ and Rekha sold an estimated 3,58,091 shares during the conditional open offer. S&P achieved its goal of acquiring a majority stake in CRISIL; it held a 56.52% stake. While ICICI Bank tendered its shares during the open offer, SBI, UTI and LIC had not. RJ had announced amidst S&P's open offer, 'I am bullish on the company.'[6] CRISIL's shares were trading at ₹1,531.75 by 30 December 2005, which was almost double S&P's offer price eight

RJ in his Nariman Bhawan office

RJ, Radheshyam Jhunjhunwala and Rajesh Jhunjhunwala at the Taj Mahal Hotel, Mumbai, in 2002

RJ with family in August 2011

RJ and Rekha, c. January 2014

Diwali, 2014 or 2015. Standing (left to right) are Rekha, Nishtha, Aryaman, and Aryavir.

RJ with his mentor, Radhakishan Damani in 2009 at the Mumbai Grand Hyatt

RJ with Amit Goela in 2014

RJ meeting students at the Nehru Science Centre, Mumbai, in 2015

Grand Canyon, US, 2018. Standing (left to right) are Aryaman, the helicopter pilot, Aryavir, Rekha and Nishtha

RJ and Rekha c. 2019 in Kenya. The lady sitting in the back is Anju, Amit Goela's wife.

Taj Mahal Hotel, Mumbai, Jan 2019
Vishal Gupta & RJ

Bhaskar Bhat and RJ in Bangalore, 2019

Prime Minister Narendra Modi and Rekha with RJ in October 2021

At the Finance Ministry, New Delhi, in 2021. Sitting (left to right) are Finance Minister Nirmala Sitharaman, Utpal Sheth, Amit Goela and RJ

RJ with students of Ashoka University in 2021

RJ at Ashoka University in 2021

RJ at his Nariman Bhawan office

RJ and Nishtha, June 2022

RJ with Amit Goela and Utpal Sheth, in 2022

RJ with Rajeev Gupta and Manmohan Gupta

With Rekha's side of the family. Standing (left to right) are Manmohan Gupta, Madhu Seksaria, Amrita Gupta, Sunil Seksaria, Rekha Jhunjhunwala, RJ, Renu Ruia, Rupal Gupta, Rajeev Gupta, Sharad Ruia and Chanda Gupta.

RJ, Rekha and their kids in January 2019

RJ and Rekha in January 2019

months ago. Despite paring down his stake by almost 40% during the open offer, the market value of RJ's and Rekha's holdings in CRISIL had appreciated from ₹62 crore on 31 March 2005 to ₹84 crore on 31 December.

There were media reports of RJ selling his CRISIL shares in 2005 for ₹27 crore to purchase an apartment in Malabar Hill, Mumbai.[7] This is precisely the sum RJ received by selling 3,58,091 shares to S&P.

Cash and Controversies

In an undated video on YouTube, an interviewer asks RJ, 'What is the opportunity you see in CRISIL?'

The investor replies, 'India's financial markets. Financial services make up 16% of US GDP. In India, it is 3–5%. So, the opportunity of CRISIL is essentially linked to India's financial markets. What is the size of India's bond market today? Who is servicing the mutual fund industry? ... Opportunity itself does not make profits for a company. It is a competitive ability. It is a business in which you cannot have new entrants. CRISIL has one of the best capabilities and reputation among rating agencies. And that gives it a competitive edge. And, what a business profile! What cash flows! It's nothing but cash, cash, cash.'[8]

Let's translate RJ's words to arithmetic. In the 28.75 years spanning 1 April 1995 and 31 December 2023, CRISIL generated ₹5,553 crore adjusted cash flow from operations (CFO), which is a robust 21% of its ₹26,393-crore revenues. Adjusted CFO is reported CFO minus interest and financial expenses, which in India are categorised as financing cash flows. After financing ₹706-crore capital expenditure and ₹1,147-crore acquisitions, and paying ₹3,244-crore dividends, CRISIL generated ₹455-crore free cash flows (FCF) (Table 12.1). Adjusted CFO minus the sum of capital expenditure, investments and dividends equals FCF. The consistent generation of FCF resulted in CRISIL's cash

Table 12.1: CRISIL's Free Cash Flow Trend

	Revenue (₹Crore)	***Adjusted CFO***	***Capex***	***Acquisitions***	***Dividends***	***Free Cash Fliws***
	A	**B**	**C**	**D**	**E**	**B-C-D-E**
FY1996–FY2003	364	97	72	-	24	1
FY2004–FY2010	2,859	665	218	98	357	-7
FY2011–FY2017	8,976	1,838	192	708	1,151	-213
FY2018–FY2023	14,194	2,953	224	341	1,713	675
FY1996–FY2023	**26,393**	**5,553**	**706**	**1,147**	**3,244**	**455**

Source: CRISIL Annual Reports

and bank balances soaring from ₹1.48 crore on 31 March 1996 to ₹370 crore on 31 December 2023.

FCFs enable businesses to build war chests to finance expansion and tide over black swan events like COVID-19 with reduced reliance on debt. CRISIL had generated positive FCF in 18.75 of the 28.75 years ending 31 December 2023. The CRA did not borrow during the ten years it generated negative FCF; it had adequate financial investments to sell. CRISIL has contracted leases. But its cash and bank deposits exceed leases by a wide margin, leaving the CRA in a comfortable net cash position.

CRISIL's first acquisition was probably that of INFAC, which occurred in 2000, three years before RJ invested in the CRA. RJ advised CRISIL to increase the pace and scale of acquisitions. CRISIL acquired minority, controlling and 100% stakes in at least ten knowledge-focused businesses by end-2023. These acquisitions comprise INFAC, NCDEX, Caribbean Information and Credit Rating Agency, Economatters, IREVNA, Pipal Research, Coalition Group, Pragmatix Services, Greenwich Associates and its most controversial investment, CARE Ratings.

On 30 June 2017, *Mint* reported, 'If you had ₹435 crore and had to choose between a 3.1% stake in Crisil Ltd and an 8.8% stake in Credit Analysis and Research Ltd (CARE Ratings), what would you choose? Here's a tip from Crisil: go for the stake in CARE Ratings. After all, it did exactly that instead of using excess cash to buy back its own shares.' *Mint* seemed to imply that CRISIL's management perceived CARE's stock to be more valuable than its own. Entities buy a part or the whole of their competitors for several reasons, including expanding their own market share and sphere of influence and earning a return by investing in an industry of which they possess a deep understanding.

Canara Bank, which owned 2.62 million CARE Ratings shares, had sought bids for selling them on 19 June 2017. CRISIL emerged as the highest bidder, quoting a price of ₹1,659.79 per CARE share, which was 16% higher than the previous day's

Figure 12.1: CRISIL's Announcement of a Stake Purchase in CARE Ratings

CRISIL
An S&P Global Company

Press Release
June 29, 2017 | Mumbai

CRISIL buys 8.9 % stake in CARE Ratings

CRISIL has purchased 26,22,430 equity shares of CARE Ratings Limited (CARE) representing 8.9% of its equity share capital. The investment has been made pursuant to a bid process conducted by Canara Bank, subsequent to their request for quotation issued on June 19, 2017.

This investment in the equity of CARE has no special rights and is in compliance with applicable rules and regulations. CARE is a SEBI registered credit rating agency and is listed on the BSE and NSE.

CRISIL continuously evaluates investment options as a part of its corporate strategy. This stake purchase is an investment in the excellent long term prospects of the credit rating sector in the country. The prospects for the sector are driven by the significant demand for capital investments and infrastructure financing in India over the long term, much of which should benefit the sector.

Ashu Suyash
Managing Director & Chief Executive Officer

For further information contact:

Amish Mehta
Chief Financial Officer
CRISIL Limited
D: +91 22 3342 3049
B: +91 22 3342 3000

Ramraj Pal
President – CRIS, Corporate Communications
CRISIL Limited
D: +91 22 3342 3036
B: +91 22 3342 3000

closing price. This, coupled with CARE having nil promoter shareholding, made CRISIL's move look like a prelude to a hostile acquisition.[9] With a 9.8% stake, Life Insurance Corporation (LIC) was CARE's largest shareholder. SEBI questioned CRISIL after CARE complained to the regulator.[10] CRISIL has not upped its stake in CARE beyond 2.62 million shares as of 31 December 2023. LIC and CRISIL are CARE's largest shareholders as of March 2024 with stakes of 9.61% and 8.78%, respectively.[11] Interestingly, CRISIL owns a single share in ICRA, which in turn holds 3,000 shares of the former as of 31 March 2024.[12]

The CARE investment was not the only controversy CRISIL was embroiled in. In January 2018, SEBI approved CRISIL's application to settle a probe into the violations of the provisions of the SEBI (Credit Rating Agencies) Regulations, 1999 'without admitting or denying the findings of fact and conclusions of law' on a payment of ₹28.37 lakh.[13]

Fortunately, CRISIL had no ratings on the heavily indebted Infrastructure Leasing & Financial Services (IL&FS) when it defaulted. IL&FS' consolidated debt as of end-March 2018 was ₹91,091 crore.[14] The CRA withdrew its rating on IL&FS Transportation Networks (ITNL), which it had rated 'A' with a stable outlook, at the request of the company and on receiving a no objection certificate from the bank on 25 July 2016; this was more than two years before IL&FS defaulted.[15] ITNL was the first constituent of the IL&FS group to default in September 2018.[16] SEBI censured ICRA, CARE, India Ratings and Brickworks, as they had assigned optimistic ratings to IL&FS and its group entities based on shareholding and had failed to adjust their assessments in a timely manner to reflect the infrastructure financier's performance, prospects and governance.

The Differentiators

CRISIL's first-mover advantage, strategic thinking and efficient execution against the backdrop of the explosive growth of India's capital markets catapulted the company to the big league. A comparison of the revenues and market caps of CRISIL, ICRA and CARE is instructive. CRISIL is a clear market leader with its ₹772-crore revenues from credit ratings in 2023 being 2.6 times and three times that of CARE's and ICRA's, respectively. Its consolidated revenues of ₹3,233 crore is 6.2 times that of ICRA's and 8.5 times that of CARE's. CRISIL's full float market capitalisation (full market cap) was ₹31,340 crore as of end-September 2024, making it a large-cap stock. ICRA is a mid-cap stock with a full market cap of ₹6,753 crore. CARE is a small-cap stock with a ₹3,330-crore full market cap.

Employee expenses are key in knowledge industries such as credit ratings, research and analytics. In FY2012, the ratio of ICRA's employee expenses to revenues was 46.6%, marginally ahead of CRISIL's 44%. CARE's employee expenses-to-revenue ratio was less than half of CRISIL's and ICRA's at 20.6%! By 2022, CRISIL's employee expenses-to-revenue ratio was the highest among the three listed CRAs at 54.1%.[17] ICRA maintained its employee expenses-to-revenue ratio at 46.1% in FY2023, while this metric more than doubled for CARE to 43.5%. CRISIL's high employee expenses-to-revenue ratio has resulted in its 20.4% PAT margin in 2023, though healthy, being lower than ICRA's 29.2% and CARE's 27.1% in FY2024.

There are a few takeaways from this benchmarking of employee expenses of the three CRAs. First, it is indeed striking that CARE had aligned its employee compensation with the other two CRAs after CRISIL acquired a stake in it. Did CRISIL play a role in CARE's improved employee compensation structure? We don't know. Second, CRISIL has the most diversified product offering and the highest employee expenses-to-revenue ratio among the three listed CRAs as of FY2024. Is this because CRISIL pays its employees more or because there exist inefficiencies it its staffing and/or compensation structures? This is for CRISIL, its shareholders and analysts tracking the CRA to ascertain.

The acquisitions diversified CRISIL's business profile and geographic footprint. Akin to RJ's most successful investment, Titan, whose jewellery business overtook watchmaking, CRISIL's research, analytics and solutions business constituted three-fourths of its consolidated revenues in 2023, while ratings accounted for a quarter. North America contributed to 40% of CRISIL's revenues, followed by India (27%), Europe (25%) and the rest of the world (8%).

Moody's subsidiary ICRA is the second most diversified CRA in India with credit ratings accounting for 58% of consolidated revenues, and consulting, knowledge and market data services contributing to 42%. ICRA earns 63% of its revenues in India and the balance 37% overseas. CARE is a pure play ratings agency whose revenues are predominantly generated in India. CARE incorporated its international ratings arm, CareEdge Global, and registered the new entity with the International Financial Services Centres Authority (India) (IFSC) in 2024.

It would be inappropriate to compare ICRA and CARE with Sensex or Nifty50, as these are large-cap indices. ICRA is a mid-cap stock and CARE, a small-cap. All three CRA stocks are constituents of the BSE Financial Services index. While the financial profile of all three CRAs is sound, CRISIL is a more expensive stock in terms of PE and PB ratios vis-à-vis CARE and the BSE Financial Services index (Table 12.2). Investors appear to be willing to pay a premium for CRISIL's stock on account of its market leadership and diversified business profile.

Table 12.2: Select Valuation Metrics of CRA Stocks

30 September 2024	**CRISIL**	**ICRA**	**CARE**	***BSE Financial Services***
Full Float Market Cap ₹ Crore	31,340	6,753	3,330	9,87,19,555
PE Ratio	55.92	57.26	27.13	17.19
PB Ratio	21.81	9.41	4.35	2.67
Promoter Stake, %	66.64	51.87	Nil	Not applicable
5-Year Price Gain (Loss), %	230.66	165.34	121.77	87.19
10-Year Price Gain (Loss), %	126.33	170.92	-26.08	235.97

Source: www.bseindia.com

Akshaya Patra

CRISIL announced a 1:10 share split in September 2011, on account of which RJ's shareholding increased tenfold to 5.50 million shares by December 2011. The CRA spent ₹79.27 crore in December 2011 buying back 9,10,000 shares at an average price of ₹871.06.[18] CRISIL announced a second buyback in July 2015. This time, the S&P subsidiary incurred ₹101.98 crore expenditure buying back 5,11,932 shares at an average price of ₹1,992.02.[19] Though RJ did not tender his shares during the two buybacks, he had reduced his shareholding to 4.0 million shares by September 2015.

RJ had purchased CRISIL shares both in his and Rekha's names. However, Rekha's name does not feature in most quarterly filings of shareholding with the stock exchanges as she owned less than 1% stake in CRISIL. According to Trendlyne, the couple, as of end-December 2015, owned 5.21 million CRISIL shares, whose market value was ₹928 crore and constituted 10.4% of their CEP. They upped their holding by 13% to 5.87 million shares by 30 June 2022. Though the market value of their holding in CRISIL rose by 92% since December 2015 to ₹1,836 crore, the CRA's share in the couple's CEP more than halved to 4.6%. The listing of their erstwhile PE investments—Star Health, Metro Brands and Nazara Technologies—was the contributory factor. RJ and Rekha earned approximately ₹106 crore dividends from their CRISIL shares between January 2016 and June 2022.

Like the Cornucopia and Akshaya Patra of Greek and Indian mythologies, the CRISIL stock has paid its investors regular dividends since the fourth year of its incorporation, that is, FY1991. Since at least 2008, CRISIL has been paying shareholders quarterly dividends. An investor who had purchased 100 CRISIL shares for ₹5,000 during its November 1993 IPO and remained invested in the CRA since would own as of 30 September 2024, 1,000 shares valued at ₹46.63 lakh. The investor would have also received ₹4.54 lakh dividends during the thirty-one-year period.

13

Potpourri

THE TATA GROUP STOCKS, CRISIL AND STAR HEALTH AND ALLIED Insurance (which was listed in December 2021) may be considered the nucleus of RaRe Enterprises' CEP at the time of RJ's demise in August 2022. This nucleus almost trebled from ₹7,761 crore (58% of CEP) to ₹22,474 crore (73%). The smaller constituents, despite declining as a percentage of CEP from 44% in end-December 2015 to 27% in end-June 2022, grew by a robust 46% in rupee terms over a six-and-a-half-year period from ₹3,439 crore to ₹8,278 crore. This component of RaRe Enterprises' CEP reveals RJ's views about industries and his attributes as an investor, trader and board member. This chapter focuses on five smaller investments of RJ's—Lupin, Aurobindo Pharma, Escorts Kubota, Aptech and NCC—to shed light on his investment personality.

Rx

India is the third-largest manufacturer of pharmaceutical products by volume, globally, and fourteenth largest by value.

India's drug and pharmaceutical exports grew at a CAGR of 5.5% and 7.5% in dollar and rupee terms from $16.89 billion (₹1.11 trillion) in FY2016 to $24.60 billion (₹1.83 trillion) in FY2022.[1] Notwithstanding Indian pharma companies' strong global market position and robust demand that propelled export growth, the BSE Healthcare index, which comprises pharma companies and hospitals, grew at a CAGR of just 4.96% from 17,310 on 1 April 2015 to 24,304 on 31 March 2022. Sensex's appreciation during this period was more than double at 11.14%.

The BSE Healthcare index's lacklustre performance between FY2016 and FY2022 was a reflection of, among other factors, the risks Indian pharma companies are exposed to—regulatory red tape, intellectual property rights issues, government-imposed price controls, counterfeit medicines, low research and development investment, pricing pressure in overseas markets, quality control and manufacturing standards maintenance, healthcare infrastructure, global trade barriers, attracting and retaining a skilled workforce, and environmental concerns.[2]

It is not surprising that the share of pharma stocks in RaRe Enterprises' CEP declined from 19% as of 31 December 2015 to 2% as of 31 June 2022. According to Trendlyne, Lupin and Aurobindo Pharma accounted for 16.4% and 6.5% of RaRe Enterprises' CEP, respectively, as of 31 December 2015. Lupin's and Aurobindo Pharma's share prices were ₹1,710.75 and ₹834.25 as of 31 December 2015, respectively. RaRe Enterprises reduced its stake in Lupin to less than 1% during the September 2021 quarter, after the pharma company's share price had declined by more than 35% in the preceding five years and nine months. Similarly, Aurobindo Pharma's share price had declined by 14% between 31 December 2015 and 30 June 2017; RJ reduced his stake in the stock to less than 1% in the September 2017 quarter. But this does not imply these stocks were loss-making investments.

According to Lupin's quarterly filings of shareholding pattern with BSE and NSE, Rekha purchased 5,00,000 shares in the

December 2002 quarter. Lupin's share price as of 31 December 2002 was ₹145.75, which translated to a market value of ₹7.29 crore. The very next quarter, RJ purchased 4,90,000 shares. The couple, who owned 9,95,000 shares on 31 March 2003, bought another 2.25 million shares in the June 2010 quarter. By 30 June 2010, they owned 3.25 million Lupin shares, whose share price had increased by more than 1,200% in the intervening seven-and-a-half years to ₹1,967.85 on 30 June 2010. The market value of their stake in Lupin was ₹639.32 crore.

Lupin announced a 1:5 stock split in August 2010. The couple's holding of Lupin shares almost increased fivefold to 15.89 million by 30 September 2010. While the share price declined to ₹388.10 by 30 September 2010 because of the share split, it rose exponentially thereafter to ₹1,710.75 by 31 December 2015. RaRe Enterprises more than halved its stake to 7.42 million shares by 31 December 2015, notwithstanding which the market value of its stake was ₹1,269 crore. RaRe Enterprises' holding fluctuated between 6.64 and 8.79 million shares between end-December 2015 and end-June 2021. RJ may have also traded in the Lupin stock. He reduced his stake in Lupin to less than 1% in the September 2021 quarter.

RJ remained invested in Lupin for almost nineteen years. As the share sales occurred over a period of almost eleven years and we do not know the prices at which the Lupin shares were sold, it is not possible to compute RJ's return on this investment. However, 100 Lupin shares bought on 31 December 2002 for ₹14,575 would have increased to 600 shares valued at ₹6.64 lakh on 30 June 2021. The investment would have appreciated by over 4,400% in 18.5 years.

RJ's investment in Aurobindo Pharma followed a similar trajectory. But he remained invested in Aurobindo for a shorter period of time—around four years. According to Aurobindo's quarterly shareholder filings, RJ purchased 3 million shares of the pharma stock in the December 2013 quarter. At the 31 December

2013 share price of ₹392.80, the market value of RJ's stake in Aurobindo was ₹117.84 crore. His holding in Aurobindo remained unchanged till the June 2015 quarter, when he purchased another 1 million shares. By 30 June 2015, Aurobindo's share price had more than trebled to ₹1,452. While Lupin had announced a share split months after RJ increased his stake, Aurobindo announced a 1:1 bonus issue in July 2015. RJ sold 5,00,000 shares that quarter, and hence owned 7.5 million shares by 30 September 2015. Aurobindo's share price had declined to ₹769.20 as of end-September 2015 on account of the bonus issue; the market value of RJ's stake was ₹577 crore.

RJ sold 1.43 million Aurobindo shares in the quarter following the bonus issue. His holding in Aurobindo ranged from 6.08 to 6.55 million shares during the period spanning end-December 2015 to end-June 2017. RJ may have, like in the case of Lupin, traded in the Aurobindo stock too. But unlike Lupin, Aurobindo's share price did not exponentially increase. By end-June 2015, Aurobindo's share price was ₹718.60—14% lower than its end-December 2015 price. RJ reduced his stake in Aurobindo to less than 1% in the following quarter.

Was Aurobindo a loss-making investment for RJ? No! He had purchased most of his holding at a price of ₹392.80 and the bonus issue served to increase his holding fivefold. As in the case of Lupin, it is difficult to estimate RJ's profit from this investment. But an investor who purchased 100 Aurobindo shares for ₹39,280 on 31 December 2013 would have owned 200 shares valued at ₹1.44 lakh by 30 June 2017. The investment would have more than trebled in 3.5 years.

Juxtaposing Lupin's and Aurobindo's financial and share price performance offers interesting insights. There was a significant improvement in Lupin's financial profile when RJ was invested in the stock. Lupin reported standalone financials in FY2001 and consolidated financials by FY2021. Consolidated financials include the performance of an entity's subsidiaries, joint ventures and associates. Standalone and consolidated financials are not comparable. In FY2001, Lupin's revenues were ₹911 and ₹60 crore, respectively. Its balance sheet leverage, that is, liabilities-to-net worth ratio was high at 2.17 times as of 31 March 2001. By FY2021, Lupin reported ₹15,299-crore revenues and ₹1,228-crore PAT. Its balance sheet leverage had improved (declined) to 0.70 times.[3] Notwithstanding, the exponential growth and stronger financials, Lupin's share price of ₹1,107.40 on 30 June 2021 was 35% lower than its 31 December 2015 share price, ₹1,710.75.

Aurobindo's consolidated revenues more than doubled from ₹5,452 crore in FY2013 to ₹15,206 crore in FY2017, while PAT grew more than fourfold from ₹496 crore to ₹2,301 crore. Balance sheet leverage improved from 1.32 times to 0.73 times.[4] Aurobindo's share price on 30 June 2017, ₹718.60 apiece, was 14% lower than its 31 December 2015 price of ₹834.25, however.

These examples indicate that the trend in share prices may be at odds with the improvement in performance due to the market's perception of risk, such as Indian pharma companies that export drugs and pharmaceuticals to the US receiving several warning letters from the country's regulator, the Food and Drug Administration, over the years.

RJ did not completely exit the pharma industry. He invested in Concord Biotech, Dishman Carbogen, Jubilant Pharmnova and Wockhardt over the years. The BSE Healthcare index almost doubled from 23,266 on 1 March 2022 to 45,278 on 31 December 2024, outperforming Sensex, which itself had appreciated by an impressive 40% during this 2.75-year period. RJ's key pharma investments after selling his holdings in Lupin and Aurobindo and the significance of pharma stocks in RaRe Enterprises' CEP is narrated in the following chapters.

Aptech

In 1986, Atul Nishar founded a computer training institute called Aptech. It soon grew to be the second largest chain of computer training institutes in India, after NIIT. In 2003, Nishar sold Aptech to the Chennai-headquartered IT training company, SSI (formerly Software Solutions Integrated). In 2005, RJ and his family, Ramesh Damani and Asit Koticha purchased a 32.19% stake in Aptech at a price of ₹56 per share.[5] Aptech was then a loss-making entity whose consolidated revenues and post-tax losses were ₹157 and ₹44 crore, respectively, in 2005.[6]

Aptech is, however, a milestone in RJ's investment career. This was the first company in which he joined the Board of Directors. In fact, RJ became Aptech's chairman on 28 October 2005. Asit Koticha, Ramesh Damani and Utpal Sheth became board members on the same day.

By FY2010,* Aptech's financial profile had improved; the company's revenues were ₹163 crore and its losses had almost halved to ₹23 crore.[7] The company had repaid all its debt and its balance sheet leverage was low at 0.20 times. In 2010, RJ purchased another 2.24% stake in Aptech for approximately ₹8 crore. In 2012, he tried to sell his stake but was unsuccessful. While he believed Aptech ought to be valued at around ₹600 to ₹700 crore, potential investors pegged the value of the training provider at not more than ₹460 crore.[8]

Aptech had turned profitable by FY2013 and reported revenues and post-tax profits of ₹182 crore and ₹31 crore, respectively. The company's consolidated cash balance had grown to ₹120 crore. The company announced a share buyback through which it purchased 8.89 million shares for ₹60 crore. All the shares that were bought back were extinguished or permanently cancelled.[9]

---

* This was a fifteen-month reporting period as the financial year ending was changed from 31 December to 31 March.

Extinguishing shares results in a permanent reduction in the issuer's authorised share capital.

On 7 September 2016, Aptech announced that it was foraying into the preschool segment. This was considered unpublished price sensitive information (UPSI). SEBI alleged that RJ and Utpal Sheth were in possession of the UPSI and had shared it with others. The regulator further accused those in possession of the information except Sheth of trading in the Aptech stock. RJ and Rekha settled the probe by paying ₹37 crore. SEBI also imposed monetary charges on Ramesh Damani and two other individuals.[10]

By FY2022, Aptech had grown into a leading provider of vocational skilling and non-formal academic curriculum-based training programmes with hundreds of global centres. It now caters to diverse industries, including IT training, media and entertainment, retail and aviation, beauty and wellness, banking and finance, and the pre-school segment. As the company has expanded through a network of franchisees, revenue and profit growth have been modest. Between FY2005 and FY2022, its revenues had grown at a modest CAGR of 2.45% to ₹237 crore and post-tax profits were healthy at 21% of revenues or ₹49 crore.

RJ often remarked in his interactions with the media that he would like to invest in small-cap stocks that would ultimately become large cap. However, Aptech has remained a small-cap stock during the seventeen years he remained invested in the company. Aptech's share price as of 30 June 2022 was ₹232, which implies a modest annualised appreciation of 8.72% over RJ's purchase price of ₹56 in 2005.

On 29 April 2021, RJ resigned as Aptech's chairman. Aptech's FY2022 annual report states, 'In order to get the benefit of his (RJ) in-depth business vision, he is retained as the Chief Mentor of the Company so that your Company achieves its desired mission and future endeavours.' An independent director, Vijay Aggarwal, was appointed as non-executive chairman, and Utpal Sheth was appointed vice-chairman.[11]

Though Aptech accounted for just 1% of RaRe Enterprises' CEP and was not among the best performing stocks, it showcases RJ's ability to turn around an ailing business. RJ steered a loss-making company into one that successfully completed a share buyback within five years. His conviction and commitment were evident in 2010, when he made a second tranche of investment in the still loss-making Aptech.

Escorts Kubota

Yudi Nanda and H.P. Nanda founded Escorts, India's fourth largest tractor manufacturer after Mahindra & Mahindra, TAFE and Sonalika Tractors, in 1944. In 1961, the company was listed on BSE. RJ purchased 5 million Escorts shares in the September 2013 quarter. At the 30 September 2013 share price of ₹84.55, the market value of his holding was ₹42.28 crore. RJ invested in Escorts just as the company was successfully completing its restructuring and its performance was improving.

In the 1980s, Escorts was India's largest tractor maker. The group then diversified into unrelated, capital-intensive businesses such as telecom and healthcare. The new businesses generated losses and borrowings escalated. Escorts reported ₹319 crore consolidated losses in FY2004, which was more than twice its FY2003 losses of ₹141 crore. Consolidated debt as of 30 September 2003 was high at ₹1,542 crore, with balance sheet leverage at a precarious 4.62 times. Escorts sold assets to repay ₹524 crore debt in FY2004; balance sheet leverage moderated to a still elevated 2.73 times.[12]

Escorts' restructuring included the sale of the motorcycle joint venture (JV) with Yamaha, auto components JV with the Mahle group, construction equipment JV with the UK's JCB, its telecom venture Escotel and Escorts Heart Institute. Between FY2008 and

FY2020, the company invested in new product development. *Business Today* reported, 'The outcome was a new range of tractors—Farmtrac, a range of high-power tractors that opened up a new market for the company, and Powertrac, with superior fuel economy.'[13]

Escorts changed its financial year ending from 30 September to 31 March in 2014. In FY2014, which was an eighteen-month period, the company reported ₹6,585-crore revenues, and its balance sheet leverage had improved to a sustainable 0.93 times. While the company had returned to profits, post-tax profits were wafer thin at ₹245 crore or 3.75% of revenues.

RJ's investment at this juncture demonstrates his positive outlook on the tractor maker. His holding in Escorts shares grew almost 2.5 times from 5 million shares in end-September 2013 to 12.48 million shares. With the company's share price rocketing by 60% since end-September 2013 to ₹135.15 in end-December 2015, the market value of RJ's holdings in Escorts grew fourfold from ₹42 crore to ₹169 crore.

As Escorts went from strength to strength, its share price grew more than fivefold to ₹713.35 by end-March 2020. It was at this juncture Osaka-headquartered Kubota Corporation, a manufacturer of agricultural machinery and construction equipment, acquired a 9.1% stake in Escorts for ₹1,042 crore.[14]

By FY2022, Escort's post-tax profits had trebled since FY2014 to ₹736 crore and the company had repaid all its debts. The ₹1,512-crore liabilities as of 31 March 2022, mostly comprising payables and advances collected from various counterparties and a few leases, accounted for just 23% of its net worth.

Kubota floated an open offer between 14 and 28 March 2022 to purchase 37.49 million Escorts shares from the public at ₹2,000 apiece and up its stake in the tractor maker. The offer price was at a 3–15% premium over the Escorts share price between 1 January and 12 March 2022, which was in the range of ₹1,741.10–1,941.85. Expectedly, the number of shares tendered during the open offer was 39% higher at 52.03 million. Kubota purchased 37.49 million shares for ₹7,498 crore.[15] Kubota also subscribed to new shares during this period, resulting in its stake in Escorts increasing to 44.8% by 30 June 2022. Escorts Limited was subsequently renamed Escorts Kubota Limited.

RJ's stake in Escorts declined from 6.4 million shares on 31 December 2021 to 1.83 million shares on 30 June 2022. *Fortune India* estimated that his cumulative investment in Escorts since September 2013 was ₹141 crore. He had tendered 4.57 million shares during the open offer, thus realising ₹914 crore cash, which is equivalent to six-and-a-half times his investment.[16] RJ's dividend income from Escorts between 1 January 2016 and 31 March 2022 was ₹11.37 crore. Escorts was the second RaRe Enterprises investee company, after CRISIL, in which a multinational acquired a stake.

NCC Limited

NCC Limited, a Hyderabad-headquartered engineering and construction company, was founded in 1978 as a partnership. It became a public limited company in 1990 and listed on BSE in 1992 as Nagarjuna Construction Company Limited.[17] The company changed its name to NCC Limited in 2011.

Rekha purchased 9,75,000 NCC shares in the March 2004 quarter. At the 31 March 2004 share price of ₹150.90, the market value of Rekha's holding in NCC was ₹14.71 crore. In the preceding financial year, that is, FY2004, NCC's post-tax profits were ₹42 crore or 4.14% of ₹762 crore. Characteristic of engineering and construction companies, which are engaged in a capital-intensive and long-gestation-period business, NCC's balance sheet leverage was high at 2.21 times. NCC's order book was a healthy ₹1,492 crore, which was equivalent to almost two years of FY2004 revenues.[18] The order book, a performance metric analysts monitor for engineering and construction companies, is the value of contracts an entity has secured and is contractually obliged to complete in the coming years. The order book position in an indicator of revenue and profit sustainability.

In the December 2004 quarter, RJ purchased 2,50,000 NCC shares, and the couple's stake increased to 1.23 million shares. NCC's share price on 31 December 2004 was ₹421.15; it had appreciated by 179% in nine months. Hence, the market value of RaRe Enterprises' stake in NCC had more than trebled since end-March 2004 to ₹51.59 crore.

NCC announced a 1:1 bonus issue in September 2006. RaRe Enterprises also purchased 11.30 million NCC shares that year. Its holding in NCC rose to 13.75 million shares as of end-December 2006, and the market value of its stake correspondingly increased to 295.56 crore. NCC's share price crashed to ₹71.90 by 31 December 2008 on account of the global financial crisis. RJ purchased more NCC shares, taking advantage of the low price, and increased his stake to 14.40 million shares.

NCC's share price was volatile between 1 January 2009 and 15 September 2014, ranging from a high of ₹198.10 on 30 April 2010 to a low of ₹16.50 on 4 September 2013. RJ's holding too fluctuated to a minimum holding of 7.73 million shares on 31 December 2011 to 29.76 million shares on 30 June 2014.

NCC's revenues by FY2014 had grown tenfold since FY2004 to ₹7,569 crore. However, it reported a loss of ₹9 crore* and its balance sheet leverage was elevated at 2.92 times. Partially offsetting these weaknesses in NCC's financial profile was its order book, which had grown fourteenfold since FY2004 to ₹20,956 crore (2.77 times FY2014 revenues) by end-March 2014.[19]

NCC announced a ₹600-crore rights issue between 29 September and 17 October 2014. The allotment ratio was 7:6, that is, shareholders had the right but not the obligation to buy

* Including the share of associates and joint ventures and before accounting for minority interests.

seven shares for every six they owned at a price of ₹20 per share. The offer price of ₹20 was at a steep discount to NCC's share price between 1 July and 26 September 2014, which ranged from ₹34 to ₹83.50.

That RJ was bullish on NCC was evident from his purchasing 40 million shares through the rights issue and another 6,50,000 from the open market. By end-December 2014, RJ's holding in NCC was 67.58 million shares, whose market value was ₹551 crore. Other shareholders were also optimistic about NCC's prospects. The rights issue was oversubscribed. The company repaid ₹719 crore debt in FY2015, which resulted in a reduction in balance sheet leverage to 2.37 times.

NCC's performance continued to improve after the rights issue. Its revenues grew by almost 50% since FY2014 to ₹11,209 crore in FY2022, while post-tax profits were 4.41% of revenues at ₹494 crore. Balance sheet leverage had improved to 1.45 times. The most impressive aspect of NCC's performance was its order book, which had more than doubled since 2014 to ₹50,244 crore (4.48 times FY2022 revenues).

Did NCC's share price reflect the improvement in its performance? The answer depends on the benchmarks chosen. As per BSE data on 23 January 2025, the ten-year share price gain of NCC was 217.45%. The ten-year gains registered by Sensex and BSE Industrials were 181.80 and 365.59%, respectively. While NCC outperformed Sensex, it clocked a lower return vis-à-vis the industry benchmark.

RJ's returns from investing in NCC are also difficult to ascertain due to the quarter-on-quarter fluctuation in the number of NCC shares RaRe Enterprises owned (Table 13.1). Given that RJ was invested in NCC for more than eighteen years (March 2004 to August 2022) and the stock's share in the RaRe Enterprises CEP ranged from 1.5% to 5.4% between 31 December 2015 to 30 June 2022, the engineering and construction firm is likely to have been a profitable investment.

Table 13.1: RaRe Enterprises' Investment in NCC Limited

	31 March 2004	**31 December 2004**	**31 December 2005**	**31 December 2006**	**31 December 2007**
Number of Shares	9,75,000	12,25,000	12,25,000	1,37,50,000	1,27,50,000
Price, ₹	150.90	421.15	256.75	214.95	352.80
Market Value, ₹ Crore	14.71	51.59	31.45	295.56	449.82
	31 December 2008	**31 December 2009**	**31 December 2010**	**31 December 2011**	**31 December 2012**
Number of Shares	1,44,00,000	1,51,50,000	1,44,00,000	77,33,000	2,10,00,000
Price, ₹	71.90	165.75	140.70	33.45	57.65
Market Value, ₹ Crore	103.54	251.11	202.61	25.87	121.07
	31 December 2013	**31 December 2014**	**31 December 2015**	**31 December 2016**	**31 December 2017**
Number of Shares	2,96,08,266	6,75,83,266	4,52,33,266	5,67,08,266	5,67,08,266
Price, ₹	33.25	81.60	135.15	83.05	122.50
Market Value, ₹ Crore	98.45	551.48	611.33	470.96	694.68
	31 December 2019	**31 December 2020**	**31 December 2021**	**30 June 2022**	
Number of Shares	6,23,33,266	7,83,33,266	7,83,33,266	7,83,33,266	
Price, ₹	54.75	33.90	75.00	58.60	
Market Value, ₹ Crore	341.27	265.55	587.50	459.03	

Source: www.trendlyne.com & www.nseindia.com

That RJ's CEP, consisting of large exposures like Titan and CRISIL and smaller ones like Escorts Kubota and NCC, was immensely profitable is not surprising. Listed entities report their operating and financial performance on a quarterly basis. So do their listed competitors. BSE and NSE report metrics like P/E, P/BV and EV/EBITDA on a real-time basis, enabling investors to decide whether to buy, sell or hold securities. Brokerages publish equity research reports, which are an additional input to support decision-making.

However, investing profitably in private equity (PE) is an entirely different ball game. The price at which a PE investor buys stakes in unlisted firms is an outcome of quantitative assessment and negotiation. PE is an illiquid asset class, that is, investors may struggle to find buyers should they want to sell their stakes in unlisted investees. PE investors ought to have the wherewithal to remain invested for several years, as it may take a long time for the investees to list on stock exchanges. NSE's inability to list after the co-location scam is an example. A successful listing is not guaranteed; IPOs can be undersubscribed and/or the newly listed entity's share price may steeply decline below the IPO price on listing. The following section analyses RJ's investments in PE, an asset class that is considerably riskier than listed equities.

Part 3

Private Equity

14

Jackpot!

RENUKA RAMNATH, THE FOUNDER, MD AND CEO OF MULTIPLES Alternate Asset Management, stated in her tribute to RJ,

> Rakeshbhai was a fine investor. He was, in fact, a private equity investor par excellence in the garb of a capital market player. I had the benefit of working with him closely on two investments—Infomedia (an acquisition of a listed company from the TATA group) and recently the buyout of the animal health division from Zydus (now named Zenex Animal Health) ... His steady faith in the Indian economy and the value creation potential of corporate India was an inspiration to many professionals and businessmen including me. He had that rare skill of quickly coming to the crux of what creates value. His ability to trust and engage the management team is what made him earn the outsized returns.[1]

Ramnath began her career at ICICI Securities and went on to lead ICICI Venture before founding the private equity firm Multiples Alternate Asset Management. In 2003, the then Ramnath-helmed ICICI Venture and RaRe Enterprises joined hands to acquire Tata Group's stake in what was known as Tata Infomedia.[2] Eighteen years later, in 2021, Multiples, RaRe Enterprises and the Canadian Pension Plan Investment Board (CPPIB) acquired the animal health business of Zydus Cadila group for approximately ₹2,921 crore.[3]

The market value of RJ's CEP zoomed by 161% in a single year from ₹16,350 crore on 31 December 2020 to ₹42,734 crore on 31 December 2021. The listings of three entities—Nazara Technologies, Metro Brands and Star Health and Allied Insurance—propelled the meteoric rise in market value. The three listings demonstrate the upside to PE investing.

Business Standard reported in August 2022 that RJ made around twenty PE investments.[4] Of these, at least six entities subsequently listed—Baazar Style Retail, Concord Biotech, Inventurus Knowledge Solutions, Metro Brands, Nazara Technologies and Star Health and Allied Insurance.

Five PE investments—Baazar Style, Concord, Inventurus, Metro and Nazara—shed light on RJ's investment persona and enhance our understanding of PE as an investment proposition. The sixth investment, Star Health, which is RJ's largest PE bet as of 2024, is the focus of the following chapter. PE firms may be categorised into at least three types—venture capital, growth equity and buyouts. RJ's PE investments fall mostly in the growth equity category.

Sector-agnostic Investments

RJ's PE investments spanned multiple industries. While Concord is a pharmaceutical firm, Baazar Style sells branded apparel, Inventurus is an IT-enabled healthcare solutions provider, Metro is a footwear chain and Nazara a digital entertainment provider. These firms (except Inventurus) share a similarity—they were poised to benefit from India's robust GDP growth, rising per-capita and disposable incomes and young population when RJ invested in them. Inventurus is an outlier, as the firm offers IT-enabled services to physician enterprises predominantly in the US and to a limited extent in Canada and Australia.

India's private final consumption expenditure (PFCE), which has been steadily growing and is projected to do so in tandem with rising GDP, drives the growth of Metro and Baazar Style. PFCE includes final consumption expenditure of households and non-profit institutions serving households, such as temples and gurudwaras.[5] India's PFCE in 1991 was $51 billion and had grown almost nineteen-fold to $966 billion in 2015. Between 2015 and 2020, PFCE grew at a CAGR of 11% to $1.64 trillion in 2020. India's PFCE as a percentage of GDP has remained steady at over 55% since at least FY2012. In calendar year 2019, India's PFCE-to-GDP ratio was 59% vis-à-vis the US' 65.5%, Brazil's 66.8%, Indonesia's 54% and China's 36.8%. With growing GDP and rising disposable income, India's PFCE-to-GDP ratio is likely to match that of the US' in the coming decades.

The composition of India's PFCE is also changing. PFCE comprises basic and discretionary spending. Expenditure on food, clothing and housing constitute basic spending. Discretionary spending includes education, healthcare, electricity, water supply, footwear, personal care products, processed foods, alcoholic and non-alcoholic beverages, tobacco, narcotics, fuel and gas, furnishing and household equipment, vehicle and personal transportation, spending on recreation and culture, communication, restaurants and hotels, financial insurance and other financial services. The share of basic spending in PFCE has declined from 46.6% in FY2012 to 40.4% in FY2020. The share of discretionary spending has correspondingly risen from 53.4% in FY2012 to 59.6% in FY2020. The rising share of discretionary spending, coupled with the top 20% of Indian households by income accounting for half of the total household consumption, bodes well for Baazar Style and Metro. The retail market in India was valued at ₹84.92 trillion in FY2024 and is projected to briskly grow at a 10.1% CAGR to ₹113.46 trillion in FY2027. The growth prospects for branded apparel sellers like Baazar Retail are favourable, underpinned by robust projected growth (CAGR) in clothes and accessories by 16% between FY2024 and FY2027.[6] India's footwear consumption at 1.9 pairs is just 60% of the global average of 3.2 pairs—this underpins Metro's growth prospects.

Nazara is a Mumbai-headquartered diversified gaming and sports media platform whose businesses span India and emerging and developed markets in Africa and North America. Nazara's favourable operating environment is evident in the rise in smartphone user penetration from 52% in 2016 to 78% in 2020, and an estimated 90% in 2023 and a corresponding increase in mobile gamers from 200 million in 2016 to 330 million in 2020, and an estimated 410 million in 2023. Smartphone users form an integral component of the gaming ecosystem, and mobile games contribute to the bulk of gaming revenues. Nazara's IPO prospectus dated 22 March 2021 states,

> Indian mobile gaming market is currently where the market in China was 8 to 10 years ago. Between 2012 and 2013, China had about 300 million mobile gamers, which is approximately the number of mobile gamers in India in 2020. Similarly, in 2012 the Chinese mobile gaming market had revenues of USD 1.3 billion, which is approximately close to the revenue for the Indian mobile gaming market in 2020. Based on how the mobile gaming market has taken off in China in the last few years, and with the Indian gaming market reflecting the Chinese gaming market of the 2010s, it is fair to assume that the Indian mobile gaming market will have a growth similar to that of China and will see an equivalent traction.

China reported mobile gaming revenues of $25.20 billion in 2020.[7]

Concord is one of the leading global developers and manufacturers of select fermentation-based active pharmaceutical ingredients (APIs) across immunosuppressants and oncology. Entry barriers for the products Concord manufactures are high. They include capital-intensive infrastructure and operational ecosystem, technological expertise, risk of contamination and raw material supply and price volatility.[8] According to Concord's IPO prospectus dated 9 August 2023, 'The potent combination of increasing domestic pharmaceutical demand, shifting of API sourcing from China to India, and growing capability and capacity of Indian manufacturers will drive the growth of the Indian API market. Domestic volume consumption of drugs is increasing given the increasing prevalence of chronic diseases and several drugs going off-patent, which will allow the introduction of new low-cost products and thus drive API volume growth.'

Inventurus is a technology-enabled healthcare solutions provider that offers a care enablement platform assisting physician enterprises in the US, Canada and Australia, with a focus on the US markets.[9] The founder-CEO of Inventurus, Sachin Gupta, is RJ's cousin. According to Inventurus' IPO prospectus dated 16 December 2024, the company performs the 'chores of healthcare, spanning administrative, clinical, and operational services through our proprietary technology platforms, so that physicians can focus on their core purpose of delivering care to patients. Combining technology, dedicated 203 resources and clinically-trained employees, our solutions enable stronger and financially sustainable healthcare enterprises'. The prospectus further states that Inventurus' growth is underpinned by widening supply–demand gap of healthcare professionals, shrinking margins of healthcare providers that are driving the adoption of technology, increase in healthcare consumerism and value-based care.

Medium-to-long Gestation Period

A key characteristic of PE investments is that investors are invested in their portfolio companies for periods ranging from a couple of years to decades. PE firms need to have access to long-term funding, as their investments in unlisted companies are illiquid. Lenders are unlikely to accept the shares of unlisted entities as collateral for loans. Further, exit routes are limited to the sale of shares to other PE investors and share buybacks by the unlisted entities themselves.

Metro was among RaRe Enterprises' early PE bets; RJ began investing in the company in 2002. The footwear retailer listed nineteen years later in 2021. The Jhunjhunwalas made their first tranche of investment in Inventurus in September 2006; the IT services firm listed more than eighteen years later in December 2024. The first tranche of investment in Concord was made in 2014; the pharma company listed almost nine years later, again in 2021. The IPO prospectus of Nazara reports that RaRe Enterprises made its first investment in December 2017. It took over three years after receiving its investment from RaRe Enterprises for Nazara to list. Star Health, the largest and most successful of RJ's PE investments as of 2024, received the first tranche of funding from RaRe Enterprises in May 2019 and listed 2.5 years later in December 2021. RJ was allotted shares in Baazar Style in October 2022; the apparel seller listed almost two years later in September 2024.

RaRe Enterprises remains invested in its six erstwhile PE investments—Baazar Style, Concord, Inventurus, Metro, Nazara and Star Health as of December 2024.

Unicorn-mukt Portfolio

A unicorn is a privately held start-up company valued at over $1 billion.[10] Four Indian unicorns—Nykaa (FSN E-Commerce Ventures), Paytm (One97 Communications), Policybazaar (PB Fintech) and Zomato (Eternal)—listed in 2021. As of 2024, Nykaa and Paytm are trading at less than half their IPO prices. The share prices of Policybazaar and Zomato too were lower than their respective IPO prices through 2022 and 2023 and recovered in 2024, a reflection of the then prevalent bull run in Indian stock markets.

Warren Buffett, an investor whom RJ admired and was often likened to, had invested ₹2,179 crore in Paytm in 2018. Buffett's firm Berkshire Hathaway, through its special purpose vehicle BH International Holdings, purchased 17.02 million Paytm shares at an average price of ₹1,279.70 per share.[11] Buffett sold 1.40 million shares during Paytm's November 2021 listing at the IPO price of ₹2,150, realising close to ₹301 crore cash. Paytm's price, however, tanked on listing, and has been declining since. *The Economic Times* reported that Buffett had sold his entire stake in Paytm by December 2023 and had realised just ₹1,272 crore in sales, thereby booking losses in excess of ₹600 crore.[12]

RJ eschewed unicorns, thereby avoiding the pitfalls of investing in overpriced stocks. Three of his six PE investments, Star Health, Inventurus and Metro, debuted as large-cap stocks. Concord was a mid-cap stock. Baazar Style and Nazara were small-cap stocks.

Performance, a Mixed Bag

The financial profiles of RJ's PE investments were a mixed bag at the time of their listing. This section analyses the financials of the five PE investments using four parameters: profitability, indebtedness, interest coverage and dividend payout. Table 14.1 provides their key financial metrics for the two reporting periods preceding their listings.

Of the five entities covered in this chapter, Concord, Inventurus and Metro had the strongest financial profiles. Their profit after tax (PAT) and adjusted cash flow from operations (adjusted CFO) margins were consistently positive. Baazar Style reported standalone FY2023 and consolidated FY2024 financials. Hence, its FY2023 and FY2024 financials are not comparable.

Baazar Style's PAT and adjusted CFO margins, though positive, were low in FY2024, as the apparel seller had leased its stores and incurred considerable lease expenses. Nazara reported post-tax losses and negative adjusted CFO. The Indian financial year spans 1 April to 31 March of the subsequent year. So, the impact of COVID-19 is evident in India Inc.'s financials in FY2021.

PAT is the contractual profit a firm earns during a reporting period and includes non-cash charges such as depreciation of tangible assets and amortisation of intangible assets such as trademarks and goodwill. Adjusted CFO, which is reported CFO minus interest expense, is the actual cash an entity generates during a reporting period and excludes non-cash charges. PAT and adjusted CFO figures diverge due to several reasons, including firms effecting sales and purchasing inputs on credit resulting in an accumulation of trade receivables and payables and inventory accumulation as entities manufacture goods for both current and future reporting periods. A sustainable firm will report positive PAT and adjusted CFO consistently. It is, however, possible for a firm to report a positive PAT but a negative CFO margin and vice versa. PAT and CFO margins are the two metrics expressed as percentages of revenues.

Two ratios are used to evaluate the entities' indebtedness—cash flow and balance sheet leverage. The ratio of net debt (debt minus cash) to the earnings before interest, taxes, depreciation and amortisation (EBITDA) is an indicator of cash flow leverage. An entity achieves a net cash position when its cash exceeds outstanding debt. The ratio of consolidated liabilities to net worth (the difference between assets and liabilities) denotes balance sheet leverage. It is important to monitor both metrics during times of stress, as it is possible for firms to maintain debt at acceptable levels in rupee terms but delay payments to vendors, resulting in an accumulation of liabilities. Jet Airways had adopted this practice during the years preceding its cessation of flying in April 2019.[13]

Table 14.1: Select Financial Metrics of RJ's PE Investments Prior to Listing

₹ Crore	*Reporting Period*	*PAT Margin*	*Adjusted CFO Margin*	*EBITDA Interest Cover*	*Dividend Payout*	*Net Debt / EBITDA*	*Liabilities / Networth*
Concord Biotech	FY2022	23.8%	27.5%	50.73	40.3%	0.02	0.19
	FY2023	27.0%	27.3%	91.43	29.4%	Net Cash	0.37
Nazara Technologies	FY2020	-10.3%	-1.1%	15.90	0.0%	Net Cash	0.32
	1H FY2021	-4.8%	-3.3%	32.90	0.0%	Net Cash	0.4
Metro Brands	FY2021	7.4%	30.1%	273.48	77.0%	1.23	0.96
	1H FY2022	12.9%	5.4%	1,061.14	69.4%	2.27	1.02
Baazar Style Retail	FY2023 [1]	0.6%	-4.18%	1.53	–	4.78	3.48
	FY2024 [2]	2.2%	3.09%	1.75	–	4.52	4.42
Inventurus Knowledge Solutions	FY2023	19.9%	80.56%	0.87	0.45	1.48	1.61
	1H FY2024	161.1%	146.11%	0.74	–	0.61	1.03

[1] & [2]: Baazar Retail reported standalone FY2023 & consolidated FY2024 financials

Source: IPO Prospectuses & author calculations

Both Concord and Nazara were in a net cash position and maintained low balance sheet leverage of below 1.0 time in the reporting periods preceding their listings. But there is a difference. Concord had achieved low cash flow and balance sheet leverage through a combination of consistent profits, most of which it reinvested in the business, and promoters' and PE investors' equity infusions. The loss-making Nazara attracted ample equity investments, as the PE investors were optimistic about its business prospects. Investor confidence was vindicated. Nazara turned profitable in FY2021 and reported year-on-year growth in PAT in FY2022 and FY2023. It maintained its net cash position and a low balance sheet leverage of 0.29 times as of 31 March 2023.

Goela observed, 'Inventurus, a business founded by Rakeshji's cousin Sachin Gupta, was close to his heart. Rakeshji was involved from the time of Inventurus' conceptualisation on a piece of paper till his demise.' The healthcare-focused IT firm's business and revenues grew robustly and PAT margin was maintained at over 15% since at least FY2024. Hence, Inventurus was able to achieve significant reductions (improvements) in both cash flow and balance sheet leverage.

Metro's cash flow leverage climbed to a moderate 2.27 times as of 30 September 2022 from a low 1.23 times in FY2021, its liabilities-to-net-worth ratio was maintained at an acceptable 1.0 time. Baazar Style's cash flow and balance sheet leverages were high at over 4.5 and 4.4 times respectively, a reflection of the liabilities incurred by leasing its stores.

EBITDA interest cover (EBITDA divided by interest expense) is a metric used to assess the adequacy of an entity's earnings to pay interest. An EBITDA interest cover of 1.0 time indicates that the entity's EBITDA is just about sufficient to pay interest; the higher this ratio, the better equipped a borrower is to pay interest. Ample equity investments enabled the then loss-making Nazara to minimise its borrowing and hence report a comfortable EBITDA cover of over 15 times during the two reporting periods preceding its listing. Baazar Style's EBITDA interest cover was adequate at 1.75 times in FY2024. The most financially stable among the entities covered in this chapter—Concord and Metro—generated EBITDAs that were in excess of 50 times their interest expense. Yet another financially stable investee, Inventurus, reported a comfortable EBITA interest cover in excess of 5 times since at least FY2024.

Dividend payments are not an indicator of financial strength. The now-defunct Infrastructure Leasing & Financial Services (IL&FS) reported losses in the years leading to its default and yet paid dividends from its reserves.[14] Dividend payment was not a key consideration for RJ while making investment decisions. As in the case of RaRe Enterprises' CEP, the investor's PE portfolio includes entities that pay zero dividends. Baazar Style and Nazara did not pay dividends in the two reporting periods preceding their listing.

Inventurus paid the highest dividends among investees in FY2024—₹165 crore, which is equivalent to 45% of its PAT. Concord paid the second-highest dividends in rupee terms—₹71 crore per annum in FY2022 and FY2023. Yet its dividend payout ratio, i.e., the percentage of PAT distributed as dividends, was moderate at over 27% in both years. Though Metro paid ₹50 crore dividends in FY2021 and ₹30 crore in the first half of FY2022, its dividend payout ratio was high at 77% in FY2021 and 69.4% in FY2022. This comparison has two takeaways for investors. First, Concord's high PAT margin in excess of 23% vis-à-vis Metro's single-digit margin enabled the former to pay higher rupee dividends while maintaining a moderate payout ratio. Second, during expansionary phases, Metro would have to finance its capital expenditures by reducing or skipping dividends if it has to maintain indebtedness at sustainable levels.

Hunting in Packs

It is not just lions that hunt in packs. For multiple reasons, PE firms are seldom the sole investors in unlisted entities. First, PE firms prudently diversify their risks by investing in several firms rather than concentrating their investments in a single entity. Second, knowledge sharing occurs when multiple PE firms jointly invest. In addition to the promoters and RaRe Enterprises, a list of entity-wise pre-IPO investors is provided in Table 14.2.

Table 14.2 indicates that domestic and overseas PE firms and corporates and high-net-worth investors (HNIs) financed Indian growth companies. The domestic PE firms include IIFL Special Opportunities Fund and Tata Capital Growth Fund. Overseas PE firms include Helix Investment Holdings and Westbridge Capital.

The pharmaceutical firm Sanofi India, previously known as Hoechst India, invested in Concord. Two reasons may have motivated Sanofi, which is listed on BSE and NSE, to invest in Concord. First, Sanofi may have wished to invest in entities operating in its industry at low prices and profit by selling its stakes at listing. Second, established firms like Sanofi may acquire minority stakes in smaller firms operating in the same industry with a view to gradually increase their stakes and/or acquire majority stakes and hence increase their market shares.

The pre-IPO investors of Inventurus, Metro and Baazar Style did not include PE firms. The promoters and several HNIs financed both firms during the years preceding their IPOs.

Utpal Sheth said, 'In the private equity space, we (RaRe Enterprises) worked with Multiples Alternate Asset Management, ICICI Venture and Blackstone. We have co-invested with these entities and also sequentially invested i.e., RaRe Enterprises and the aforesaid entities invested in the same companies at different points of time.'[15]

Table 14.2: Entity Wise Pre-IPO Investors

Entity	***Pre-IPO Investors***
Nazara Technologies	IIFL Special Opportunities Funds
	Westbridge Ventures I
	Kae Capital Fund
	Kalysta Capital Fund
Star Health	Oman Insurance Company PSC
	India Advantage Fund S3 I
	Tata Capital Growth Fund I
	Alpha TC Holdings Pte Ltd.
	Alpha FDI Holding Pte Ltd
	Apis Growth 6 Limited
	Westbridge AIF I
	Madison India Opportunities Fund
Concord Biotech	Helix Investment Holdings Pte. Limited
	Hoechst India Limited
	Sudman Consultants LLP

Source: IPO Prospectuses

Rockstar Backers and Successful Listings

Having high-profile HNIs investing in unlisted firms does not necessarily guarantee their success at the time of listing. Two metrics used to gauge the success of an IPO are subscription and listing day pop, which is the extent of share price appreciation on the day a stock debuts on the stock exchange. The response to IPOs floated by entities backed by RJ as a PE investor vary from Nazara, which garnered a subscription of over 175 times its IPO

Table 14.3: Performance of Jhunjhunwala-Backed IPOs

	Subscription (Times)				
	QIB	**NII**	***Retail***	***Employee***	***Overall***
Nazara Technologies	103.77	389.89	75.29	7.55	175.46
Star Health	1.03	0.19	1.10	0.10	0.79
Metro Brands	8.49	3.02	1.13	-	3.64
Concord Biotech	67.67	16.99	3.78	24.48	24.87
Baazar Style Retail	81.83	59.41	9.07	35.08	40.63
Inventurus Knowledge Solutions	80.64	23.25	14.55	-	52.68

Source: IPO prospectuses

size (₹583 crore), to Star Health, which was undersubscribed. Star Health received bids equivalent to just 79% of its ₹6,400 crore IPO (Table 14.3). In India, quotas are allotted to qualified institutional buyers (QIB), non-institutional investors (NIIs are retail investors who place bids of over ₹2 lakh in an IPO), retail investors (place bids up to ₹2 lakh) and employees of the entity floating the IPO. The data in Table 14.3 indicates that retail investors did not rush to subscribe to the Star Health IPO, though the media and social media relentlessly publicised the fact that RJ had backed the insurer as a PE investor.

Similarly, Baazar Style's share price rose by a modest 2.78% while Star Health's share price inched up by less than 1.0%. Metro's share price dipped by a marginal 1.36%. Three entities (Nazara, Inventurus and Concord) delivered significant listing day pops. This does not imply that high-profile backers do not have any impact on an IPO's performance. Statisticians would recommend a minimum sample size of 25–30 entities for reliable conclusions to be drawn.

The House (Almost) Always Wins

An IPO typically comprises two components—an offer for sale (OFS) and a fresh issue. The entity floating the IPO collects the proceeds from the fresh issue and the selling shareholders collect the OFS proceeds. RaRe Enterprises was not a selling shareholder in the IPOs covered in this chapter. Selling shareholders are pre-IPO investors who partially or completely divest their stakes in an IPO. PE backers sell their stakes during an IPO if the listing price is attractive enough for them to clock a profitable exit and deploy the sale proceeds in other businesses. Those firms that remain invested post an entity's listing are optimistic about the firm's prospects and hence share price appreciation, and/or their investment strategy is to invest in listed and unlisted businesses.

Concord, Inventurus and Nazara were entirely OFS; the issuing entities did not receive any cash from the IPOs. Metro and Star Health comprised both OFS and fresh issues (Table 14.4).

Table 14.4: IPO Sizes, OFS and Fresh Issues, ₹ Crore

	IPO Size	***Use of Proceeds***	
		OFS	***Fresh Issue***
Nazara Technologies	582.69	582.69	–
Star Health	6,400.44	4,400.44	2,000.00
Metro Brands	1,367.51	1,072.51	295.00
Concord Biotech	1,550.52	1,550.52	–
Baazar Style Retail	834.68	686.68	148.00
Inventurus Knowledge Solutions	2,497.92	2,497.92	–

Source: IPO prospectuses

SEBI requires entities floating IPOs (henceforth referred to as issuers) to report the prices at which they allocated shares to the pre-IPO investors in the prospectus. SEBI also requires issuers to report the weighted average acquisition cost (WAAC) of shares allotted to the selling shareholders. Table 14.5 provides entity-wise WAAC and the listing day pop.

The table indicates that the listing pop IPO investors earned paled in comparison to the handsome profits selling shareholders earned. Investors who subscribed to the Metro IPO experienced a marginal depreciation in their investment on the listing day.

Analysing the trajectory of RJ's PE investments in Baazar Style, Concord, Inventurus, Metro and Nazara will shed light on the modus operandi and magnitude of profits this asset category can generate. Ascertaining the profits RJ made in his PE investments is complicated, as he purchased shares both from the entities he

Table 14.5: Promoters and PEs Profits vis-à-vis Listing Day Pop

Column	**A**	**B**	**C**	**[B / A] - 1**	**[C / B] - 1**
Entity	***Selling Shareholder's WAAC, ₹ [1]***	***Issue Price, ₹***	***Closing Price on Listing Day, ₹***	***Selling Shareholders Gross Profit***	***Listing Day Pop***
Nazara Technologies	0 – 730.95	1,101	1,584.40	At least 51%	43.91%
Star Health	47.00 – 175.69	900	906.85	412% to 1,815%	0.76%
Metro Brands	0 – 14.16	500	493.45	At least 3,431%	-1.31%
Concord Biotech	227.14	741	942.33	226%	27.17%
Baazar Style Retail	0 – 124.50	389	399.83	At least 212%	2.78%
Inventurus Knowledge Solutions	0 – 65.73	1,329	1,886.65	At least 1,922%	41.96%

[1] WAAC - Weighted average acquisition cost

Source: IPO prospectuses, chittorgarh.com & author calculations

invested in and from other PE investors. This is standard practice, and transactions between PE investors in unlisted entities are not reported and are hence difficult to track.

Between 1 November and 13 December 2004, RaRe Enterprises purchased 335,000 Concord shares at an average price of ₹329.70, thereby investing ₹11.53 crore in the pharma company. Five years later, on 4 December 2009, Concord bought back 232,237 shares or close to 70% of RaRe Enterprises' holdings at ₹873 per share for ₹20.27 crore. RJ had not only recovered his investment but had also booked an ₹8.74 crore gross profit (₹20.27 crore buyback proceeds minus ₹11.53 crore share proceeds) in five years. Gross profit, which does not include the cost of raising funds, administration expenses, the time value of money on account of remaining invested in the firm and taxes, translates to a modest annualised return of 12%. Sensex's annualised return during this period was 24.4%.

So, why did RJ remain invested in Concord? For starters, he had recovered his investment, which gave him the funding to invest in other ventures, and had earned an annualised return of 12%. Had RJ invested in an ETF that tracked Sensex, he would have earned a 24.4% return annually but would not have recovered his investment. Further, Concord sweetened the deal by declaring a 1:1 bonus issue on 1 November 2010 and 25 November 2013. On 8 July 2022, i.e., a year before listing, Concord effected a 1:10 share split. Three days later on 11 July, the company announced a 1:10 bonus issue. Bonus issues and share splits are essentially free shares an issuer allots to its investors. The 102,763 shares RaRe Enterprises owned on 4 December 2009 after the Concord buyback would have grown to over 41 million shares had RaRe Enterprises not sold its shares. But RJ's shareholding in Concord as of the date of the IPO prospectus, 9 August 2023, was over 25 million shares. The Big Bull had profited by selling close to 16 million zero cost shares Concord had allotted to him through multiple bonus issues and a share split. Concord listed on 18

August 2023. RJ's listed equities portfolio appreciated by 7.15% or ₹5,143 crore in the September 2023 quarter, of which Concord's listing accounted for 56% or ₹2,895 crore.

A slew of new economy stocks including Paytm, Policybazaar, Nykaa, Zomato and the RJ-backed Nazara listed in 2021. Their IPOs were oversubscribed, as optimistic investors believed that these growth companies powered by technology and digital infrastructure would deliver superior returns. While Nazara did deliver a handsome listing day pop of close to 44%, its share price declined subsequently and, as of 2024, continues to trade at lower than the ₹1,101 issue price. The selling shareholders and IPO investors who sold on the listing day have profited from investing in Nazara. IPO investors who sold their holdings subsequently booked cash losses, while those who remain invested as of 2024 have experienced a depreciation in investment value. What about RJ?

Interestingly, RJ purchased the 263,545 Nazara shares on 8 December 2017 not from the issuer but from another PE investor, Westbridge Capital. RaRe Enterprises' CEO, Utpal Sheth also purchased 2,780 shares from Westbridge Capital. The price at which the sales were conducted is not reported in Nazara's IPO prospectus. Barely a fortnight after RaRe Enterprises purchased the Nazara stock, the issuer announced a 2:5 share split. Exactly one month later, on 8 January 2018, Nazara declared a 1:4 bonus issue. Within a month of purchasing the stock, RaRe Enterprises' holding in Nazara was 17.5 times its purchase or over 4.6 million shares. Of these 4.6 million shares, Nazara's share split and bonus issue resulted in the issuer allotting close to 4.35 million shares free of cost. Also, the share split and bonus issue implied that RaRe Enterprises, average acquisition cost (share purchase in rupee terms divided by number of shares) of Nazara shares had declined by 90%! As of the date of the IPO prospectus, 22 March 2021, RaRe Enterprises owned over 3.29 million shares.[16] This meant that RJ's investment vehicle had sold over 1.3 million of the 4.35 million shares before the IPO. The market value of RaRe Enterprises' holding in Nazara was ₹286 crore when the issuer listed on 31 March 2021. RaRe Enterprises' listed equities appreciated by close to ₹4,340 crore in the quarter ended 31 March 2021, of which Nazara accounted for 6.6%.

RaRe Enterprises invested ₹43.48 crore in the footwear retailer Metro at an average price of ₹1,234.46 to acquire 352,250 shares on 4 January 2008, almost thirteen years before its December 2021 IPO. Metro's IPO prospectus states, 'We have also been supported by our investors, including Mr. Rakesh Jhunjhunwala since 2007.' This statement may imply that RJ purchased Metro shares from pre-IPO investors in 2007. Metro announced a 2:1 bonus issue in October 2008 and a 1:2 share split in March 2021. This meant that RJ ought to have owned over 2.09 million shares as of the prospectus date. However, Metro's IPO prospectus reports that he owned 39.15 million shares by December 2021.[17] Hence, RaRe Enterprises had purchased Metro's shares from other pre-IPO investors, and the share split and bonus issue amplified its holding. This is indeed a testimony to the faith RJ had in the business and its promoters. While we do not know the quantum and prices of shares RJ purchased from other pre-IPO investors, my calculations indicate that the average acquisition price of the tranche of shares RJ purchased on 4 January 2008 declined by over 83% from ₹1,234.46 to ₹207.50 in March 2021.

RaRe Enterprises' holding in Metro was valued at ₹3,973 crore by end December 2021, nine days after its December 2021 listing. The December 2021 quarter has been RaRe Enterprises' most remunerative to date, when the market value of its listed equities appreciated by 47% or ₹13,662 crore. The addition of Metro accounted for 29% of the portfolio appreciation. The cumulative price appreciation of shares RJ owned since at least 30 September 2021 contributed to another ₹578 crore or 4% of the quarterly portfolio appreciation.

So, what contributed to the balance 67% or ₹9,110 crore portfolio appreciation by end December 2021? The listing of Star Health and Allied Insurance did.

The Challenges of PE Investing

There prevails a view in the market that PE is an asset class that generates supernormal profits. However, it is important to recognise the elevated risks that accompany high returns. The bumper profits PE backers earn in successful deals offset their losses in unsuccessful transactions. Part of the high returns of PE deals is compensation for the long gestation period and illiquid nature of the asset class; it is difficult for investors to sell their stakes till the investee is listed. Responsible PE investors provide inputs regarding strategic direction and sound corporate governance practices to investees.

Inventurus' Sachin Gupta acknowledged, 'In the last 16 years of his (RJ's) short life, we spoke every two days, if not more. And we met in person at least once a week when I was in India. Every conversation with him was like a drug. It would either leave me with a dramatic high or feeling like a total idiot. I cannot remember any encounter that didn't need me to think on my feet. Several years into this deeply personal and professional relationship, I realised this was his way to teach and mentor. There was nothing formal about it but it was deliberate and the learning was profound.'[18]

PE investors may also finance their investees during crises. Rajiv Agarwal, the Managing Director of PE investments at RaRe Enterprises, observed, 'Inventurus was in financial stress a few years before listing and needed ₹80 crore. Rakeshji loaned the money and did not use the opportunity to increase his stake at a low share price.'[19]

There was even an instance of RaRe Enterprises upping its stake in a PE investment due to the change in ownership of another investor. Agarwal observed, 'RaRe Enterprises first invested in Concord Biotech in December 2004. In 2005, the Hyderabad-based Matrix Labs bought a 58% stake in Concord. In 2006, Mylan NV acquired Matrix and was desirous of exiting the investment in Concord. The promoters and RaRe Enterprises bought Mylan's stake in Concord.'[20] Agarwal is on the boards of several companies including Aptech, Concord, Hungama Digital Media, Nazara and Alchemy.

I was surprised that RJ was not a PE backer for his mentor R.K. Damani's flagship enterprise—D-Mart. Ramesh Damani explained, 'A few years before R.K. Damani took Avenue Supermart (D-Mart) public, he gifted family and friends including me and Rakesh shares of the retailer. It was an extraordinarily generous gift. While Rakesh wanted to buy D-Mart shares, R.K. Damani did not want to dilute his stake.'[21]

'My strike rate is not high. I would have made 20 private equity investments by now, but 10 of them would be duds, dead and written off,' the Big Bull remarked at the Times Network India Economic Conclave 2021.[22] Notwithstanding the losses, RJ backed unlisted companies as a PE investor. It is evident that the significant appreciation in RaRe Enterprises' successful PE investments offset the losses from the duds by a wide margin. The story of one such immensely profitable investment for RaRe Enterprises is narrated in the following chapter.

15

Janus Stock

INSURANCE STOCKS, ESPECIALLY THOSE OF PROPERTY AND casualty (P&C) insurers known as general insurers in India, are a favourite with value investors across the globe. A key reason is that insurance is a defensive industry, that is, even during a cyclical downturn—or rather, especially during a recession—the insured (referred to as insurance policy holders or policyholders in India) continue paying their premiums. Most policyholders would like to at least maintain, if not enhance, their insurance cover during downturns. Hence, insurance premiums tend to be stable even during recessions.

Another attractive feature of insurers is their unique business model, aptly described in the 2022 annual report of the Warren Buffett-helmed Berkshire Hathaway. 'Our property/casualty ("P/C") insurance business has been the engine propelling Berkshire's growth since 1967, the year we acquired National Indemnity and its sister company, National Fire & Marine, for $8.6 million. Today, National Indemnity is the largest P/C company in the world as measured by net worth. Insurance is a business of promises ... One reason we were attracted to the P/C business was the industry's business model: P/C insurers receive premiums upfront and pay claims later .... This collect-now, pay-later model leaves P/C companies holding large sums—money we call "float"—that will eventually go to others. Meanwhile, insurers get to invest this float for their own benefit. Though individual policies and claims come and go, the amount of float an insurer holds usually remains fairly stable in relation to premium volume. Consequently, as our business grows, so does our float.' Berkshire goes on to report that its float has increased 4,208 times over a period of fifty-two years, from $39 million in 1970 to $164.11 billion in 2022. It is this float money that has fuelled the explosive growth in Berkshire's assets from $30 billion in 1995 to $948 billion in 2022.[1]

The insurance business is even more attractive in the world's fifth-largest economy, as the country's insurance penetration and density are lower than not just the four countries whose nominal GDPs are larger than that of India's—the US, China, Japan and Germany—but also the global average and the mean of emerging Asian economies (Table 15.1). This implies that the growth prospects of India's insurance industry, underpinned by a rapidly growing economy and improving disposable incomes, are promising. Insurance penetration is defined as premiums as a percentage of GDP while insurance density is premiums per capita.

Table 15.1: Insurance Penetration and Density, 2022

	US	*China*	*Japan*	*Germany*	*India*	*Emerging Asia [1]*	*World*
Insurance penetration	11.60%	3.90%	8.20%	5.90%	4.00%	3.60%	6.80%
Insurance density, $	8,885	489	2,690	2,881	92	229	853

[1] Including India and China

Source: sigma 3/2023, Swiss Re Institute

It is these favourable industry dynamics that led to the proliferation of private sector players in the life and general insurance sectors after the government-appointed Malhotra Committee recommended the opening up of the insurance industry in 2000. The Insurance Regulatory and Development Authority of India (IRDAI) was tasked with overseeing the industry.[2] At this juncture, the state-owned players dominated the industry. Life Insurance Corporation of India (LIC) was a virtual monopoly, with a market share of 99.5% in FY2001. New India Assurance, with a market share of 34%, United India Insurance (22%), Oriental Insurance and National Insurance (20% each) controlled 96% of the P&C / general insurance sector.[3]

By 31 March 2019, there were twenty-four life insurers, thirty-four general insurers and two reinsurers operating in India. The intense competitive landscape and India's GDP growing at the second-highest rate among major economies resulted in the country's life insurance premium growing tenfold during the eighteen-year period ending 31 March 2019 to ₹508,100 crore and gross direct premium of general insurers grew fourteenfold to ₹1,72,500 crore. LIC retained its leadership position, with a market share of 66% in FY2019. But the combined market shares of the four state-owned general insurers had more than halved to 42%, though New India Assurance held on to its leadership position with a market share of 16%. The aggregate market shares of the private general insurers exceeded that of the state-owned insurers by FY2019.

Seven private players led the charge to overtake the businesses of the four state-owned general insurers. This spirited seven were led by ICICI Lombard, with a market share of 8% in FY2019, Bajaj Allianz (6%), HDFC Ergo (5%), Tata AIG (4.5%), Reliance General (3.6%), Star Health and Allied Insurance (3.1%) and Cholamandalam MS (2.6%). Of these seven, Star Health was an outlier for two reasons. First, it was neither backed by a financial institution nor a conglomerate.

ICICI Bank and HDFC Limited (which merged with HDFC Bank in July 2023) held controlling stakes in ICICI Lombard and HDFC Ergo, respectively. Conglomerates such as Bajaj, Tata, Anil Dhirubhai Ambani Group (ADAG) and the Murugappa Group are the largest shareholders of Bajaj Allianz, Tata AIG, Reliance General and Cholamandalam MS, respectively. Second, Star Health is a monoline insurer selling health insurance, referred to as standalone health insurer (SAHI) in India. The remaining six sold fire, marine, motor and health insurance. Another interesting aspect is that Star Health and Reliance General are not joint ventures with overseas insurers, whereas ICICI Lombard, Bajaj Allianz, HDFC Ergo, Tata AIG and Cholamandalam MS are.

The Trailblazer

Venkatasamy Jagannathan, a former chairman and managing director of the state-owned United India Insurance, founded India's first SAHI—Star Health, which is headquartered in Chennai. Jagannathan aspired to provide competitively priced and comprehensive health insurance to India's large and growing middle-income group. ETA Star Group (a Dubai-headquartered investment joint venture between Al Ghurair and the Tamil entrepreneur B.S. Abdur Rehman), Oman Insurance Company PSC, Jagannathan and a few HNIs subscribed to Star Health's initial equity of ₹10.50 crore (around $2.3 million in 2006).

In May 2006, Jagannathan and twelve employees began Star Health's operations in a modest office at Madha Church Road in Chennai, the monthly rent of which was ₹30,000. A journalist, who did not wish to be named, observed, 'Jagannathan is married to the sister of the Tamil politician, Vaiyapuri Gopalsamy, better known as Vaiko, the founder of MDMK—a Tamil Nadu-based political party. MDMK has mostly been an ally of the DMK, one of the two political parties that have dominated Tamil Nadu's political landscape since 1969; the other being AIADMK. Star Health's founding coincided with the DMK being voted back to power in the 2006 state elections. The Indian National Congress, an ally of the DMK, was in power in the neighbouring state of Andhra Pradesh at this point of time.'

Star Health was viewed with scepticism till it secured a health insurance programme each in Tamil Nadu and Andhra Pradesh.[4] These two contracts served to strengthen the brand's visibility among its target clientele and kick-started the SAHI's growth, which attracted more PE investors. ICICI Venture invested in Star Health through its India Advantage Fund S31 since 2010, Tata Capital Growth Fund 1 and the Singapore-headquartered private equity firm Alpha TC Holdings since 2013.

In FY2019, Star Health reported ₹128-crore post-tax profits, which were an eye-watering 57% of its ₹226-crore revenues. Insurers earn profits from two key sources—underwriting insurance and investing. Underwriting may generate profits or losses; this is a function of the insurer's risk assessment prowess and the quantum of claims incurred. It is imperative for insurers to invest prudently so that investment income offsets underwriting losses, if any. By FY2019, there were seven SAHIs in India—Aditya Birla, Care Health, HDFC Ergo, Manipal Cigna, Niva Bupa, Reliance Health, and Star Health. Of these, Star Health was the sole entity that reported an underwriting profit. Of the thirty-two general insurers operating in India, only five, including Star Health, reported underwriting profits in FY2019. All four state-owned general insurers—National Insurance, New India Assurance, Oriental Insurance and United India Insurance—reported underwriting losses.[5]

Star Health's robust performance incentivised existing investors, attracted new investors and encouraged employees to subscribe to its equity. In FY2019 and FY2020, investors subscribed to ₹350 crore and ₹147 crore of Star Health's equity, respectively. The new investors included RJ, WestBridge AIF

I, Madison India Opportunities Trust Fund, MIO Star, Apis Growth 15 Limited.

RJ made his first investment in Star Health on 16 May 2019; he purchased over 4.9 million shares for ₹70 crore, which translates to a share price of ₹142.68. Prior to the 16 May investment, Star Health's book value per share was ₹30.57. Hence, RJ and the other investors, in FY2020, paid a price that was 4.67 times the book value per share. The premium investors paid over the book value reflected in Star Health's sustained robust performance, with its market share improving from 3.13% in FY2019 to 3.57% in FY2020 and post-tax profits more than doubling from ₹128 crore to ₹268 crore. Star Health's equity mobilisation in FY2021 was the highest in its sixteen-year history as an unlisted insurer—a record ₹2,639 crore. But it was compulsion and not investors' enthusiasm to finance a rising star that impelled this equity injection.

Black Swan

India Ratings and Research (Ind-Ra), the Indian arm of Fitch Ratings, has assigned credit ratings on Star Health since August 2017. The credit rating agency (CRA) has emphasised Star Health's 'monoline revenue stream' or business concentration risk linked to selling just health insurance as a rating constraint in all its rating rationales published since August 2017.

The validity of this observation became apparent during the COVID-19 outbreak; health insurance claims sky-rocketed by 42% in FY2021 and 95% in FY2022. Consequently Star Health, which reported underwriting profits in FY2020, generated 73% of SAHIs' underwriting losses in FY2021 and 63% in FY2022. Though investment income partially offset underwriting losses, it was not adequate to insulate Star Health from post-tax losses (Table 15.2).

Table 15.2: Star Health's Select Metrics Before and During COVID-19

₹ Crore	FY2020	FY2021	FY2022
Claims incurred	3,087	4,369	8,540
Underwriting Profit / (Loss)	155	-1,732	-2,062
Post-tax Profit / (Loss), PAT	1	-1,086	-1,041

Source: Star Health annual reports and IPO prospectus

The recurring losses resulted in Star Health's solvency ratio plunging from 2.22 in March 2021. Solvency ratio is a measure of capital adequacy that indicates the sufficiency of an insurer's assets to repay liabilities and debts; the IRDAI requires general insurers to maintain a minimum solvency ratio of 1.5 times.

What was Star Health's solvency ratio in September 2021 after the insurer had reported eighteen months of losses? Here is where things get interesting. While Star Health's IPO prospectus dated 7 December 2021 reports that its solvency ratio was 1.52 in September 2021, IRDAI's 'Handbook on Indian Insurance Statistics 2021-22' pegs the figure at 0.03! According to IRDAI, by September 2021, Star Health's solvency ratio had not just breached the regulatory minimum to the second-lowest among general insurers (with the state-owned National Insurance reporting the lowest solvency ratio of 0.01); it was practically non-existent!

Quixotic Rating Upgrade

The weakening of Star Health's financial performance coincided with Ind-Ra upgrading Star Health's credit rating from 'IND AA-' to 'IND AA'. The CRA cited seven key rating drivers—sustained leadership position in the health insurance segment, adequate liquidity, established claim processing and underwriting practices, experienced management, COVID-19-induced volatility in operating and capital buffers, single line of business, and diversified shareholding.[6] The CRA did not deem it necessary to opine on Star Health's year and a half of losses, their impact on the solvency ratio and whether the insurer's solvency ratio complied with the regulatory minimum of 1.5.

A table summarising key financials at the end of the rationale reported Star Health's losses and negative return on net worth for FY2021, though.

The rating rationale dated 20 September 2021 reported the solvency ratios of 1.65 on 30 June 2021, 2.21 on 31 March 2021 and 1.88 on 31 March 2020. The CRA further stated, 'As per Ind-Ra's stress case scenerio,* the company's solvency margin would continue to be adequate to meet the regulatory requirements post factoring infusion of primary capital raised through IPO, which would be around INR20 billion along with issuance of subordinated debt of about INR5 billion depending upon market conditions in FY22.'

Credit ratings are supposed to be forward-looking exercises, wherein CRAs take into account current and projected performance to assess an entity's debt servicing ability. Further, rated entities like Star Health are contractually obliged to provide non-public information like interim financials and their impact on solvency ratios to CRAs. That Ind-Ra in September 2021 chose to look at Star Health's solvency ratios only up to 30 June 2021 and Star Health's pipeline IPO and subordinated debt issue to bolster solvency ratio is puzzling. Did Ind-Ra imply that it expected Star Health's IPO to be a success?

Fortunately for Star Health and Ind-Ra, investors and the media did not question the rationale of a rating upgrade against the backdrop of mounting losses and their impact on the insurer's solvency ratio. Star Health's IPO subscribers seem to have overlooked how critical the listing was for the insurer

---

* Scenario was spelt as 'scenerio' in the rating rationale.

to shore up its solvency ratio—an imperative to remain in business and comply with regulations—and did not exercise their bargaining power.

Peer-less IPO

Star Health's rather aggressive pricing belied its precarious situation. In December 2021, Star Health floated a ₹7,249-crore IPO, comprising a ₹2,000-crore fresh issue whose proceeds would accrue to the insurer and a ₹5,249-crore OFS by several pre-IPO investors referred to in India as the selling shareholders.* RJ was not among the selling shareholders. RJ and Westbridge AIF remained invested in Star Health after its IPO and are categorised as promoters in the insurer's IPO prospectus.[7] This demonstrates his optimism about the long-term prospects of Star Health.

A cursory examination of the 'Basis for the Offer Price' section of Star Health's IPO prospectus indicates that the IPO price was untenable at best and over-ambitious at worst. The company reported that its earnings per share (EPS), price-earnings (P/E) ratio and return on net worth (RONW; post-tax profit expressed as a percentage of an entity's assets minus liabilities) were all negative for FY2021 and the six months ending 30 September 2021, as the insurer had reported losses. The IPO prospectus then listed ICICI Lombard General Insurance and New India Assurance as peers with P/E ratios of 46.66 and 15.30, respectively, and stated, 'ICICI Lombard General Insurance Company Ltd. is not strictly comparable with the Company as they operate under general insurance with health insurance not forming a significant

* The selling shareholders were Apis Growth 6 Limited, MIO IV Star, University of Notre Dame DU LAC, MIO Star, ROC Capital Pty Limited, Venkatasamy Jagannathan, Sai Satish, Konark Trust, Berjis Minoo Desai and MMPL Trust.

component, whereas the Company is a standalone health insurance provider.'[8*]

Valuing or pricing an entity's stock is a subjective exercise, and several multiples may be used for this purpose, including P/E, price-to-book value (P/BV), price-to-sales and enterprise-value-to-EBITDA ratios. Also, while Star Health was the first SAHI to list in India, estimating the share price based on the P/BV ratio of India's listed insurers is appropriate given the commonalities in the macroeconomic environment, regulatory oversight, risk factors and business models of most types of insurance companies—life, general, reinsurance and SAHI.

Star Health was the seventh insurer in India to be listed. A week ahead of the listing, that is, on 1 December 2021, the asset-weighted average P/BV ratio of the six listed insurers—New India Assurance (NIA), General Insurance Corporation (GIC), SBI Life, ICICI Prudential, ICICI Lombard and HDFC Life—was 8.76, which translates to a listing price of ₹181 for Star Health. The P/BV ratios of the state-owned insurers, NIA and GIC, at around 1.0 was much lower than those of the private insurers, which ranged from 8.81 to 16.23. The asset-weighted P/BV ratio for the private insurers, which may be considered more apposite peers for Star Health, was 11.84, based on which Star Health's listing price would have been ₹244. These are rather optimistic estimates, as no haircut has been assigned for the losses Star Health reported in the eighteen months preceding the IPO and its ambiguous solvency ratio. At the listing price of ₹900 per share, Star Health's P/BV ratio was 43.65, which was 5 times and 3.69 times the metric for all insurers and private insurers, respectively! The workings are provided in Appendix 6.

Star Health's pricing did not reflect three red flags. First, investor sentiment was negative in the aftermath of the ₹18,300-crore Paytm IPO, which was India's largest IPO in 2021 and the

* New India Assurance, also a general insurer, was omitted in this statement.

third largest to date. On listing day, 18 November 2021, Paytm's share price had crashed by 27.25%. Second, Star Health was the smallest insurer and one with the weakest financial metrics in the period preceding the listing. In fact, it was the sole loss-making Indian insurer at the time of listing as of 2024 (Table 15.3). Though LIC listed five months after Star Health, its performance has been included in Tables 15.3 and 15.4 to present a complete picture.

Third, all insurer listings, except HDFC Life, were lacklustre—they failed to garner large subscriptions and achieve a listing-day pop. HDFC Life was subscribed 4.89 times and its share price rose by 19% on listing day. While the IPOs of NIA, GIC, SBI Life, ICICI Prudential and ICICI Lombard garnered subscriptions ranging from 1.20 to 10.48 times, the share prices of NIA, GIC and ICICI Prudential declined on the listing day. The share prices of ICICI Lombard and SBI Life registered modest listing day pops of less than 5%. In May 2024, Go Digit General Insurance floated a successful IPO that garnered 9.60 times subscriptions and registered a listing day pop of 12.45%.

Star Health ignored the warning signals and priced its stock at ₹900 per share. Retail investors and qualified institutional buyers (QIBs include banks, mutual funds and foreign portfolio investors) fully subscribed to their respective quota. The insurer received bids equivalent to just 19% of its non-institutional investor (NII comprising retail investors, non-resident Indians and trusts who apply for more than ₹2,00,000 worth shares) quota. Employees placed bids equivalent to just 10% of their quota. The IPO had garnered bids equivalent to just 79% of the issue size; Star Health had no option but to prune its IPO size from ₹7,249 crore to ₹6,400 crore. While the insurer received the ₹2,000 crore that was critical to strengthen its capitalisation, the OFS component was reduced to ₹4,400 crore.

Star Health earned the dubious distinction of being the sole IPO in 2021 and the only insurance listing to be undersubscribed. The

Table 15.3: Star Health's Weak Financials Ahead of Listing

	Listing Date	*Key Metrics*				
		FY	***Revenue* [1]**	**PAT *Margin***	**SR [2]**	***Mkt Share* [3]**
LIC of India	17 May 2022	FY2021	685,100	0.8%	1.77	61.60%
New India Assurance	13 November 2022	FY2017	20,600	4.1%	2.27	15.00%
GIC of India	25 October 2017	FY2017	29,300	10.7%	1.83	60.00%
HDFC Life	17 November 2017	FY2017	30,600	2.9%	2.01	4.70%
SBI Life	3 October 2017	FY2017	30,300	3.2%	2.11	5.00%
ICICI Prudential Life	29 September 2016	FY2016	20,200	8.2%	3.21	5.22%
ICICI Lombard General	27 September 2017	FY2017	7,200	8.9%	2.13	8.40%
Star Health & Allied	10 December 2021	FY2020	5,300	-15.6%	0.03 / 1.52 ?	4.65%

[1] Revenue denominated in ₹ Crore
[2] SR - Solvency Ratio
[3] Mkt Share - Market Share

Source: IPO Prospectuses, Handbook on Indian Insurance Statistics, IRDAI and author calculations

SAHI being an RJ portfolio company did not offset an exorbitant pricing and weak financial performance of the preceding eighteen months. The listing day ended with Star Health's share price inching up by less than 1% to close at ₹907. IPO investors must have heaved a sigh of relief.

Different Strokes for Different Folks

There was another category of investors, though, who were laughing on their way to the bank. The pre-IPO investors who were selling their stakes paid anywhere from a minimum ₹47 to a maximum of ₹175.69 per Star Health share. At the IPO price of ₹900, these investors reaped pre-tax capital gains* ranging from 412% to 1815%! A group of ten pre-IPO investors, including Star Health's CEO and chairman, Jagannathan, had paid ₹1,572 crore to acquire 128.25 million shares. These investors sold 38% of their holding in the IPO for ₹4,400 crore cash. By selling just 38% of their holding, they had received cash equivalent to 2.8 times their investment.

By December 2021, RJ owned 118.62 million Star Health shares. Of these, he purchased 82.88 million shares from the insurer itself at a price of ₹155.28 per share. He purchased another 73.13 million Star Health shares from other PE investors before the IPO. The prices at which he bought these shares is not disclosed in the Star Health IPO Prospectus. RJ also sold an estimated 37.39 million Star Health shares before the IPO, leaving him with 118.62 million shares, which he did not sell during the IPO.

While the prices at which RJ purchased Star Health shares from other investors before its listing is not known, the maximum price at which shares were allotted before the IPO according

* Capital gains: The difference between the sale price and purchase price of a share expressed as a percentage of the purchase price.

to the insurer's prospectus was ₹488.96. Assuming that RJ's net purchase of 35.74 million shares from other investors (73.13 million purchased minus 37.39 million sold before the listing) was at the peak price of ₹488.96, he invested ₹3,035 crore to purchase 118.62 million Star Health shares; the weighted average acquisition cost is ₹255.82 apiece. At the IPO price of ₹900, the value of his holdings in Star Health had more than trebled to ₹10,756 crore. The market value of 1,000 Star Health shares investors purchased during its IPO for ₹9 lakh would have declined to ₹7 lakh.

The timing of an investment and the holding period are, among others, key factors that determine whether investors make a profit or loss by investing in a stock. However, subscribing to an IPO in India, especially in overpriced listings such as Star Health, is not a combination of skill and being at the right place at the right time; it is a Janus investment.

In Roman mythology, Janus is the god of beginnings and endings, gates, transition, time, doorways, passages and ... duality. This deity is usually represented as having two faces—one looking at the past and the other at the future. Similarly, shares listed at inflated prices are Janus investments, wherein the pre-IPO investors are guaranteed to earn exorbitant returns while IPO investors face considerable downside risk.

Star Health turned profitable in FY2023 after two consecutive years of losses, and its solvency ratio improved to 2.14. In June 2023, the founder-CEO, the seventy-eight-year-old Jagannathan, resigned from the board and was succeeded by Anand Roy, who has been with Star Health since 2006.[9, 10] Though Jagannathan oversaw the insurer's recovery, he was unable to prevent its share price dipping. It was the worst performing insurance stock between its listing in December 2021 and November 2024. Star Health's share price had dipped to ₹460 by 22 November 2024, translating to an annualised loss of over 20% in the three years since listing (Table 15.4).

Table 15.4: Key Performance, Valuation and Return Metrics of Listed Indian Insurers

Business		***Key Metrics, FY2024***				***IPO Size, ₹ Crore***	***Subscription, Times***
		Premium, ₹ Crore	***PAT Margin, [1]***	***Solvency Ratio, %***	***Market Share, %, [2]***		
Reinsurance	GIC of India	32,250	20.18%	3.25	65.09	11,176	1.38
Life Insurance	LIC of India	476,831	8.58%	1.98	60.66	21,008	2.95
	SBI Life Insurance	81,431	2.33%	1.96	8.60	8,386	3.55
	HDFC Life	63,082	2.50%	1.87	7.35	8,695	4.89
	ICICI Prudential Life	43,236	1.97%	1.92	5.10	6,057	10.48
General Insurance	New India Assurance	34,187	3.19%	1.87	14.40	9,467	1.20
	ICICI Lombard General	25,594	7.50%	2.62	8.08	5,701	2.98
	Star Health & Allied	15,254	5.54%	2.21	4.98	6,400	0.79
	Go Digit General	9,016	2.02%	1.61	2.37	2,615	9.60

Business		Listing		Listing Day Gain/(Loss)	YTD Gain/ (Loss), [3]	P/E	P/BV
		Day	Price, ₹				
Reinsurance	GIC of India	25-Oct-17	912	-4.13%	-2.60%	8.84	1.07
Life Insurance	LIC of India	17-May-22	949	-7.77%	-2.54%	13.43	5.71
	SBI Life Insurance	3-Oct-17	700	1.08%	11.07%	67.91	9.11
	HDFC Life	17-Nov-17	290	18.83%	13.07%	85.69	9.30
	ICICI Prudential Life	29-Sep-16	334	-10.91%	9.24%	151.07	8.47
General Insurance	New India Assurance	13-Nov-17	800	-9.11%	-11.09%	20.92	0.92
	ICICI Lombard General	27-Sep-17	661	3.06%	15.35%	40.39	6.56
	Star Health & Allied	10-Dec-21	900	0.76%	-20.33%	31.60	3.84
	Go Digit General	23-May-24	272	12.45%	37.08%	202.03	6.72
		Sensex	**Annualised 5-year Return**		**19.21%**	**22.04**	**3.91**
			Annualised 10-year Return		**17.92%**		
		BSE Financial Services	**Annualised 5-year Return**		**13.68%**	**16.79**	**2.68**
			Annualised 10-year Return		**19.38%**		

[1] Profit after tax (PAT) expressed as a percentage of revenues

[2] As of FY2023 and in terms of gross premium

[3] YTD - Year to date, the period spanning the stock's listing day and 22 November 2024. The returns are annaulised

Source: Insurers FY2024 annual reports, IRDAI FY2023 annual report, www.bseindia.com and chittorgarh.com

The Insurance Stocks Puzzle

IPO investors have burnt their fingers not just by investing in Star Health but also GIC, LIC, SBI Life, HDFC Life, ICICI Prudential, New India Assurance and ICICI Lombard. In other words, none of the eight listed Indian insurance stocks have delivered returns at least on par with Sensex's returns since their listing. At the time of writing this chapter in November 2024, Go Digit General has been listed for just six months. As all other insurers have been listed for at least two-and-a-half years, it is not appropriate to examine Go Digit General's annualised returns.

Analysing listed insurers' key performance metrics, valuation ratios (P/E and P/BV), and annualised returns since listing offers several insights to investors and analysts alike.

First, Indian insurer listings have not been unequivocal successes. Three metrics are used to assess an IPO's success—subscriptions, listing-day pop and long-term returns that at least match, or better still outperform, the market returns (Table 15.4).*

Even the annualised share price increase of one of the two successful insurance listings, HDFC Life, is lower than Sensex's return. During the seven years spanning HDFC Life's listing on 17 November 2017 and 22 November 2024, its share price appreciated by an annualised 13.07%. Sensex's five-year and ten-year annualised returns as of 22 November 2024 were 19.21% and 17.29%, respectively. BSE Financial Services index's five-year and ten-year returns were 13.68% and 18.38%, respectively. There is no insurance stock index in India as indices comprise at least twenty-five to thirty stocks. Hence, it is apt to benchmark the listed insurer's share price performance with the BSE Financial Services index. As of November 2024, GIC, LIC, HDFC Life, SBI Life and Go Digit General Insurance are constituents of the

* Listing-day 'pop' is the rise in share price on the day the stock debuts on stock exchanges, resulting in an instant appreciation in the value of the IPO investors' holdings.

BSE Financial Services index. ICICI Lombard, whose share price appreciated by an annualised 15.35% since its September 2017 listing, is the best-performing insurance stock. However, its share price rise has also lagged those of Sensex and the BSE Financial Services index.

Second, despite insurers reporting stable operating and financial performance, their stocks underperformed indices. As of FY2024, all nine listed insurers were profitable, and their solvency ratios were well above the regulatory minimum of 1.50 times. Included in the nine listed insurers are three market leaders—GIC, with a market share of 65%, LIC (61%) and NIA (14.40%). All other insurers have a significant market share of at least 5% except Go Digital General, which has a modest 2%.

Third, the valuation metrics (P/E and P/BV) of the market leaders are lower than those of Sensex, the BSE Financial Services index and private insurers! This is despite the government owning majority stakes of 82.40% in GIC, 96.5% in LIC and 85.4% in NIA. The exceptions to this undervaluation are NIA's 20.92 times P/E ratio being higher than the BSE Financial Services index's 16.79 times and LIC's 5.71 times P/BV comparing favourably with Sensex's 3.91 times and BSE Financial Services index's 2.68 times. The phenomenon of government-backed market leaders' P/BV trailing those of the private insurers prevailed even at the time of Star Health's listing in 2021. (Refer to Appendix 6 for details.)

It is indeed ludicrous that the government-backed reinsurer with a dominant market share of 65%—GIC, which is the most profitable and has achieved the highest solvency ratio among listed insurers—should trade at a discount, in P/E and P/BV terms, to Sensex, the BSE Financial Services index and private insurers. The second absurdity is another government-backed market leader's—NIA's—P/BV being lower than 1.0 time, while the recently listed Go Digital General's P/BV is 6.72 times. This is despite NIA's profitability and solvency ratio being higher than

Go Digital General's. The share prices of both GIC and NIA, which listed in 2017, are trading at lower levels than their issue prices even after adjusting for these entities' 1:1 bonus issues in 2018!

Fourth, the P/E and P/BV ratios of private-sector insurers are exponentially higher than those of Sensex and the BSE Financial Services index and the three public sector market leaders. The sole exception to this phenomenon is Star Health's P/BV of 3.84 times, which is higher than the BSE Financial Services index's 2.68 times and a shade lower than Sensex's 3.91 times. SBI—in which the government shareholding is 57.51%—holds a 55.39% stake in SBI Life, and the market values the entity as a private sector insurer.

The valuation of insurer stocks in India, in my view, reflects investor irrationality. Investors and promoters or controlling shareholders stand to lose due to this disconnect between listed insurers' profile and performance, past returns and valuation. According to IRDAI's FY2023 annual report, there are twenty-four life insurers and thirty-three general insurers in India. Should the listed insurers wish to expand organically or acquire smaller players, like HDFC Life's acquisition of Exide Life in 2022, a follow-on public offering and/or private placement with domestic and overseas institutional investors may be necessary. Investor response to future equity raises by insurers is likely to be lukewarm should the current incongruities in pricing and valuation persist.

The government is adversely affected by the undervaluation of GIC, NIA and, probably, LIC. At their current valuations, diluting the government stake in these three insurers is not an attractive proposition, even though the proceeds could be used to reduce India's high fiscal deficit.

The stage is set for activist investors to purchase insurance stocks and bring a semblance of rationality to their pricing.

Though Star Health's share price continued to decline after RJ's demise, it has been a profitable investment for the investor.

RaRe Enterprises continued to own slightly over 100.75 million shares of the insurer as of end-December 2024; it has not pared its stake since Star Health's listing. The decline in Star Health's share price may be attributed to several factors—its overpriced IPO, the incongruities in Indian insurance stocks valuations, share prices declining by end-2024 due to high valuations, and the Trump tariff threat. Whether RaRe Enterprises will remain invested in Star Health remains to be seen.

PART 4

Epiphany

16

Mahalaxmi Race Course and Arthur Road Jail

A TALE THAT RJ OFTEN NARRATED GOES: 'I WAS DRINKING AT Geoffrey's when a pretty girl walked up to me and asked, "Give me a tip to double my investment in three years." I told her, "Go to Mahalaxmi Race Course."'

Yet another frequently repeated voice byte was, 'All those who thought they were gods of the stock market went to Arthur Road Jail.'

RJ was not just an entertaining but also an astute communicator. He used the Geoffrey's incident to explain capital risks and the Arthur Road Jail analogy to explain reputational risks—two hazards which, if not monitored and mitigated in real time, destroy lives and businesses.

Capital risk is the risk of an investor losing their investment corpus—an unfortunate event that is often an outcome of a very high-risk appetite, ignorance, greed, fraud or a black swan event. RJ made a distinction between investing and gambling. He often stated that investing was a full-time job that required knowledge and practice, while one ought to set aside a sum for 'fun' or betting on risky ventures that were tantamount to gambling.

Reputational risk, on the other hand, is defined as 'a threat or danger to the good name or standing of a business or entity' that occurs due to the actions of the company / entity, acts of employee(s), and activities of other stake holders such as associates, joint venture partners, and suppliers'.[1] In India, the risk of SEBI debarring investors from operating in capital markets for years and being imprisoned are real. Hence, even if investors are amoral, it pays to be law-abiding to pursue their chosen career.

Being a law-abiding, knowledgeable and trained investor is a non-negotiable prerequisite for managing one's personal monies and/or operating as a professional investor. This is because the three domains RJ operated in—listed equities, trading of shares, commodities and currencies, and private equity—are exposed to multiple risks, both systematic and idiosyncratic.

Systematic risk refers to the risk inherent to the entire market. Systematic risk, also known as undiversifiable risk, volatility risk or market risk, affects the overall market, not just a particular stock or industry.[2] Political developments, legislative changes, natural disasters, weather events, terrorism, inflation and changes in interest rates and exchange rates are examples of systematic risks. The COVID-19-induced 28% decline in the market value of RaRe Enterprises' CEP from ₹12,657 crore on 31 December 2019 to ₹9,080 crore on 31 March 2020, which mirrored the 29% decline in Sensex during this period, is an example of systematic risk.

Interest rate fluctuations impact both the assets and liabilities of RaRe Enterprises. On the assets side, investments in banks account for more than 5% of RaRe Enterprises' CEP. Moderate increases in interest rates improve banks' earnings and, consequently, their stock prices. However, most of the corporates whose stocks RaRe Enterprises is invested in are borrowers. Higher interest rates depress corporates' profits and thus their share prices. The impact of interest rate changes on RaRe Enterprises' listed equity investments is mixed as a result.

The impact of interest rate changes on RaRe Enterprises' listed equities portfolio may be estimated but not on its liabilities. This is because RaRe Enterprises is an unlisted entity and hence not required to make its financials available in the public domain. RaRe Enterprises itself is not a single entity, but an agglomeration of multiple entities. One of its constituents is Rare Equity Private Limited (REPL), on whose ring-fenced assets Acuité Ratings has assigned a AA+ (CE) rating. Ring-fencing refers to the creation of a virtual barrier that segregates a portion of a company's assets from the rest.[3] The 'CE' abbreviation that follows the rating stands for 'credit enhancement'.

Acuité has assigned the second-highest rating on REPL's borrowing. A pool of shares owned by the company is the collateral for the debt. This pool of shares is called the 'pledge portfolio'. The conditions that the ring-fenced portfolio needs to comply with include BSE100 constituents accounting for 80% of the pledge pool, security cover ranging from 1.75 to 2.45 times, and REPL paying principal and interest at least seven days before the due date. Should REPL fail to pay seven days ahead of the due dates, the trustee has the option to sell the shares in the pledge pool and pay principal and interest. The security cover is the ratio of the market value of the pledge pool to outstanding principal and accrued interest.[4]

The takeaway for investors is that the credit enhancement of ring-fencing a pool of shares that comply with the three aforesaid conditions, among others, has enabled REPL achieve an AA+ (CE) rating despite the company reporting losses for at least two consecutive years: FY2023 and FY2024 (Table 16.1).

Table 16.1: REPL – Select Financial Metrics

Particulars	*Unit*	*FY2023*	*FY2024*
Total Assets	₹ Crore	907.9	998.51
Total Income [1]	₹ Crore	-43.42	36.35
PAT	₹ Crore	-43.86	-13.61
Net Worth	₹ Crore	223.01	209.4
Return on Average Assets	(%)	(4.84)	(1.43)
Return on Average Net Worth	(%)	(17.91)	(6.30)
Debt/Equity	Times	2.77	2.99

[1] Total Income = Net interest income + Other income

Source: Acuité Ratings and Research

Acuité's rating reports indicate that REPL has used the aforesaid structure to issue ₹200–500-crore non-convertible debentures over the year. This borrowing is less than 2% of the market value of RaRe Enterprises' (the consolidated entity) CEP. RJ evidently adopted this credit-enhanced structure to reduce RaRe Enterprises' borrowing costs. But we do not know what RaRe Enterprises' capital structure is, the quantum of its interest expense, the proportion of fixed and floating rate debt, and if the company hedged interest rate risk using derivatives such as swaps.

Though RaRe Enterprises invests in Indian companies, the assets side of its balance sheet is not immune to exchange rate fluctuations. Investees such as Tata Motors, Tata Communications, Indian Hotels and CRISIL, among others, have overseas operations and export their products and services. Hence, a depreciation of the Indian rupee will result in an increase in the rupee equivalent of their revenues, and vice versa. Similarly, there are importers of commodities, inputs and services amongst the investees. The rupee-denominated expenses of importers will increase when the Indian rupee depreciates, and vice versa. RJ also traded in foreign exchange (FX). Exchange rate fluctuations would have impacted the open FX positions and impacted the performance of RaRe

Enterprises' investees and, consequently, their share prices and dividend payouts.

I was unable to find videos and interviews in which RJ spoke about RaRe Enterprises' use of derivatives to hedge the whole or part of interest rate and exchange rate risks. Most, if not all, interviewers asked him about the more visible and high-profile activity of stock picking rather than the behind-the-scenes but essential function of risk management. RJ, however, spoke at length about the idiosyncratic risks RaRe Enterprises is exposed to, especially capital and concentration risks.

Capital Risk

RJ mentioned in an April 2015 interview with the Association of Investment Bankers of India, 'The two investments where I misjudged the quality and character of the entrepreneur were A2Z Maintenance and Engineering Services and Bilcare. I had blind faith in both the companies but I have learned from my mistakes.'[5]

A2Z Maintenance & Engineering Services is an engineering, procurement and construction (EPC) company engaged in power distribution and facility management services (FMS). RJ, who was a private equity investor in A2Z, purchased 4,74,898 shares between July 2006 and 2007 for ₹20.26 crore at an average price of ₹426.63. A2Z declared a 1:1 bonus issue in August 2007 and a 3:2 bonus issue in March 2010.[6] The two bonus issues resulted in RJ's holding increasing to 2.37 million shares and the average purchase price declining to ₹85.33 per share.

A2Z floated a ₹675-crore IPO between 8 and 10 December 2010 and listed on BSE and NSE on 23 December 2010. RJ offloaded a part of his stake in the IPO. A2Z's listing price was ₹400, which translated to a PE ratio of 26 times. Analysts highlighted that A2Z's stock was overpriced, as the average PE ratio for EPC companies then was 15 times.[7] A2Z's IPO was undersubscribed; it received subscriptions equivalent to 96% of the issue size.[8]

I was unable to find A2Z's final IPO prospectus in the public domain. While A2Z's red herring prospectus dated 3 December 2010 stated that RJ was selling 5,00,000 shares in the IPO, an 11 May 2013 *Outlook Business* column reported that he sold a million shares.[9] Had RJ sold 5,00,000 shares in the IPO, he would have realised ₹20 crore cash, which is slightly lower than his ₹20.26-crore investment. Had he sold a million shares, he would have realised ₹40 crore cash, which is almost twice his investment.

However, the IPO investors certainly lost money. On listing day, A2Z's share price declined by 18% to ₹328.75. To instil confidence in investors, RJ spent ₹48 crore to purchase 1.375 million shares at ₹350.77 a share. This could not stymie A2Z's share price decline. In May 2012, RJ purchased 2.65 million shares for ₹26 crore at ₹100 a share. On 15 October 2012, he resigned from directorship of A2Z.[10]

A2Z's aggressive expansion resulted in the company reporting losses after listing. The company, which had started off as an FMS provider, moved on to installing power distribution lines and sub-stations. Moreover, A2Z deployed a significant proportion of the IPO proceeds to construct 60MW biomass plants, which faced delays in execution and signing power purchase agreements.

According to A2Z's quarterly filing of shareholding with the stock exchanges, RJ divested his entire stake in the company in January 2015, when the share price ranged from ₹15.50 to ₹23.15. Nine years later, in 2024, A2Z's share price languished between ₹12.25 and ₹26.52. A2Z continued to be a loss-making entity, though its losses narrowed from ₹126 crore in FY2023 to ₹7 crore in FY2024.

RJ may have also booked a loss on Bilcare, a Pune-headquartered pharma packaging company, in which RJ and Rekha first purchased 1.15 million shares equivalent to a 10.22% stake in the March 2004 quarter.[11] At the then prevalent share price of ₹117.85, the market value of their investment was ₹13.55 crore. Bilcare inducted RJ as an independent director on its board on 31 March 2004. That year, Bilcare reported ₹11-crore post-tax profits on to ₹110-crore revenues, which translated to a healthy profit margin of 10%. Balance sheet leverage was moderate at 1.12 times as of 31 March 2004.[12]

Between FY2004 and FY2008, Bilcare's revenues and post-tax profits had skyrocketed sixfold and by seven-and-a-half times to ₹670 crore and ₹82 crore, respectively. Profit margin had improved from 10% in FY2004 to 12% in FY2008. As this expansion was funded by debt, balance sheet leverage was elevated; it had almost doubled since FY2004 to 2.16 times as of 31 March 2004. Bilcare's impressive growth and profit margin propelled its share price to an all-time high of ₹1,596 in December 2007. Pharma is a defensive industry, that is, demand for most pharma products is unaffected by cyclical downturns. Hence, Bilcare's revenue momentum and profit margins were healthy and its share price peaked even amidst the 2007–08 global financial crisis.

Bilcare's revenues grew by 59% in the next two years to ₹1,066 crore in FY2010. Profit margin continued to be healthy at 11%, while balance sheet leverage improved to 0.99 times. In FY2011, Bilcare purchased the plastic film-making business of the Swiss chemicals company, Ineos, for ₹607 crore. While this acquisition doubled Bilcare's revenues to ₹2,329 crore in FY2011, post-tax profits grew by just 28% and profit margin declined to 6.42%. As the acquisition was debt-funded, balance sheet leverage rose sharply to 1.80 times as of 31 March 2011.[13]

The situation was exacerbated by accusations of 'dubious accounting' of the incremental ₹750-crore borrowing in FY2013, failure to write off non-remunerative assets and capitalising software expenses instead of expensing them.[14] Capitalising expenses instead of expensing them results in an overstatement of profits. The deterioration in Bilcare's performance and accusations of window-dressing accounts resulted in a crash in its share price.

RJ, who ceased to be on the Bilcare board in FY2010, remained invested in the company till his demise. RaRe Enterprises reduced its stake in Bilcare to less than 1% during the March 2023 quarter, when its share price ranged from ₹38 to ₹59.15, that is, it was not more than half the price at which RJ had bought the stock nineteen years ago. Further, Bilcare had paid dividends annually only between September 2007 and 2012, ceasing thereafter. By FY2023, Bilcare was a shadow of its former self. Revenues and post-tax profits had dwindled to ₹992 crore and ₹50 crore, respectively, which translated to a profit margin of 5%. Balance sheet leverage was manageable at 1.26 times, however.[15]

Besides A2Z and Bilcare, there were other stocks whose prices declined during the period RJ owned them. These include Heads UP Ventures, Indiabulls Housing Finance, Jaiprakash Associates, Orient Cement, Prozone Realty, SAIL, TV18 Broadcast and Viceroy Hotels. RJ owned these stocks for the whole or part of the period spanning 31 December 2015 and 30 June 2022. While the aforesaid companies' stock prices declined during this seven-and-a-half-year period, RJ need not have necessarily made a loss. He may have simultaneously executed profitable trades in these stocks and/or purchased some of these at a much lower price before 31 December 2015. However, the share of each of these stocks in RaRe Enterprises' CEP was less than 1%. The exceptions are TV18 Broadcast, whose peak share in RaRe Enterprises' CEP was 2.6%, and SAIL (4%). The market value of RaRe Enterprises' CEP continued to appreciate despite the share prices of certain stocks declining. This is because RJ's larger investments were mostly multibaggers, and the performance of his smaller investments was a mixed bag. The practice of spreading one's investment corpus over a number of stocks is known as diversification, the absence of which results in concentration risks.

Concentration Risk

RJ acknowledged in his interactions with the media that the Tata Group stocks, led by Titan, accounted for a significant proportion of his CEP. Hence, the performance of RaRe Enterprises' listed equities is tied to the performance of the five Tata Group stocks—Indian Hotels, Rallis, Tata Communications, Tata Motors and Titan. Of these, Rallis, whose share in RaRe Enterprises' listed equities was 1.3% on 30 June 2022, is an underperformer. In choosing to allocate a large portion of his corpus to the Tata Group stocks, RJ consciously or subconsciously reduced two other risks—governance and social risks.

Assessing the ESG (environmental, social and governance) impact of investments is a relatively recent trend. For long, investors considered only financial outcomes while making investment decisions. However, with increasing pollution, global warming and rising sea water levels—situations that were caused and/or exacerbated by political and business decisions—the practice of assessing the environmental, social and governance aspects of investments has become prevalent. Tata Sons adopted the motto 'Humata, Hukhta, Huvarshta'—good thoughts, good words, good deeds—decades before ESG became a buzzword. The Tatas' commitment to governance and social causes may have been one of the reasons for RJ investing heavily in the group.

Concentration risk is characteristic of the portfolios managed by successful professional investors. According to Trendlyne data, Mukul Agarwal's holding in BSE accounted for 13.5% of the market value of his listed equities portfolio as of 31 December 2024, Glenmark Pharma constituted 22% of Ashish Dhawan's investments, and Choice International's share in Madhusudan Kela's holdings was 46%.

Two factors underpin the lumpy portfolios of professional investors. First, some of the investments professionals make may become multibaggers, and their share in the portfolio becomes disproportionately large. Second, investing is the vocation of professional investors. They are trained, knowledgeable, and monitor their portfolio almost in real time. Hence, they are far more equipped than amateur investors to handle concentration risks. Wealth managers advise retail investors, who are usually not as knowledgeable as professionals and/or are strapped for time, to invest in multiple stocks or a mutual fund instead.

Share Trading and Private Equity Related Risks

RJ revealed that he generated capital through leveraged share trading to invest in medium- to long-term assets. Leveraged trading is a high-risk activity that amplifies both profits and losses. In the absence of proper risk management strategies like stop-loss, traders are likely to face a double whammy of accumulating trading losses and having to repay the loans borrowed to trade.

Liquidity and market risks are associated with private-equity investments. Liquidity refers to the ease with which investors may buy or sell assets. As private-equity investments are unlisted, investors ought to have the wherewithal to remain invested in the medium to long term. Selling stakes in unlisted companies is much more difficult than divesting holdings of listed entities. Further, profitable exits through successful listings or acquisition by a larger entity is not a certainty for private-equity investments.

The Official Line

Utpal Sheth observed that RaRe Enterprises had adopted a three-pronged strategy of risk management to mitigate the firm's trading, borrowing and investment risks.

Sheth remarked, 'First was the risk management of trading positions in the futures and options market. Here, risk management was entirely price-driven. We were not arbitrage players; we were not hedgers. Every trading position was a view-based position.'

Sheth used the past tense while speaking of managing trading risks. This is because RJ used to trade stocks, currencies and commodities to raise capital for the firm. RaRe Enterprises has ceased trading after RJ's demise. Sheth further explained that RJ traded in stocks, currencies and commodities based on his views of and outlook for these assets. RJ did not trade to exploit arbitrage opportunities or hedge.

Arbitrage is the simultaneous purchase and sale of the same or similar asset in different markets / stock exchanges in order to profit from tiny differences in the asset's listed price. It exploits short-lived variations in the price of identical or similar assets in different markets or in different forms.[16] Hedging is a risk management strategy employed to offset losses in investments by taking an opposite position in a related asset. The reduction in risk provided by hedging also typically results in a reduction in potential profits. Hedging strategies typically involve derivatives, such as options and futures contracts.[17]

Sheth further explained, 'The second aspect of risk management was in relation to leverage. The bulk of the leverage was on account of our trading positions. There, our risk management was in the context of leverage as a percentage of total assets. We also ensure diversification in terms of number of lenders and no concentration on the liabilities side.'

The profit margins associated with trading in stocks, commodities and currencies are wafer-thin. Hence, the volume of trades has to be high to earn meaningful profits in rupee terms. RJ used to borrow to trade. He mentioned, 'My net capital employed in trading is ₹1 lakh. Even if I make ₹1 crore, you cannot imagine my return on equity. Everything else is borrowed and I pay interest on it. Trading is based on pure leverage.'[18]

Though RaRe Enterprises financed its trading business predominantly through borrowing, the investor ensured that outstanding debt was a fraction of its assets. This is a prudent practice, as RJ himself acknowledged that good traders get around

40% of their trades right.[19] Hence, maintaining outstanding loans at a level commensurate with the borrower's liquid assets and cash flows is essential to absorb trading losses, minimising margin calls when asset values depreciate and growing the business.

Yet another strength of RaRe Enterprises' risk management culture is that the firm did not rely on any one lender or even just a few. RaRe Enterprises borrowed from a wide array of lenders to ensure it had multiple sources to raise funds in a quick and cost-effective manner, and nurture relationships with capital market participants who would partner its expansion plans.

Sheth remarked that the third aspect of risk management related to the investment portfolio. He stated, 'Risk management is conviction-driven and probability-driven. It is not driven by price, nor is it driven by liabilities. Here, there was no constraint on the degree of concentration we would have so long as the degree of conviction was disproportionately high.'[20]

In addition to financial and economic analysis, RJ used two qualitative metrics to make medium- to long-term investments. First was conviction, that is, his views of the management, the investee's current and projected performance, and industry dynamics. The second was his estimate of the probability of the investee flourishing. As a seasoned investor, he understood that sound due diligence does not guarantee a 100% success in investing and that investees tend to outperform (Titan and CRISIL), underperform (A2Z and Bilcare) and perform in line with expectations. Hence, RJ's 'guestimation' of the probability of an investment being a profitable one was a key input in decision-making. In other words, he was comfortable with uncertainty.

It is this conviction and a sixth sense to gauge the probability of a medium- to long-term investment generating profits—along with a deep knowledge of the industry, skills to trade and invest, and an extensive network—that enabled RJ, and other successful professional investors, to make big-ticket investments. This is a case of what's sauce for the goose ***not*** being sauce for the gander.

Successful professional investors are well-equipped to assume concentration risks. Retail investors are not. Hence, wealth managers advise retail investors to diversify their investments or invest in mutual funds.

The Known Unknowns

RJ's business model was to generate capital through leveraged trading of shares, currencies and commodities, and borrowing to invest in listed equities and private equity. This chapter lists some of the key risks the three segments he operated in—leveraged trading, listed equities and private equity. However, we do not know how RaRe Enterprises measures and mitigates risks. Is all of RaRe Enterprises' debt denominated in Indian rupees or does it borrow foreign currency-denominated debt? We don't know. The consistent growth in RaRe Enterprises' listed equities portfolio and successful listings of its private equity investments are indicative of an organisation with a robust risk management culture.

17

The Show Goes On

ALMOST TWO-AND-A-HALF YEARS HAVE PASSED, AS OF 31 December 2024, since RJ's demise on 14 August 2022. The media reported that RJ had planned his succession meticulously even as his health deteriorated during the eight months preceding his demise. Berjis Desai drafted a will at the behest of the ace investor, bequeathing most of his assets to his wife Rekha and their three offspring—Nishtha, Aryaman and Aryaveer. Rekha, her brother Rajeev Gupta, RJ's nephew Vishal Gupta, Berjis Desai, Amit Goela and Utpal Sheth were appointed trustees. Radhakishan Damani, Kalpraj Dharamshi and Amal Parikh were advisors.[1]

The most traceable component of RaRe Enterprises' business is its investments in listed equities, which grew by an impressive 67% from ₹30,752 crore as of 30 June 2022 (the last complete quarter RaRe Enterprises was helmed by RJ) to ₹51,242 crore as of 31 December 2024.

Portfolio Growth Versus Return

This 67% growth over a two-and-a-half-year period is not synonymous with return. Three of RaRe Enterprises' PE investments listed during this period—Concord Biotech in August 2023, Baazar Style Retail in September 2024 and Inventurus Knowledge Solutions in December 2024. In the absence of the three PE investments, the market value of RaRe Enterprises' CEP would have been ₹45,043 crore as of 31 December 2024, which represents a still robust 46% increase since 30 June 2022.

As was the case during RJ's lifetime, the trajectory of growth in the listed equities portfolio has not been unidirectional. The market value of the CEP declined in three of the ten quarters of the period spanning 1 July 2022–31 December 2024; the average rate of depreciation was 6.05%. The average rate of portfolio appreciation in the seven quarters of the aforesaid period was 10.58%. If all PE listings are excluded, the average rate of quarterly appreciation and depreciation was 11.28% and 5.08%, respectively.

RaRe Enterprises has sustained RJ's track record of profit-making quarters exceeding loss-making ones and average quarterly profit being significantly higher than loss by a wide margin.

What Has Not Changed

RaRe Enterprises' CEP retains its 'triple L' characteristics—large-cap-focused and lumpy, with low dividend yield. Large-cap stocks dominated the portfolio, though their share declined from 89% on 30 June 2022 to 72% on 31 December 2024. With the listing of Concord Biotech and Inventurus Knowledge Solutions, the share of mid-cap stocks correspondingly rose from 8% to 25%. The share of small-cap stocks remained unchanged at around 3%.

Tata Group stocks accounted for 45–50% of the portfolio during the period spanning 1 July 2022–31 December 2024.

The market value of Titan stock was the highest among RaRe Enterprises' listed equities, though it declined from 34% on 30 June 2022 to 29% on 31 December 2024. Concord Biotech's listing and its share price almost doubling between September 2023 and December 2024 resulted in the share of the pharma company's stock in RaRe Enterprises' listed equities portfolio surging from 6.8% to 11%. There was a resultant decline in the portfolio shares of most other stocks, including Titan and Star Health Insurance. The addition of Concord Biotech was not the sole factor that led to the share of Star Health more than halving from 24.5% in June 2022 to 9.3% in December 2024; the insurer's share price declined by 36% between June 2022 and December 2024. CRISIL bucked the trend with its share in the portfolio increasing from 4.1% to 4.9%, despite RaRe Enterprises selling 2,01,000 shares (5% of its holding in the credit rating agency) between January and September 2024, as its share price had more than doubled between June 2022 and December 2024.

The estimated dividend income from the CEP rose from ₹174 crore in 2022 to ₹212 crore in 2023, and further to ₹217 crore in 2024. The dividend yield continued to decline (Table 17.1) both in absolute terms and as a percentage of MSCI India. RaRe

Table 17.1: Sustained Decline in Dividend Yield

	2020	**2021**	**2022**	**2023**	**2024**
Dividend Receipts (₹ Crore)	76.31	140.07	174.23	211.83	216.73
Dividend Yield					
Listed Equities	0.66%	0.60%	0.54%	0.51%	0.43%
Listed Equities excl PE		0.68%	0.74%	0.66%	0.59%
MSCI India	1.09%	1.00%	1.18%	1.22%	1.16%

Source: Author calculations, Trendlyne and https://en.macromicro.me/collections/5738/msci-index-dividend-yield/48221/msci-dividend-yield

Enterprises' dividend yield declined from an estimated 46% of MSCI India in 2022 to 37% in 2024. This is a consequence of the presence of several multi-baggers in RaRe Enterprises' listed equities portfolio.

What Has Changed

RaRe Enterprises ceased trading in stocks after RJ's demise. Rekha Jhunjhunwala observed in an interaction with *The Economic Times*, 'We don't trade anymore ... only he (Rakesh) could handle trading. That secret sauce only belonged to him.'[3]

RaRe Enterprises reduced its stake in Indiabulls Housing Finance, which accounted for a minuscule 0.2% of the listed equities portfolio, to less than 1% during the quarter ended 30 September 2022. I was unable to ascertain if the stock was sold before or after RJ's demise. RaRe Enterprises also reduced its stakes in nine stocks to less than 1% after RJ's demise—Anant Raj, Autoline Industries, Bilcare, Dishman Carbogen, Edelweiss Financial Services, Man Infraconstruction, Orient Cement, Prozone Realty and Rallis India. RJ had purchased Dishman Carbogen in the June 2020 quarter and Orient Cement in the March 2016 quarter. The remaining seven stocks were part of RaRe Enterprises' CEP since at least 31 December 2015.

Rallis was RaRe Enterprises' largest holding among the nine stocks sold; it accounted for 1.3% of the market value of listed equities as of 30 June 2022. Each of the remaining eight stocks accounted for less than 0.5% of the portfolio's market value. The aggregate market value of the nine stocks was ₹731 crore or 2.4% of the portfolio as of 30 June 2022. The dividend yield of these stocks was higher than that of the remaining stocks in the listed equities portfolio at over 1% between 2016 and 2021, except in 2020 (0.80%).

The purchase consideration is not known for the six stocks RJ purchased before 31 December 2015—Anant Raj, Bilcare,

Edelweiss Financial Services, Man Infraconstruction, Prozone Realty and Rallis India. RaRe Enterprises may have sold Anant Raj and Man Infracon at a profit, as these stocks had appreciated by 600% and 250%, respectively, since 31 December 2015. Edelweiss and Rallis share prices had appreciated by 30% each since 31 December 2015, thereby underperforming the multi-baggers in RaRe Enterprises' CEP and Sensex. The share prices of Bilcare and Prozone Realty were 60% and 20% lower, respectively, than their end-December 2015 share prices at the time of their sale. RaRe Enterprises may have sold Dishman Carbogen and Orient Cement at a loss; their share prices were 60% and 10%, respectively, lower than the prices at which they were purchased.

Selling these stocks was a step in the right direction, in my view, as it allowed RaRe Enterprises to focus on its larger and potentially more profitable investments. According to Trendlyne data, Sun Pharma, a leading manufacturer of specialty generics globally, is the sole listed equity added to RaRe Enterprises' CEP after RJ's demise and before 31 December 2024.[4]

With the sale of Lupin and Aurobindo Pharma, the share of pharma stocks had declined from 23% of listed equities in December 2015 to 2% in June 2022 under RJ's watch. With the listing of Concord and addition of Sun Pharma, however, this share rose from 2% in June 2022 to 15% in December 2024.

Listed PE Portfolio Performance Is a Mixed Bag

The number of PE investments that floated IPOs and were constituents of RaRe Enterprises' listed equity portfolio rose from three (Metro Brands, Nazara Technologies, and Star Health and Allied Insurance) as of 30 June 2022 to six (the aforesaid three entities, plus Concord Biotech, Baazar Style Retail and Inventurus) by 31 December 2024.

The market value of RaRe Enterprises' holdings in successfully listed PE investments (S-PE) rose by 42% from ₹10,382 crore in

June 2022 to ₹14,788 crore in December 2024. The September 2023 listing of Concord Biotech and Baazar Style Retail's IPO a year later added ₹2,895 crore and ₹104 crore in the respective quarters to the market value of RaRe Enterprises' listed equities portfolio. Inventurus listed in December 2024, which augmented RaRe Enterprises' CEP by ₹545 crore that month. Yet, the share of S-PE declined from 34% of the CEP in June 2022 to 29% in December 2024.

The trends in the share prices of and RaRe Enterprises holdings in the six S-PEs unravel the puzzle of an increase in listings and a simultaneous decline in their share (Table 17.2).

A key factor that caused the decline in the S-PE was Star Health and Allied Insurance's share price almost halving since it was listed in December 2021. The insurer has paid nil dividends since listing. Nevertheless, RaRe Enterprises remains invested in this entity; it had purchased Star Health's share before the IPO at an average price of ₹155.28 per share and at undisclosed prices from other investors.[5] Assuming RJ's average acquisition cost of Star Health shares is ₹255.82 (explanation provided in the chapter titled 'Janus Stock'), RaRe Enterprises' unrealised capital gains is a handsome 85% even at a considerably lower share price of ₹474.50 per share as of 31 December 2024.

Though Nazara Technologies' share price declined by an annualised 2% since its March 2021 listing, RaRe Enterprises purchased another 2.89 million shares of the digital entertainment company. Between its September 2024 listing and 31 December 2024, Baazar Style Retail's share price declined by a steep 20%, which may in part be attributed to a 4% decline in Sensex during this period. Inventurus Knowledge Solutions successfully listed on 19 December 2024, that is, the IPO was oversubscribed and its share price rose on listing day and till end-2024. As RaRe Enterprises remained invested in Inventurus' stock for twelve days after its listing as of 31 December 2024, the annualised return is eye-popping at over 70,00,000%. Inventurus' share price

Table 17.2: Performance of RaRe Enterprises' Successfully Listed PE Investments

Entity	*IPO Size, ₹ Crore*	*Issue Price, ₹*	*Listing Day*	*As of 31 December 2024*		*Annualized Return*
				Holding Period [1]	*Price, ₹*	
Nazara Technologies	582.69	1,101	30 March 2021	3.76	1,015.10	-2%
Star Health & Allied Insurance	6,400.44	900	10 December 2021	3.06	474.50	-19%
Metro Brands	1,367.51	500	22 December 2021	3.03	1,217.75	34%
Concord Biotech	1,550.52	741	18 August 2023	1.37	2,210.70	122%
Baazar Style Retail	834.68	389	06 September 2024	0.32	309.70	-51%
Inventurus Knowledge Solutions [2]	2,497.92	1,329	19 December 2024	0.03	1,919.50	71,84,794%

Entity	*Dividends, ₹ Crore*			*Holding, Number of Shares*		
	2022	**2023**	**2024**	***Listing Day***	**31 December 2024**	***Purchase/(Sale)***
Nazara Technologies	-	-	-	32,94,310	61,83,620	28,89,310
Star Health & Allied Insurance	-	-	-	10,07,53,935	10,07,53,935	-
Metro Brands	8.81	13.70	5.00	3,91,53,600	2,61,02,394	-1,30,51,206,
Concord Biotech	-	-	8.75	2,51,99,240	2,51,99,240	-
Baazar Style Retail	-	-	-	27,23,120	27,23,120	-
Inventurus Knowledge Solutions [2]	-	165.48	-	10,25,78,205	8,50,18,326	-1,75,59,879

[1] Holding period in years
[2] Holding on listing day is after deducting 3.38 million shares the Jhunjhunwala family sold during Inventurus' IPO

Source: chittorgarh.com and bseindia.com

moderated to ₹1,417.10, which is still higher than its listing price, by 18 April 2025.

The annualised returns indicated in Table 17.2 are what the IPO investors have earned up to 31 December 2024. RaRe Enterprises invested in the six aforesaid companies at considerably lower prices than their listing prices before their IPOs. These investments may be immensely profitable for RaRe Enterprises even if the investees' share prices decline. Star Health and Baazar Style are cases in point.

Akasa Air

On 7 August 2022, RJ inaugurated Akasa Air's maiden flight from Mumbai to Ahmedabad. The investor, who was accompanied by Rekha, attended the inauguration in a wheelchair. The Union Civil Aviation Minister Jyotiraditya Scindia flagged off the inaugural flight virtually from Delhi. RJ lit a lamp and ate a slice of cake. At the inauguration, RJ quipped with his characteristic optimism, 'They say India has a very bad bureaucracy. But the cooperation that the ministry of civil aviation has given us is unparalleled. Nowhere in the world is an airline conceived in 12 months!'[6]

RJ acquired a 40% stake in Akasa Air for $35 million (approximately ₹259 crore in 2021). Vinay Dube, who was previously the CEO of Jet Airways and GoAir, was appointed CEO of Akasa. By FY2024, Akasa's market share both in terms of revenue per kilometre (RPK) and passengers carried was 4.5%, just behind SpiceJet's market share of over 5%. IndiGo is the undisputed leader with a market share of over 60%. The airlines of the Tata Group (Vistara, Air India, AIX Connect and Air India Express) had garnered an aggregate market share of 28% and 27% in RPK and passenger terms, respectively.[7] Akasa reported losses of ₹744.53 crore in FY2023 and ₹1,670 crore in FY2024. Akasa's CFO Ankur Goel observed, 'The foundational years of any airline are dedicated to investing in its people, fleet, training, operating infrastructure, and network, and hence no airline registers P&L profits in these years.'[8]

Airlines are a cyclical and capital-intensive industry globally. Operating an airline in India is even more challenging due to the high taxes on aviation turbine fuel and quixotic regulation. All these factors did not dampen RJ's fascination for airlines. He remained invested in Jet Airways, SpiceJet and IndiGo for short periods in the past and, in my view, sold his stakes as they did not meet all the criteria he had in mind for his key investments. He, like Indigo's promoters, correctly conceptualised Akasa Air as a budget airline. That his favourite investees—the Tata Group—had re-entered aviation did not deter him. It is a pity that RJ is not around to see his pet project take wings.

Real Estate Foray

Rekha informed *The Economic Times*, 'I have started to invest in real estate, though he [Rakesh] showed no interest in property investments. Following his passing away, I recognised the importance of investing in tangible assets.' RaRe Enterprises has invested ₹1,000 crore in offices at Mumbai's Bandra Kurla Complex and Chandivili and residential properties at upscale Walkeshwar. Deutsche Bank is among the tenants of RaRe Enterprises' office properties.[9] A ₹1,000-crore ($116 million) investment, though sizeable, is equivalent to just 2% of the market value of RaRe Enterprises' CEP.

The Vision Outlives the Visionary

The composition of the CEP is mostly unchanged. RaRe Enterprises' management team remained invested in RJ's three PE investments that he oversaw: Concord Biotech, Style Baazar and Inventurus. The new leadership has ceased the risky share trading operations and streamlined the listed equities portfolio by reducing their stakes in at least eight minor investments to less than 1%. The foray into real estate, if well-executed, will increase recurring revenues and enhance borrowing capacity. Lenders typically lend up to 80% of the value of the property pledged.

It is not by accident that RJ's influence on RaRe Enterprises survives even after his demise. Utpal Sheth divulged, 'I had pitched to Rakeshji that institutionalisation was imperative. We had both worked on a shareholder value creation engagement for Apollo Hospitals, in which we used a phrase: "The vision has to outlive the visionary." I used the same phrase with him. He was initially sceptical and said, "'Institutionalisation is all good. But I don't think I am the kind of person who can function in an institutionalised environment. We're such a small team. Do we need to be institutionalised?"' We discussed and pitched institutionalisation to Rakeshji. He agreed.'[10]

Ramesh Damani opined, 'He created a very methodical succession plan. You had to give him full marks for his vision.'[11]

It is premature to compare the new leadership's performance with RJ's, however. Rekha lamented, 'When my husband discussed investments at home, I would pay no attention ... I regret I didn't listen to him. I should have taken some interest at that time.'[12] She is certainly not the only person at RaRe Enterprises and amongst India's investors to miss RJ.

18

Ten Commandments

I WROTE THIS CHAPTER BEFORE I VISITED RARE ENTERPRISES' office at Nariman Bhawan in Mumbai. Vishal Gupta showed me around the premises. Amit Goela had a freewheeling conversation with me, notwithstanding the long telephonic interview I had conducted from Singapore. The office manager, Pawan, lent me the sole copy of the Ashoka University publication, *Rakesh Jhunjhunwala: The Man Who Believed in India*, RaRe Enterprises possessed. Pawan then pointed me to a DTP shop across the road where I could get the book scanned. As I walked around the office, the collegiate environment and collaborative spirit was palpable. RJ is no longer in our midst, but RaRe Enterprises is one of the many testimonies of the vision outliving the visionary.

Several investors have lauded RJ's intelligence quotient. R.K. Damani, an investor extraordinaire himself, remarked, 'He was always alert, probably even when he was sleeping … He was the most intelligent man I knew.'[1] Notwithstanding his exceptional brainpower, RJ had two posters titled 'Ten Commandments for Trading' and 'Ten Commandments for Investing' on the walls of his office.

Ten Commandments

Ten Commandments for Trading	*Ten Commandments for Investing*
1. Be realistic. Make trading price-dependent, not opinion dependent. 2. Trading is a full-time profession, not a part-time job. It cannot be half-hearted. 3. Know the rules and verify them for they may not be what you assume. 4. Never aspire to be the market's master. It's best to be its slave. Leverage your skills, not your capital 5. Have a broad idea of direction. Remember trend is your friend. 6. Don't be afraid to make a mistake. Only ensure that you can make one that you can afford so that you may live to make another. 7. Play 'Seen', not 'Blind'. For the market offers many an opportunity even after the cards are open. 8. Know what and how much to risk. Assess risk. 9. Take a loss. The first loss is your best loss. Pyramid your profits. 10. Good judgement comes from experience. Experience comes from bad judgement. Trading can only be learned; it can't be taught.	1. Be an optimist. The necessary quality for investing success. 2. Expect a realistic return. Balance fear and greed. 3. Caveat emptor. Never forget this four-letter word R-I-S-K. 4. Invest on broad parameters and the larger picture. Make it an act of wisdom, not intelligence. 5. Be disciplined. Have a game plan. 6. Be flexible. For investing is always in the realms of possibilities. 7. Contrarian Investing. Not a rule, not ruled out. 8. It's important what you buy. It's more important at what price you buy. 9. Have conviction. Be patient. Your patience may be tested, but your conviction will be rewarded. 10. Make exit an independent decision, not driven by profit or loss.

Even a phenomenon like RJ deemed it necessary to continuously remind himself of the principles of trading and investing. Most of us are not endowed with RJ's intellectual prowess and mindset. Hence, we are unlikely to match his performance. But the lessons from his career are essential to internalise and adhere to should we aspire to be upright and successful investors.

1. Be law-abiding.

RJ emphasised abiding by the law. Notwithstanding this, the income tax department raided his premises at least twice. He also had to settle charges of alleged insider trading in the shares of Geometric Ltd in November 2018 and Aptech in July 2021, paying penalties of ₹2.49 lakh and ₹21.70 crore, respectively.[2,3] These incidents underscore the regulatory risks the investment industry is exposed to and subjectivity in the interpretation of laws that could result in upright professionals getting embroiled in legal cases.

2. Be aware.

Awareness, an attribute common to all successful investors including RJ, consists of three traits. First, RJ's training as a chartered accountant endowed him with the knowledge to embark on an investment career. Second, cultivating a network of mentors and collaborators came naturally to him thanks to his affable nature. He learnt the nitty-gritty of professional investing and the soft skills essential to be successful from this network. Third, a passion for investing and a curious mind drove him to keep his ears close to the ground. He was thus able to synthesise political, economic, legislative and business events to arrive at sound investment decisions.

Table 18.1 lists the five-year (31 January 2020–30 January 2025) and ten-year (31 January 2015–30 January 2025) share price returns registered by the twenty-seven stocks RJ owned as of 30 June 2022. The returns are as of 30 January 2025 and span the period preceding and the two-and-a-half-year period (14 August 2022–30 January 2025) following RJ's demise. The list excludes RaRe Enterprises' erstwhile PE investments (Metro Brands, Nazara Technologies and Star Health and Allied Insurance) and entities were listed for less than ten years as of 30 January 2025 (Jubilant Ingrevia and Dishman Carbogen).

The share prices of nine of the twenty-seven entities clocked higher returns than Sensex both on a five-year and ten-year basis. The nine entities are Escorts Kubota, Anant Raj, Titan, Indian Hotels, Man Infracon, Tata Communications, Fortis Healthcare, NCC and CRISIL.

Twelve entities' share prices clocked higher returns than Sensex on a five-year basis, but their ten-year returns were lower than the index. This implies that their share prices underperformed during the period 31 January 2015–30 January 2020, but have improved in the subsequent five years. The twelve entities are Federal Bank, Karur Vysya Bank, Geojit Financial Services, Valor Estate, Orient Cement Va Tech Wabag, Autoline, Tata Motors, Wockhardt, Bilcare, Prozone and Canara Bank.

Two entities' share price returns, Jubilant Pharmova and Aptech, outperformed Sensex on a ten-year basis but underperformed on a five-year basis. The underperformance in the preceding five years (31 January 2020–30 January 2025) was partially on account of their stock prices skyrocketing between January 2015 and 2020. More analysis is required to ascertain whether systematic and/or idiosyncratic factors caused the last five years' underperformance and are likely to adversely impact these companies' prospects.

Table 18.1: Share Price Performance of RJ's Stock Picks as of 30 January 2025 (a non-exhaustive list)

Entity	***10-Year Return***		***5-Year Return***	
	%	***Performance [1]***	%	***Performance [1]***
Sensex	**157.85**	-	**85.77**	-
Escorts Kubota	2,556.60	Outperform	375.80	Outperform
Anant Raj	2,242.97	Outperform	3,205.78	Outperform
Titan Company	665.48	Outperform	186.52	Outperform
Indian Hotels Company	617.92	Outperform	477.77	Outperform
Man Infraconstruction	594.20	Outperform	889.61	Outperform
Jubilant Pharmova	502.84	Outperform	73.56	Underperform
Tata Communications	496.79	Outperform	263.64	Outperform
Fortis Healthcare	439.97	Outperform	309.99	Outperform
NCC	215.87	Outperform	311.10	Outperform
Aptech	200.57	Outperform	31.79	Underperform
CRISIL	164.54	Outperform	218.39	Outperform
Federal Bank	157.73	Underperform	86.99	Outperform
Karur Vysya Bank	124.40	Underperform	380.34	Outperform
Geojit Fin Serv	116.18	Underperform	276.02	Outperform
Valor Estate	86.70	Underperform	1,440.67	Outperform
Orient Cement	77.05	Underperform	314.07	Outperform
Va Tech Wabag	68.51	Underperform	495.56	Outperform
Edelweiss Financial	50.03	Underperform	14.31	Underperform
Autoline Industries	30.22	Underperform	287.37	Outperform
Tata Motors	27.33	Underperform	275.30	Outperform
Wockhardt	21.70	Underperform	303.66	Outperform
Agro Tech Foods	15.58	Underperform	15.11	Underperform
Rallis	4.41	Underperform	4.84	Underperform

Entity	*10-Year Return*		*5-Year Return*	
	%	*Performance [1]*	%	*Performance [1]*
Bilcare	7.09	Underperform	271.02	Outperform
Prozone Realty	2.94	Underperform	88.99	Outperform
Canara Bank	0.65	Underperform	127.73	Outperform
Sammaan Capital [2]	-72.47	Underperform	-48.10	Underperform

[1] Vis-à-vis Sensex
[2] Formerly Indiabulls Housing Finance
Source: bseindia.com

Four entities underperformed Sensex both on a five-year and ten-year basis. These are Edelweiss Financial, Agro Tech Foods, Rallis and Indiabulls Housing Finance (subsequently renamed Sammaan Capital). RaRe Enterprises sold Edelweiss Financial, Rallis and Indiabulls Housing Finance after 30 June 2022.

The returns provided in Table 18.1 would have accrued to an investor should they have made a one-time purchase of the stock and remained invested for a decade. RJ, however, purchased stocks in multiple tranches, occasionally engaged in bottom fishing and traded in some of these stocks too. Hence, his returns are very different from a vanilla investor's. It is indeed impressive that the share prices of nine of the twenty-seven entities consistently outperformed Sensex for a decade and twelve entities improved since January 2020. That the returns of two entities decelerated and four have been underperformers is evidence of past performance not guaranteeing future success and even the best of investors not getting all their calls right.

3. Monitor investments.

The performance of RaRe Enterprises' listed equities is a reflection of RJ's awareness and him being a hands-on investor. His quizzing the Federal Bank management is narrated in the 'Banking on Banks' chapter. It demonstrated his in-depth knowledge of banking. From the following conversation he had with the management of his favourite company, Titan, in November 2018, it is evident that RJ was well aware of the goings-on in the industries in which his investees operated.

> RJ: What about that party which has failed in Madras (Chennai), some very large jeweller?
>
> Titan: Nathella.
>
> RJ: Are you taking them over?
>
> Titan: No. Such jewellers, the only thing you can take over, if at all, is their retail outlets. You can't take over the franchise because the practices of such jewellers—the customers are used to those practices. That way a whole lot of jewellers are available in that sense. But it would be quite impossible for us to continue with their name or their skill or franchise, as in customer base. It is better if the customers actually migrate to us.[4]

RJ was a non-executive director on the boards of several companies including Hungama Media, Aptech, Bilcare, Viceroy Hotels, Concord Biotech, Provogue India and Geojit Financial Services.[5] Many of these companies benefitted from his expertise, though he did admit that Bilcare did not heed his counsel. RJ's interactions with the senior managements of Titan and Kotak Mahindra Bank motivated them.

4. Diversify.

It is well known that RJ was a superb stock-picker, in whose listed equities portfolio Tata Group stocks, led by Titan, were the largest constituents. Counterparty concentration is characteristic of most professional investors' portfolios, as demonstrated in the chapter titled 'Mahalaxmi Race Course and Arthur Road Jail'.

What has not been widely discussed is RaRe Enterprises' granular industry exposure and diversified business profile. RaRe Enterprises' CEP and PE investments that have been listed thus far operate in diverse industries, which imparts an element of stability to the organisation's cash flows. While the multi-baggers in the portfolio depress dividend yield, dividend income in rupee terms almost quadrupled from ₹55 crore in 2016 to ₹217 crore in 2024 (Appendix 5).

5. Borrow cautiously.

RJ asserted that he engaged in leveraged trades to raise capital for RaRe Enterprises' listed equities and PE verticals. Rare Equity Private Limited issuing non-convertible debentures with its shares as collateral demonstrates that RaRe Enterprises borrowed for other businesses too. However, RJ cautioned investors about the risks of borrowing and urged them to borrow in moderation. His astuteness was evident when he stated, 'You should know when to leverage and when not to. Though my wealth was much higher in 2008 than in 2003, my leverage was not even 10% of what it was in 2003.' Sensex, which had opened at 13,828 in January 2007 plunged by 30% in the following two years to end at 9,647 in December 2008 amidst the global financial crisis.

6. Manage risks.

Risk management is the least discussed aspect of RJ's operations. Practically nothing is known about how Rare Enterprise measures and mitigates its risks. Atul Suri observed,

> For someone with his wealth and his size, it is very easy to get arrogant. It often happens with retail investors that very often trading becomes delivery and long term. Rakeshji never let that happen. He had great ability to manage risk—I have seen him exit losing positions, get back the next day, go through

> that immense amount of pain because he believed in risk management. The problem is that when you become very rich and you have a lot of liquidity, you can let that risk management go because you can afford it. He never let that happen till the last moment .... Whether he had ₹100 in his pocket or ₹100 crore, for Jhunjhunwala, the discipline with which he managed his positions was phenomenal. I used to wonder that someone like him could take losses, he had that ability but the ruthlessness with which he sold and exited his positions was fantastic. That kept him afloat. That is why most successful traders will do well in a phase but when the phase changes, all these rules go haywire and they are unable to recover and stand. He was able to do it cycle after cycle, for 30 years. Risk management kept him afloat.[6]

7. Do not time the market.

All one has to do to profit in capital markets is to buy low and sell high, that is, purchase securities when their prices are low and sell when their prices are high. However, this is a deceptively simple adage. Academics and investors assert that predicting the peaks and troughs of markets and executing trades during these inflexion points consistently is practically impossible. RJ's timing of his divestment of the luggage manufacturer V.I.P. Industries' stock is an example.

RJ purchased 1.26 million shares in V.I.P. in the September 2009 quarter. At the 30 September 2009 share price of ₹150.80, his stake was worth ₹19 crore. V.I.P.'s share price touched a lifetime high of ₹1,025 on 21 September 2011. In October 2011, V.I.P. announced a 1:5 stock split, and RJ's holding rose to 9.09 million shares by December 2011. V.I.P.'s share price by end-December 2011 was ₹77.20 on account of the stock split. By end-December 2020, V.I.P's share price had risen more than fourfold to ₹362.50.

RJ sold some of his holdings in V.I.P. between October 2011 and December 2015. His stake ranged from 5.22 to 7.50 million shares between December 2015 and 2020. RJ reduced his stake to less than 1% in the first half of 2021. An investor who had purchased 100 V.I.P shares on 30 September 2009 for ₹15,800 would have owned 500 shares worth ₹1.72 lakh; the market value of their holding would have grown at a CAGR of 24%. As RJ's holding in V.I.P. fluctuated, computing his return is not straightforward.

Like most stocks in RJ's portfolio, V.I.P.'s share price had also declined by 16% in 2020 due to the COVID-19 outbreak. He had predicted that share prices would rebound in 2021, which they did. RJ had exited V.I.P. when its share price ranged from ₹304.60 to ₹423 in the first half of 2021. V.I.P.'s share price rose to ₹668.85 on 9 November 2021. However, I was puzzled that RJ offloaded his entire stake in V.I.P., a multi-bagger that paid regular dividends, while retaining the four underperforming stocks. The market value of RaRe Enterprises' holding in V.I.P. was ₹204 crore, while that of four underperforming stocks—Edelweiss Financial, Agro Tech Foods, Rallis and Indiabulls Housing Finance—was ₹688 crore as of 31 December 2020.

Goela explained, 'Rakeshji spoke to the management. He believed that with the entry of competitors, the share price was stagnating and that the stock had completed its journey. So, he sold the stock. Rakeshji made the buy and sell decisions independently and did not compare (in this instance) V.I.P.'s performance with other stocks and then decide.'[7] While RJ did not sell V.I.P shares at their peak price in 2021, he certainly sold them on the upswing. Meeting a target rate of return or limiting losses are more realistic strategies than 'buy low, sell high'.

8. Do not imitate.

The Times of India, in January 2021, and *Mint*, in August 2022, identified some of the best-performing stocks on BSE and NSE.[8, 9] The fifteen stocks identified by the two publications, along with their returns, are listed in Table 18.2. RJ had invested in two of the fifteen stocks—Titan and CRISIL. Three IT stocks were included in the list of best performing stocks—Wipro, Infosys and TCS—in which RJ hadn't invested, as he admitted that he didn't understand the industry.

Table 18.2: Select Large-Cap Multi-baggers

Entity	*Period*	*Return*
Banks & Financial Services		
HDFC Bank	1995–January 2021	36,900.00%
Bajaj Finance	1993–January 2021	29,900.00%
HDFC Limited	1993–January 2021	19,900.00%
CRISIL	1994–January 2021	10,900.00%
Bajaj Finserv	2008–January 2021	1,900.00%
IT Stocks		
Wipro	1995–January 2021	35,900.00%
Infosys	February 1993–August 2022	13,651.08%
Tata Consultancy Services	August 2004–August 2022	2,727.23%
Pharma		
Dr. Reddy's	1991–January 2021	2,19,900.00%
Divi's Labs	2003–January 2021	46,900.00%
Sun Pharma	1994–January 2021	30,900.00%
Other Corporates		
Titan	September 2004–August 2022	57,806.32%
Asian Paints	1992–January 2021	42,900.00%
Reliance Industries	1977–August 2022	10,499.24%
Hindustan Unilever	July 1995–August 2022	1,460.84%

Source: Times of India, 23 January 2021 and *Mint*, 14 August 2022

Does this imply RJ failed to invest in most of the best-performing stocks? No! Stock prices fluctuate. A high return since listing does not imply that an entity's share price has appreciated smoothly. The share price of Dr. Reddy's Laboratories is a case in point. The share price of this pharma company appreciated by 2,19,900% between 1991 and January 2021, making it the best-performing stock among the fifteen entities listed in Table 18.2. However, Dr. Reddy's underperformed Sensex during the ten-year period January 2015 to 2025. Its share price rose by 76%, which is less than half of the increase registered by Sensex, that is, 158%.

RJ often acknowledged that R.K. Damani was his mentor, from whom he learnt about investing and life. He also acknowledged that he learnt the importance of research from Nemish Shah. Ramesh Damani was a long-time friend who invested with RJ in Aptech. Madhusudan Kela, Atul Suri and Manish Gupta were some of RJ's protégés. Comparing the portfolio composition of RJ, Radhakishan Damani, Ramesh Damani, Nemish Shah and Madhusudan Kela is illuminating (Table 18.3). Atul Suri and Manish Gupta do not feature in this analysis as Trendlyne does not report their portfolio composition.

There is only one stock that both RJ and R.K. Damani own—Aptech. There are no commonalities between RJ's listed equities portfolio and those of Ramesh Damani, Nemish Shah and Madhusudan Kela. Further, there is a significant variation in the market value of these five investors' listed equity holdings, ranging from Ramesh Damani's ₹68.60 crore to R.K. Damani's ₹1.54 lakh crore as of 30 June 2024.

If the market value of R.K. Damani's listed equities is five times that of RJ's CEP, why is the latter more renowned as a stock picker? One reason is that the personalities of RJ and Radhakishan Damani are polar opposites. Whereas RJ was outspoken, R.K. Damani is taciturn. The second and more important reason is that the promoter group led by R.K. Damani held a 74.9% stake in Avenue Supermarts, the listed retail chain he founded, as of 30

Table 18.3: Listed Equity Holdings as of 30 June 2022

Rakesh Jhunjhunwala	***Radhakishan Damani***	***Ramesh Damani***
Market Value of Listed Equities as of 30 June 2022, ₹ Crore		
30,752.44	1,53,875.00	68.00
Listed Equity Holdings		
Aptech	Avenue Supermarts	Goldiam Intl
Star Health	VST Industries	Vadivarhe Speciality
Metro Brands	India Cements	Panama Petrochem
NCC	Advani Hotels	Garden Reach Shipbuilders
Nazara Technologies	Aptech	
Rallis	Sundaram Finance	
Bilcare	Mangalam Organics	
Agro Tech Foods	Sundaram Finance	
VA Tech Wabag	3M	
Geojit Fin Serv	Trent	
Jubilant Pharmanova	Blue Dart Express	
CRISIL	BF Utilities	
Titan Company	Andhra Paper	
Jubilant Ingrevia	United Breweries	
Autoline Industries	Metropolis Healthcare	
Karur Vysya Bank	Astra Microwave	
Fortis Healthcare		
Federal Bank		
Anant Raj		
Dishman Carbogen		
Indian Hotels		
Prozone Reality		
Wockhardt		
Canara Bank		
Valor Estate		
Edelweiss Financial		
Escorts Kubota		
Sammaan Capital		
Man Infraconstruction		
Orient Cement		
Tata Communications		
Tata Motors		

Nimesh Shah	*Madhusudan Kela*
Market Vaue of Listed Equities as of 30 June 2022, ₹ Crore	
1,243.80	220.70
Listed Equity Holdings	
Lakshmi Machine	Mkventures Capital
Bannari Amman Sugars	IRIS Business
Elgi Equipments	CSL Finance
Zodiac Clothing	
EID Parry	
Rane Engine Valve	

Source: www.trendlyne.com

June 2022. R.K. Damani's stake in Avenue Supermarts was worth ₹1.49 trillion on 30 June 2024 and constituted 97% of his listed equity holdings. His listed equity investments, excluding Avenue Supermarts, was ₹4,877 crore or 16% of RJ's portfolio.

Retail investors tend to mimic successful investors by buying the shares the latter purchased much earlier and/or by investing in unlisted entities in the grey market. Following this strategy is unlikely to yield as much profit. In certain cases, retail investors facilitate the profitable exits of professional investors. An even riskier strategy is purchasing unlisted shares in the grey market. In December 2024, I received a WhatsApp message from my brokerage announcing that NSE shares were available for purchase. Retail investors lapped up these shares with much gusto. I spoke to a few of these investors to understand why they purchased the shares of an entity that was the epicentre of the co-location scam, whose CEO was arrested and which was struggling to get listed for years. Their unanimous response was, '(R.K.) Damani is a NSE shareholder. The IPO is bound to be a success. We will profit.'

Damani purchased 7.82 million NSE shares, equivalent to a 1.58% stake in the stock exchange, in the March 2020 quarter.[10]

The Economic Times reported that the value of Damani's stake in NSE ranged from ₹650 to ₹800 crore, which implies that the share price varied between ₹832 and ₹1,023.[11] According to unlistedzone.com, a platform that facilitates the trading of unlisted shares, NSE's share price was ₹740 in September 2021; this is the earliest available quote.[12] In September 2024, NSE announced a 4:1 bonus issue, which resulted in the number of NSE shares R.K. Damani owned growing fivefold to 39.08 million shares and his average purchase price declining by 80% and probably ranging from ₹166 to ₹205.[13] NSE's share price rose from ₹1,240 before the bonus issue to ₹1,900 from October 2024 onwards.[14] While pre-IPO investors, including R.K. Damani, are likely to clock handsome gains if and when NSE lists, it remains to be seen if IPO investors will also profit.

9. Be emotionless.

What is the difference between share trading and investing? Aswath Damodaran, professor of finance at New York University's Stern School of Business, observes, 'The prices of stocks can move towards infinity or towards zero, depending on where mood and momentum take them. Value on the other hand has both upper and lower bounds, with both bounds being set by expected cash flows, growth and risk .... Price is reactive, Value is proactive!'[15] Traders take long and short positions in stocks to profit from day-to-day volatility, which is a reflection of the market's mood and momentum. Investors analyse business models, financials, economic and competitive landscapes, risks, and growth prospects to purchase stocks, which they hold for the medium to long term.

Hence, traders and investors usually have very different personalities. Traders are quick-thinking and clinical in adjusting their positions to limit losses or maximise gains. Investors are patient and analytical and are usually willing to ride through short-term volatility to achieve their target rate of return in the medium to long term. The fascinating aspect about RJ was that he was both a skilled trader and investor. Suri states that RJ could exit positions with remarkable alacrity and yet remain invested in stocks like Titan for more than three decades* despite its share price more than halving three or four times during this period.[16]

RJ often quipped, 'Emotions are reserved for wife, children, mistress, and religion.' But was he always Zen? This doesn't seem to be the case. Goela observed, 'I will not deny that Rakeshji's moods were affected by the markets. He constantly evaluated whether his judgement was right.'[17]

10. Decide amidst uncertainty.

Functioning in capital markets is an art, a science and an assessment of human behaviour that requires decisions to be made on the basis of incomplete information and amidst uncertain and fluctuating market conditions. This applies to all segments of capital markets—stocks, debt, private equity, commodities, rates, FX, real estate, etc. RJ's success as an investor is the outcome of the comfort he developed in dealing with this uncertainty, willingness to accept losses, diversifying his bets, and learning from his mistakes and moving on.

Sheth stated, 'Rakeshji never felt regret even when he missed opportunities. For example, investing in software stocks. He was very clear that not investing in software stocks was a mistake and that we should learn from mistakes. He would say: *Yah to satta mat karo, yah aphsos mat karo*.'[18] (Either don't bet or don't regret).

RJ once remarked, 'My strike rate is not high. I would have made 20 private equity investments by now, but 10 of them would

---

* RJ started purchasing Titan shares from 1991.

be duds, dead and written off.'[19] He also opined, 'I think a good trader does not initiate more than 40% of trades that are right.' Most tellingly he often counselled, 'We invest in the future and that future is uncertain ... Don't try to be too predictive. Try and understand the general direction.'

19

Thus Spake RJ

AN OLD QUATRAIN GOES:

> 'Mussolini with his black shirts, backs against the wall,
> Hitler with his brown shirts, heading for a fall,
> Churchill in his dress shirt dominates them all,
> Three cheers for Gandhi—no shirt at ALL!'

Simplicity is the hallmark of astute minds. Think of Steve Jobs and his black turtlenecks; Warren Buffett, as of 2024, continuing to live in a house he had purchased for $31,500 in 1958; and closer home, Azim Premji.

RJ's career is awe-inspiring. He was a trader, investor and a private-equity backer for whom borrowing was a significant source of financing. Despite this, he was a very simple human. RJ loved Amchi Mumbai and often averred, 'I cannot live without Bombay.' While he loved Italian and Chinese cuisines, his favourite was Indian fare, especially dal chawal. Guru Dutt's magnum opus *Sahib, Bibi aur Ghulam* was his favourite film, while Titan was his beloved stock.

I watched more than a hundred YouTube videos featuring RJ while researching for this book. The pithy aphorisms he used to drive home ideas shed light on his character and his approach to investing. I have listed the statements that he often repeated in this chapter. Most of his statements are self-explanatory. The ones with explanations are in text boxes.

This chapter aims to shed light on RJ—the human and the investor—in his own words.

Howard Marks: 'Volatility is not risk, permanent decline in value is.'[1]

Volatility can be a symptom of risk but is not synonymous with it ... Investors should focus on potential losses and how to mitigate them, not just fluctuations in prices.... Risk cannot be quantified in advance, as the future is inherently uncertain.... Therefore, investors must rely on their judgment and understanding of the underlying factors influencing an investment's risk profile, rather than focusing on historical data alone.[2]

Peter Drucker: 'Culture eats strategy for lunch/breakfast.'

A business' culture determines its success, regardless of how effective its strategy may be. Culture refers to employee behaviour under pressure, how they respond to various challenges and how they treat stakeholders including vendors, customers, investors, lenders and each other.[3]

Winston Churchill: 'We make a living with what we get. We make a life with what we give.'[4]

Wealth

'Wealth allows me not to be worried. Money means security, achievement. It gives me power to grow. It is important as a means to an end. Wealth is not happiness. Wealth is comfort and independence. The quest to earn wealth has subsided. Success and wealth are transitory.'[5]

Mindset

'Means are as important as the ends.'

'Only a tolerant mind can accept change.'

When asked what he would have been if not an investor, RJ replied, 'I cannot do anything but invest. Markets are my passion.'

'You do not succeed without obsession.'

'Buy when the market is rising, sell when the market is falling.'

'Nothing is sacrosanct in investment. At a price everything is investible.'

'Be a realistic investor. See reality as what it is and not what you'd like it to be. Don't be too pessimistic and don't get too optimistic.'

'I was dogmatic. Markets proved me wrong.'

'No investment can give a linear return. Some years, it will underperform. Both CRISIL and Lupin have underperformed during the last few years.'

'Don't be afraid to make a mistake. Rely on your intuition and judgement.'[6]

'I don't mind losing money or when an individual fails. Emotionally it hits me if a person's character is not good. I made all films with Balki. I don't mind making mistakes but I don't like being cheated. I trust Balki.'[7]

'A good investor is like a chameleon and changes as circumstances change.'

'Emotions are reserved for wife, children, mistress and religion.'

'Why have an opinion on everything? I don't want to have an opinion on other people's standards and conscience. I don't want others to have an opinion on my ... I am a liberal.'

'We invest in the future and that future is uncertain ... Don't try to be too predictive. Try and understand the general direction.'

'I don't want to be anyone's clone. I am not in any rat race.'

When asked what drew him to a career in investing, RJ replied, 'I am my own boss. I go to the office when I want to and do not go when I don't feel like it. My dividend income is enough for my expenses and charitable causes. God has given me wealth. He has given me far more than I need.'[8]

Capital Markets

'Markets are like weather. You may not like it but you have to bear with it.'

'Markets are like women—commanding, mysterious, always exciting, always volatile, always uncertain.'

'The stock market is a lady ... You cannot have a good relationship with a woman by browbeating her. You have to accept her; you have to respect her; you have to learn from her.'

'Stock markets are as much about psychology as about reality. Markets are not just about money; they are also about knowledge, ego and the satisfaction of being right.'

'Most bull markets begin at the depth of pessimism.'

'You cannot be taught about markets; you have to experience it. It is like sex.'[9]

Trading and Investing

'If you have a wife and a mistress and you can manage both well, then you can do trading and investing both well ... You keep them apart ... One should not know anything about the other.'

'You want to trade, you trade. You want to invest, invest. Don't confuse the two. Trading is for creating the capital. Investing is for growing the capital.'

'In trading, risk is extreme. In investment, risk is not extreme.'

'Trading is about momentum and following the trend. Trading gives me capital to invest. Trading skills teach me that stocks can remain overvalued.'

'Trading is all about price. You should know the broad direction of the market, what to stake and when to take a loss.'

'Trading gives you the highest ROE [return on equity]. It is the largest source of my wealth. Trading profits finance my investments.[10]

'I think a good trader does not initiate more than 40% of trades that are right. We traders follow a pyramidal structure. We buy when a stock is at ₹100. We buy more when it rises to ₹105 and buy again at ₹110. If the market goes down, we sell. As a trader, I will never ever average. A trader needs to know when to take a loss as no one can predict momentum.'[11]

RJ advised traders to determine a stop-loss price (a pre-determined price at which a security is sold to limit losses) and stick to it while trading. Certain traders have a tendency to purchase more shares as price declines; their rationale is that they are reducing their average purchase price. However, this is risky, as it is difficult to predict if and when the share price may appreciate. Hence, abiding by the stop-loss price is essential.

'Price is the indicator of what is coming. I made trading profits in spurts—1989–92, 2003–07, 2009–11. Between 1994 and 1999, I did not make any trading income.'

'The worst of mistakes are made in the best of times.'

'Be more opinionated while investing and less opinionated while trading.'

'Trading, investing and cooking cannot be taught, they have to be learnt.'

'My worst investment has been in my health. I would encourage everyone to invest in their health.'[12]

Guiding Principles of Investing

'I have no written laws or rules of investment because there are no laws or rules.'

'Tips are hazardous to your financial health. You can't make money on borrowed knowledge.'

'When you invest in a small company, you are backing an individual.'

'I don't invest in start-ups—highest risk. Lots of start-ups are me too, very few have original ideas. [I am interested in] differentiated start-ups with clear paths to profitability. I invested [in start-ups] in 2000 and 2007 and lost money both times.[13]

Investment Framework

Yogesh Shah asked, 'Should I invest in small caps or large caps?' RJ replied, 'Invest in small caps that are going to become large caps.'

'There are two parts of data—analysis and interpretation.'

'[My] parameters for investment are opportunity, competitive advantage, ability to grow and financial profile, [which comprises] input–output analysis, working capital cycle and valuation.'

'While assessing a company, I think of opportunity, productivity, scalability, management and corporate governance, that is, how the company treats all shareholders.'

'The criteria I use to identify investible companies are capital investment and profitability ratios. These ratios should be good. Companies should buy on credit and sell in cash. Such companies have the highest P/Es. Of the fifty top companies, forty-five will meet these characteristics.'

'Cash flows are the ultimate means of valuation. Always look at the cash flow statement.'

'Apart from my house, I own no real estate. I invest in real estate funds.'

The key elements that determine a company's success: 'People, patience, technology, frugality and governance.'

'We invest out of informed ignorance and intuition.'

'[I] began with financial analysis; now I focus on business models.'

'[The] two most difficult things in world—riding the stock and beauty in a girl. It's personal.'[14]

Leverage

'If I have bank balance, I cannot sleep. If I pay interest, I sleep well .... Leverage is akin to smoking and drinking. It is pleasurable in moderation and becomes problematic when overdone. I built wealth through leverage ... (but) you should live to make another mistake.[15]

Traders and/or investors have at least four sources of funds to carry out their trading and investment activities: their own funds; investment income such as rent, interest and dividends; divestment proceeds; or cash realised by selling investments and borrowing. Of these, borrowing to trade or invest is the riskiest. Borrowing to trade and/or invest is a spread game, that is, players borrow monies anticipating that the returns from their activities are significantly higher than interest expense. Borrowers are required to pledge their listed investments as collateral to borrow. Lenders in India's organised sector such as banks and NBFCs usually lend a maximum of 50% of the market value of the borrower's listed investment portfolio. This is known as the loan-to-value ratio (LTV).

The risk of financing trading and investments with borrowing or leverage arises when the returns are inadequate to service the debt or, much worse, when a loss is incurred. Traders and/or investors face a double whammy when the market value of their collateral declines, resulting in the LTV exceeding 50%. Lenders would then require borrowers to offer additional listed securities as collateral so that the LTV moderates to below 50%. This is known as margin call. The double whammy of trading and/or investment returns being negative or lower than borrowing cost and facing a margin call frequently occurs during cyclical downturns.

Hence RJ's warning, 'You should live to make another mistake.'

'[The stock] market took off between March and April 2003. In the next twelve to fifteen months, I carried the highest leverage of my life ... You should know when to leverage and when not to. Though my wealth was much higher in 2008 than in 2003, my leverage was not even 10% of what it was in 2003. Be emotionless.'[16]

Views on Select Companies

'Start-ups are good if they do something original. I do not want to invest in me-too start-ups. Lyft and WeWork are examples.'[17]

Lyft is a ride-hailing company like Uber and Ola founded in 2012. It operates in the US and Canada. Lyft listed in 2019 through a $2.34 billion IPO that valued the company at $23.40 billion. Recurring losses, lay-offs and discontinuation of rental services resulted in Lyft's share price declining by more than 82% from $78.29 in end-March 2019 to $13.57 on 20 December 2024.

WeWork is a provider of co-working spaces founded in 2010 by Adam Neumann and Miguel McKelvey. WeWork's incorporation coincided with high vacancy rates in office properties at New York City. The start-up doubled in size between 2010 and 2011, and grew exponentially thereafter. Early investors included those involved in commercial real estate and a venture capital firm called Benchmark. By 2015, WeWork quadrupled its valuation to $10 billion, had a customer base of 23,000 across thirty-two locations and was renting desks for as little as $45 per month. SoftBank first invested in WeWork in 2017, which resulted in a doubling of the company's valuation in two years to $20 billion. SoftBank's investment enabled WeWork to expand globally. Between 2017 and 2018, SoftBank invested around $8 billion in the company. In 2019, SoftBank floated a potential $16 billion investment in WeWork that would give the investor a controlling stake in the start-up. Despite SoftBank scaling back its incremental investment to $2 billion, it resulted in WeWork's valuation more than doubling to $47 billion. WeWork aggressively expanded its core business, invested in unrelated businesses, including a company that manufactured indoor wave pools and another than produced superfoods, and even opened an elementary school in New York. WeWork announced its intention to float an IPO in August 2019.

WeWork's IPO prospectus reported that Neumann had personally purchased the trademark to the word 'we' and sold it to WeWork for $5.9 million. Bloomberg reported that this was one of the many instances of WeWork's corporate leadership seemed to enrich themselves at the expense of the shareholders and the company.[18]

That WeWork's $47 billion valuation was irrationally inflated vis-à-vis its UK-incorporated competitor IWG's (formerly Regus) $3.7 billion was evident when the performance of the two co-working space providers was juxtaposed. While IWG's 50 million square feet catered to 2.5 million customers, WeWork's 4.5 million square feet was rented to a clientele of 5,00,000. IWG operated in 3,000 locations spread across 120 countries. WeWork's geographic spread was a fraction of IWG's, at 528 locations in 29 countries. IWG earned $500 million profits from $3.4 billion revenues. WeWork's $1.9 billion loss exceeded its $1.8 billion revenues.

Investor interest in WeWork's IPO was lacklustre, and the company postponed its listing. Neumann resigned as CEO. Two senior WeWork executives, Sebastian Gunningham and Artie Minson, were appointed as co-CEOs. Amongst their tasks on assuming charge of WeWork was selling Neumann's $60 million private jet, divesting the numerous acquisitions the company had earlier made, close down the elementary school, lay off thousands of employees and indefinitely postpone the IPO. SoftBank bailed WeWork out by investing another $9.5 billion, which exceeded the investee's $8 billion valuation. WeWork is an example of a 'company that got too much money too fast with no effective oversight on how to spend it.[19]

'SoftBank is a Ponzi scheme.'[20]

Tokyo-headquartered SoftBank, a technology-focused conglomerate with a global footprint, was founded by Masayoshi Son in 1981 as a software distributor. Ranked 325 among Fortune Global 500 companies as of 2024, it has fuelled its expansion by gargantuan investments. In 2006, SoftBank purchased Vodafone Japan (Vodafone K.K.) from the UK-headquartered Vodafone Group PLC for approximately $15 billion, which is one of the largest M&A transactions in Japan to date. Interestingly, Vodafone Group PLC extended a loan to SoftBank to purchase Vodafone K.K. In 2000, SoftBank acquired a stake in the Jack Ma-founded Alibaba, a year after its incorporation, for $20 million. When Alibaba listed in 2014, the market value of SoftBank's stake in the e-commerce company was $55 billion.[21]

In 2017, SoftBank joined hands with Saudi Arabia's Public Investment Fund (PIF), the Abu Dhabi Investment Authority (ADIA) and other investors to create the $100 billion Vision Fund—the world's largest technology fund. PIF's injection of $45 billion made it the largest investor in the Vision Fund, followed by SoftBank ($28 billion), ADIA ($15 billion) and other investors ($12 billion).

Vision Fund's profitable investments include the UK-headquartered chip design firm ARM, the China-headquartered ride hailing firm DiDi, the South Korean e-commerce company Coupang and the Indian electric motorbike manufacturer Ola Electric.[22] Its unsuccessful investments comprise WeWork, Wirecard and One97 Communications (Paytm). These are non-exhaustive lists. In September 2020, the *Financial Times* reported that SoftBank was 'the "Nasdaq whale" that has bought billions of dollars' worth of US equity derivatives in a series of trades that stoked the fevered rally in big tech stocks before a sharp pullback'.[23]

A Ponzi scheme is an investment scam that pays early investors with money taken from later investors to create an illusion of big profits. SoftBank's practice of raising large sums of equity against the backdrop of a complex organisation structure, volatile cash flows, high indebtedness and questionable corporate governance practices prompted RJ to liken the conglomerate to a Ponzi scheme.

Limitations and Mistakes

'I must limit my optimism.'

'[I] misjudged peoples' characters. Biggest mistakes I made was in trusting people.'

'I was a late entrant into software because I did not understand technology.'

'I am bad at confirmation bias. If I am convinced, I do not listen to others. Sometimes confidence pays; sometimes it does not.'[24]

Prognosis

'A country has to be transparent, non-aggressive and democratic for its currency to be accepted. Hence the Chinese Yuan (CNY) will not supplant the USD.'

In a 20 January 2021 'Off the Cuff' episode, RJ predicted, 'In twenty to twenty-five years, India will surpass China. When I came to the market, thousands were richer than me. It does not mean I cannot get ahead. China's debt to GDP is the highest in the world.'[25]

Advice for Retail Investors

'Speculation (trading) is done with a passbook and not a cheque book.'[26]

Before the proliferation of online banking, banks issued customers a passbook and a cheque book. Customers visited their bank branches periodically to update their passbooks with transactions. The branch provided customers with a withdrawal slip should they wish to withdraw a modest sum of money, say ₹500. Customers filled the withdrawal slip and handed it to the branch official with their passbook to withdraw cash. Cheque leaves were used or withdrawing larger sums of money and transferring money to others. RJ advised investors to allocate a small sum of money for trading.

'If you are not a professional investor, opt for mutual funds (MFs) or portfolio management schemes (PMS). Investment is not easy; it is a full-time job. A lot of people want to invest for excitement. Keep 10% of the money for excitement.'

'Invest in MFs through systematic investment plans (SIPs). It is difficult to time the market.'

'There is a lot of froth in the IPO market ... Stay away.'[27]

This was RJ's comment at the Reuters Global Investment 2018 Outlook Summit held in November 2017. This warning was accurate during the 2021–22 IPO rush, too, when there were mammoth listings, such as LIC (₹21,008 crore) and Paytm (₹18,300 crore). LIC listed at ₹949 on 4 May 2022 and is trading at ₹821.80 on 22 April 2025. Paytm's performance is even worse; its share price on 22 April 2025, ₹882.60, is 59% lower than its listing price of ₹2,150 on 8 November 2021. Those who invested in the 2021-22 IPOs have witnessed their portfolios depreciate in value. Most Indian IPOs floated in the last five years have tended to be overpriced.

However, the rationale for RJ eschewing IPOs is very different. Utpal Sheth explained, 'RaRe Enterprises did not invest in IPOs as we were not recognised as institutional investors, though we are larger than several institutional investors. Therefore, there was no mechanism for us to get meaningful allotments like anchor investors and qualified institutional buyers (QIB) did. If we participated as high-net-worth investors (HNI), we would get a proportionate allotment. The very act of Rakeshji subscribing to an IPO as a HNI meant that the offering would be hugely oversubscribed. With proportionate allotment, he would be acting against his own interests.'[28]

India

'India is chaos … America is chaos … Growth and prosperity come from where there is chaos and not order.'

'India is greater than personalities. I would very much like that Mr. Modi becomes Prime Minister … BJP tally will surprise on the upside … India grows not because of politicians but in spite of them.'

'[India faces] two risks—the safety of our leaders and Pakistan's nuclear bomb. I will not trust a failed state with a nuclear bomb.'

'We settle faster than the NYSE. India does not need government spending. India needs a platform. India needs ease of doing business. Indian manufacturing is impeded by lack of infrastructure and laws. [There is] no right to hire and fire. Give us freedom. *Hum duniya ko dikha denge*! (We will show the world).'[29]

Politics

'Only two Indian prime ministers have experienced poverty—Narendra Modi and Lal Bahadur Shastri.'

'I'm an out and out BJP supporter.'

'P. Chidambaram has most been the most capital market-friendly finance minister. Yashwant Sinha's pension reforms were unbelievable. New employees were moved to NPS (National Pension Scheme).'

'Demonetisation was an effort that did not succeed.'

'[I take] pride in India and Indian-ness and not Hindu and Hindu-ness.'[30]

Epilogue

Platonic Principles

IN THE NETFLIX SERIES *THE CROWN*, THE FOUNDER AND THEN headmaster of Gordonstoun School, Kurt Hahn, advises the young Philip Mountbatten (later Duke of Edinburgh and consort to Queen Elizabeth II) after the latter engages in fisticuffs with his bullies that he ought to follow Platonic principles and argue without quarrelling, quarrel without suspecting and suspect without slandering.

These principles when extended to capital markets would, I suppose, be 'to analyse without anticipation, to anticipate without excitement and to be excited without avarice'. Analysing with an open mind is essential to make an unbiased assessment of an investment opportunity. As investment is a forward-looking exercise, anticipating possibilities calmly is a prerequisite for comprehensive risk assessment and management. It is natural for humans to get excited when events unfold in a manner they envisage. However, investors who are motivated by the satisfaction of being proven right, and pride in building a viable business, wealth, and fame are more likely to have an unblemished track record than those who are driven by just riches and prominence.

Image credit: GCMMF

Successful professional investors with clean reputations, including RJ, have abided by the aforesaid principles. Yet RJ's contribution to and influence on India's investment landscape extends beyond investing. Uday Kotak evocatively remarked, 'Rakesh Jhunjhunwala's other big passion was Indians investing in our capital market. He and I did not like our capital markets being excessively dependent on foreigners. He played a major role in the development of the market. Foreign investment is welcome, but India has to build its own capital market. He instilled trust in people that the capital market is not a gambling den but a platform that facilitates investment in and profiting from assets with fundamental value. A lot of credit to Rakesh for that. I shared his belief. I observed in the 1990s that Indian capital markets are being exported. It is so gratifying for me to observe fifteen to twenty years later that we have a domestic market which has the potential to be the most vibrant place after the US. We have now evolved from being a nation of savers to a nation of investors.'[1]

Several first-generation investors, some of whom are profiled in this book, have amassed immense wealth ethically. Few have inspired millions of novices to become financially literate and instilled in them the confidence to invest. These retail investors, too, have prospered and provided a rapidly growing nation with the much-needed stable capital to sustain its development momentum.

However, a person who is both an inspiration and a virtuoso who trades, invests, backs unlisted ventures and successfully executes bespoke transactions, including mergers and acquisitions and distressed buyouts, is unusual. The fortune that RJ built is indeed rare and difficult, if not impossible, to replicate. It is for this extraordinary achievement that the government awarded RJ India's fourth highest civilian award, the Padma Shri, posthumously in 2023. Rekha received the award from President Draupadi Murmu at Rashtrapati Bhavan.

It is apt to conclude this narrative with Ramesh Damani's observation, 'Rakesh broke all the rules of being a good investor—don't talk the book, don't take leverage, don't be opinionated. Good investors were looking at MNC businesses in India. He looked at homegrown business. It is said about Henry Kissinger, "The story of his life is the history of our times." I feel the same way about Rakesh. The story of his life is the history of India's capital markets.'[2]

Glossary

Algorithmic trading or algo-trading	Algo-trading uses a computer program that follows a defined set of instructions (an algorithm) to place a trade. The trade, in theory, can generate profits at a speed and frequency that is impossible for a human trader to replicate. The defined sets of instructions are based on timing, price, quantity or any mathematical model. Algo-traders frequently employ high frequency trading (HFT) technology. While it provides advantages, such as faster execution time and reduced costs, and is more systematic by ruling out the impact of human emotions on trading activities, algo-trading can also exacerbate the market's negative tendencies by causing flash crashes and immediate loss of liquidity.
Anchor investor	Prominent investors who invest in IPOs ahead of listing to lend credibility to the issues
Basis point(s)	One basis point equals one-hundredth of a per cent or 0.01%
Bid, ask and mid (exchange) rates	Bid rate is the rate which a foreign exchange dealer is willing to pay for the currency, while the ask price is the rate at which a dealer will sell the same currency. Mid rate is the average

	of the bid and ask rates. The dealer earns a profit or spread from the difference between the bid and ask rates.
Bonus shares	Offer of free additional shares to an entity's existing shareholders. For example, a 1:5 bonus issue implies the company will allot one free share for every five shares owned by investors. Listed entities announce bonus issues as an alternative to dividend and to distribute accumulated reserves. There is no cash outflow for listed entities on account of bonus issues.
Book value	The book value of a share is calculated by dividing the difference between a company's assets and liabilities by the number of outstanding shares
Buyout firms	A category of private equity firm that purchases a mature and typically listed entity and delists it. A variation of this model is when the management of a listed firm purchases all outstanding shares and delists the entity. When a buyout occurs, all of the company's previous shareholders sell their stakes to the PE firm or management team.
Capital adequacy ratio (CAR)	An indicator of a bank's ability to meet its obligations. Regulators of most countries stipulate and monitor the minimum CAR of banks in their jurisdiction.
Cash reserve ratio (CRR)	The percentage of net demand and time liabilities (NDTL), which include current and savings account and fixed deposits, banks maintain with the Reserve Bank of India (RBI) as cash. The RBI pays zero interest to banks on CRR balances. The RBI stipulates the CRR, which is one of the monetary tools the central bank uses to control credit growth, flow of liquidity and inflation in the economy.

Circular trading	A fraudulent practice in which several entities, usually related or known to each other, buy and sell shares among themselves to push up prices and trading volumes, making the stock appear more liquid than it actually is.
Compound annual growth rate (CAGR)	The rate of return that an investment would need to have every year in order to grow from its beginning balance to its ending balance, over a given time interval. The CAGR assumes that profits are reinvested at the end of each period of the investment's life span. While the CAGR measures the smoothed rate of return, it does not reflect investment risk.
Co-location	Locating computers owned by high frequency trading (HFT) firms and proprietary traders in the same premises where a stock exchange's computer servers are housed. This enables HFT firms to access stock prices a split second before the rest of the investing public. Co-location is a lucrative business for exchanges, which charge HFT firms millions of dollars for the privilege of 'low-latency access'. Latency is the time that elapses from the moment a signal is sent to its receipt. Since lower latency equals faster speed, high frequency traders spend heavily to obtain the fastest computer hardware, software and data lines so as to execute orders as speedily as possible and gain a competitive edge in trading.
Custodian	A custodian bank is a financial institution that holds customers' securities for safekeeping to prevent them from being stolen or lost. The custodian may hold stocks, bonds or other assets in electronic or physical form on behalf of its customers. Custodians also manage customers' accounts and the settlement of transactions, account for the status of assets and ensure compliance with tax regulations.

Front running	Trading of stock or any other financial asset by a person/entity in possession of inside knowledge of a future transaction that is about to affect its price substantially. The seller may also front-run based on insider knowledge that their firm is about to issue a 'buy' or 'sell' recommendation to clients that will almost certainly affect the price of an asset. This exploitation of information that isn't yet public is illegal and unethical in almost all jurisdictions.
Growth equity	A private equity strategy that focuses on investments in established and growing companies.
High frequency trading or HFT	A method of trading that uses powerful computer programs to transact a large number of orders in fractions of a second. Typically, the traders with the fastest execution speeds are more profitable than traders with slower execution speeds. While HFT may enhance market liquidity, it is criticised for allowing larger traders, who usually have access to co-location facilities, to gain an upper hand in trading.
Money market dealer	Money market refers to trading in short-term debt instruments continuously and in large volumes between institutions and wholesale traders. Money market dealers are brokers who facilitate money market trading.
New economy stocks	Stocks of companies that leverage on technology and the internet to deliver goods and services. Usually, companies operating in the new economy are in their growth phase which incur a high level of capital expenditure financed by debt, and hence pay low dividends. In India, Paytm, Policybazaar, Nazara Technologies, Nykaa and Zomato are categorised as new economy stocks.

Non-performing assets (NPA)	Loans or advances that are in default or in arrears. A loan is in arrears when principal or interest payments are late or missed. A loan is in default when the lender considers the loan agreement to be broken and the debtor is unable to meet their obligations.
Portfolio management firm	An entity that selects and manages investments that meet the long-term financial objectives and risk tolerance of retail clients, companies and institutions.
Private equity (PE)	Investment partnerships that buy, manage, and sell companies. Private equity firms operate investment funds on behalf of institutional and accredited investors. Private equity funds may acquire private companies or public ones in their entirety, or invest in such buyouts as part of a consortium. They typically do not hold stakes in companies that remain listed on a stock exchange. Private equity is often grouped with venture capital and hedge funds as an alternative investment. Investors in this asset class are usually required to commit significant capital for years, which is why access to such investments is limited to institutions and high-net-worth individuals.
Provision or loan loss provision	An income statement expense set aside by lenders as an allowance for uncollected loans and loan payments.
Return on assets	A company's post-tax profits expressed as a percentage of its assets.
Share splits	A corporate action in which a company issues additional shares to shareholders, based on a specified ratio. A 1:2 share split implies every share is split to two shares, resulting in a halving of the face value of shares. Listed entities announce share splits to increase

	share liquidity, reduce share price and make it affordable for more shareholders.
Short or short position	This is created when a trader sells a security first with the intention of repurchasing it or covering it later at a lower price. A trader may decide to short a security when they believe that the price of that security is likely to decrease in the future.
Statutory liquidity ratio (SLR)	The minimum percentage of deposits banks maintain in their own vaults in the form of liquid cash, gold and other securities. The RBI stipulates the SLR, which is one of the monetary tools the central bank uses to control credit growth, flow of liquidity and inflation in the economy.
Venture capital	A private equity strategy that invests in early-stage start-ups. Venture capitalists (VCs) acquire a stake in start-up in exchange for seed capital. The founders of start-ups find this mode of financing attractive as VCs do not require a majority stake of over 50%.

Sources: Business Standard, Investopedia, https://online.hbs.edu/blog/post/types-of-private-equity, https://groww.in/p/difference-between-bonus-issue-and-stock-split

Appendices

Appendix 1: Berkshire Hathaway's Listed Equity Holdings as of 30 June 2024

Appendix 2: RaRe Enterprises' Listed Equity Holdings as of 30 June 2024

Appendix 3: Harshad Mehta's Investments as Reported in https://www.harshadmehta.in/ (reproduced verbatim)

Statement showing losses suffered by Shri Harshad Mehta and his family members and corporate entities by premature sale of their shares in blue chip companies at throw away prices even before the liabilities against them were crystallized. The false claims made by income tax department since stand deleted but a huge loss of Rs. 20,677.28 crores now cannot be recouped

Appendix 4:
Performance of Select Stocks Harshad Mehta Reportedly Invested In

Appendix 5:
Rakesh Jhunjhunwala's Listed Equities Portfolio: 31 December 2015 to 2024

I made the following assumptions in presenting and computing various metrics related to RJ's listed equities portfolio

- RJ invested both in his and his wife Rekha's names. Trendlyne reported Rekha's holdings separately and as a subset of RJ's portfolio till the last complete quarter (the one ending 30 June 2022) preceding his demise on 14 August 2022. Viceroy Hotels is the sole stock, according to Trendlyne, which Rekha owned and RJ did not own. I have included Rekha's holdings in Viceroy Hotels in the list of stocks RJ owned.
- Trendlyne did not report RJ's holdings for certain quarters. The quarters of missing data are indicated in cells with a grey background colour in the following table.

Missing Shareholding Data (Number of Shares)

Bikare	30-Jun-22	30-Sept-22	30-Dec-22		
	1,997,925	1,866,675	1,735,425		
Escort Kubota	31-Dec-21	31-Mar-22	30-Jun-22		
	6,400,000	4,115,194	1,830,388		
Federal Bank	31-Mar-16	30-Jun-16	30-Sept-16		
	27,071,060	32,946,060	38,821,060		
Fortis Healthcare	31-Dec-16	31-Mar-17	30-Jun-17	30-Sept-17	
	5,000,000	6,000,703	7,001,405	8,002,108	
Fortis Healthcare	30-Sept-17	31-Dec-17	31-Mar-18	30-Jun-18	30-Sept-18
	8,002,108	9,126,581	10,251,054	11,375,527	12,500,000
Jaiprakash Associates	30-Jun-17	30-Sept-17	31-Dec-17	31-Mar-18	
	25,000,000	26,666,667	28,333,333	30,000,000	

Source: Trendlyne & author calculations.

- One quarter data is missing in the case of Bilcare, Escorts Kubota, and Federal Bank. For these entities, I have estimated RJ's holding in the missing quarter as the average of his shareholding in the preceding and succeeding quarter
- There are two quarters of missing data for Fortis Healthcare (March and June 2017) and Jaiprakash Associates. I have estimated RJ's shareholding for the missing quarters as his holding in previous quarter plus 33% of the difference in shareholdings between the first and fourth quarters.
- There are three quarters of missing data for Fortis Healthcare (December 2017, March and June 2018). I have estimated RJ's shareholding for the missing quarters as his holding in previous quarter plus 25% of the difference in shareholdings between the first and fifth quarters.

RJ's Quarterly Shareholdings

Appendix 6:
Star Health's Estimated P/BV at Listing

Notes

Introduction

1. Nazneen Karmali, 'India's 100 Richest:2024', *Forbes*, 9 October 2024, https://www.forbes.com/lists/india-billionaires/.

Chapter 1: Dalal Street

1. Sachin P. Mampatta & Rajesh Bhayani, 'How Abraham Lincoln triggered India's first stock market crash', *Business Standard*, 11 July 2015, https://www.business-standard.com/article/beyond-business/150-years-later-115071001354_1.html.
2. Ashishkumar Chauhan and Archana Jain, *The Temple of Wealth Creation: A 143-Year Journey*, *BSE*, https://www.bseindia.com/downloads1/CTB.pdf.
3. Securities and Exchange Board of India, https://www.sebi.gov.in/.
4. James Chen, 'Free-Float Methodology and How to Calculate Market Capitalization', *Investopedia*, 8 November 2023, https://www.investopedia.com/terms/f/freefloatmethodology.asp.
5. 'What is Sensex | How is the Sensex calculated | Sensex and Nifty Difference', *Business Standard*, https://www.business-standard.com/about/what-is-sensex.
6. Jyotindra Dubey, 'Disinvestment got boost under Vajpayee-led NDA govt', *India Today*, 6 July 2019, https://www.indiatoday.

in/diu/story/disinvestment-got-boost-under-vajpayee-led-nda-govt-here-s-how-public-sector-companies-fared-post-privatisation-1563694-2019-07-06.

7. Debashis Basu and Sucheta Dalal, 'GV Ramakrishna, the Man Who Created a Modern Regulatory Framework for Stock Market, Passes Away', *Moneylife*, 20 March 2021, https://www.moneylife.in/article/gv-ramakrishna-the-man-who-created-a-modern-regulatory-framework-for-stock-market-passes-away/63277.html.
8. Pratip Kar, 'Remembering GV Ramakrishna and the Early Days at SEBI', *Moneylife*, 19 May 2021, https://www.moneylife.in/article/remembering-gv-ramakrishna-and-the-early-days-at-sebi/63914.html.
9. Shiv Taneja, 'Pherwani Committee report recommends setting up of NSE in New Bombay', *India Today*, 30 September 1991, https://www.indiatoday.in/magazine/economy/story/19910930-pherwani-committee-report-recommends-setting-up-of-nse-in-new-bombay-814863-1991-09-29.
10. National Stock Exchange, www.nseindia.com.
11. 'Defunct stock exchanges of India: A journey cut short for Delhi Exchange, Calcutta Exchange, others', *Financial Express*, 30 June 2023, https://www.financialexpress.com/market/defunct-stock-exchanges-of-india-a-journey-cut-short-for-delhi-exchange-calcutta-exchange-others-3149555.
12. 'ETD Tracker', *FIA*, https://www.fia.org/fia/etd-tracker.
13. Nandini Vijayaraghavan, *Unfinished Business, Evolving Capitalism in the World's Largest Democracy*, Penguin Random House India, 2023.
14. Saurav Mukherjee, 'NSE co-location case: SC rejects CBI plea, Chitra Ramkrishna's bail to continue', *Mint*, 13 February 2023, https://www.livemint.com/news/india/nse-co-location-case-sc-rejects-cbi-plea-chitra-ramakrishna-bail-s-to-continue-11676303917798.html.
15. Shailesh Menon, 'What listing of BSE and NSE means for the exchanges and investors', *The Economic Times*, 26 January 2017, https://economictimes.indiatimes.com/markets/stocks/news/what-listing-of-bse-and-nse-means-for-the-exchanges-and-investors/articleshow/56787104.cms?from=mdr.

16. 'BSE Limited IPO Prospectus' dated 28 January 2017, downloaded from sebi.gov.in.
17. 'National Stock Exchange of India Limited's Draft Red Herring Prospectus' dated 28 December 2016, downloaded from sebi.gov.in.
18. 'BSE Ltd. IPO (BSE IPO) Detail', *Chittorgarh*, https://www.chittorgarh.com/ipo/bse-limited-ipo/611/.
19. 'NSE's Shareholding Pattern Under Regulation 31 of SEBI Regulations, 2016' dated 31 March 2024, downloaded from nseindia.com.
20. Laura Gray, 'How to boost GDP stats by 60 percent', *BBC News*, 9 December 2012, https://www.bbc.com/news/magazine-20639775.
21. 'Kenya's economy grows by 25% after recalculation', *BBC News*, 30 September 2014, https://www.bbc.com/news/business-29426575.
22. Diane Coyle, *GDP: A Brief but Affectionate History*, Princeton University Press, 2015.
23. Thomas Butler-Bowdon, *50 Economics Classics: Your Shortcut to the Most Important Ideas on Capitalism, Finance, and the Global Economy*, Nicholas Brealey Publishing, May 2017.
24. Shyam Sekhar, 'Elections and Markets', iThought Wealth, 7 May 2024 accessed at https://www.youtube.com/watch?v=bRTZUM7VmNA.

Chapter 2: The Early Years

1. 'Five lesser-known facts about stock market expert Rakesh Jhunjhunwala', *India Today*, 5 July 2021, https://www.indiatoday.in/business/story/birthday-special-rakesh-jhunjhunwala-5-lesser-known-facts-about-him-1824019-2021-07-05.
2. *Rakesh Jhunjhunwala: The Man who Believed in India*, Ashoka University, 2023.
3. 'Rakesh Jhunjhunwala: Making of the Legend', YouTube: ET Now, 6 July 2020, https://www.youtube.com/watch?v=x8-houvaP0s.
4. My interview with Vishal Gupta, 20 May 2025.
5. *Rakesh Jhunjhunwala: The Man who Believed in India*, Ashoka University, 2023.
6. My interviews with Rajiv Agarwal on 30 April 2025, Vishal Gupta on 20 May 2025, and Rekha Jhunjhunwala on 6 June 2025.

7. *Rakesh Jhunjhunwala: The Man who Believed in India*, Ashoka University, 2023.
8. Ibid.
9. My interview with Renuka Ramnath, 14 August 2024.
10. My interview with Bhaskar Bhat, 3 June 2025.
11. *Rakesh Jhunjhunwala: The Man who Believed in India*, Ashoka University, 2023.
12. 'Deepika Padukone and Rakesh Jhunjhunwala in a candid conversation', YouTube: ETNowLite, 1 October 2013, https://www.youtube.com/watch?v=MjdP1HSABBc.
13. 'Backstory: Rakesh Jhunjhunwala's first punt, and the clients who trusted him with their money', CNBC TV18, 8 September 2021, https://www.cnbctv18.com/market/stocks/backstory-rakesh-jhunjhunwalas-first-punt-and-the-clients-who-trusted-him-with-their-money-7494831.htm.
14. *Rakesh Jhunjhunwala: The Man who Believed in India*, Ashoka University, 2023.
15. 'Tribute to Rakesh Jhunjhunwala | FLAME Investment Lab | 2009', YouTube: FLAME University, 16 August 2022, https://youtu.be/ySZ1G4-cZJ8.
16. 'Off the Cuff with Rakesh Jhunjhunwala', YouTube: The Print, 20 January 2021, https://www.youtube.com/watch?v=rLxv5w-q68A.
17. 'Rakesh Jhunjhunwala: Making of the Legend', YouTube: ET Now, 6 July 2020, https://www.youtube.com/watch?v=x8-houvaP0s.
18. Reena Zachariah, 'Successor to "Big Bull" plays to her strengths', *The Economic Times*, 27 November 2024, https://economictimes.indiatimes.com/markets/stocks/news/successor-to-big-bull-plays-to-her-strengths/articleshow/115712844.cms?from=mdr.
19. *Rakesh Jhunjhunwala: The Man who Believed in India*, Ashoka University, 2023.
20. My interview with Vishal Gupta, 20 May 2025.
21. 'The thrill of being proved right in the market is what drives me: Jhunjhunwala', *The Economic Times*, 30 October 2016, https://economictimes.indiatimes.com/markets/expert-view/i-came-to-trade-in-mumbai-with-rs-5000-rakesh-jhunjhunwala-to-katrina-kaif/articleshow/55133418.cms?from=mdr.

22. Krishna Veera Vanamali and Puneet Wadhwa, 'How did Rakesh Jhunjhunwala make his billions?', *Business Standard*, 16 August 2022, https://www.business-standard.com/podcast/current-affairs/how-did-rakesh-jhunjhunwala-make-his-billions-122081600056_1.html.
23. 'Rakesh Jhunjhunwala Talks About His Trading Style', YouTube: Yogesh Desai, 1 May 2017, https://www.youtube.com/watch?v=r8nl0NTQ0NY.
24. 'Tribute to Rakesh Jhunjhunwala | FLAME Investment Lab | 2009', YouTube: FLAME University, 16 August 2022, https://youtu.be/ySZ1G4-cZJ8.
25. James Chen, 'Short Position: Meaning, Overview, and Example', *Investopedia*, 29 May 2024, https://www.investopedia.com/terms/s/short.asp.
26. 'Mood in Share Market Turns Downbeat', *India Today*, 15 February 1990, https://www.indiatoday.in/magazine/economy/story/19900215-mood-in-share-market-turns-downbeat-812355-1990-02-14.
27. Remya Nair, 'The Making of Budget 1991', *Mint*, 9 February 2016, https://www.livemint.com/Home-Page/AhZbrw8aLWlbE558h9ofxL/The-making-of-Budget-1991.html.
28. Puja Mehra, 'Ten Budgets that Changed India', *Business Today*, 20 March 2011, https://www.indiatoday.in/india/photo/ten-budgets-that-have-had-the-most-impact-on-the-nation-s-economy-365272-2011-03-04/2.
29. 'GDP growth (annual %) – India', *World Bank Group*, https://data.worldbank.org/indicator/NY.GDP.MKTP.KD.ZG?locations=IN.

Chapter 3: Catalysts

1. Definitions of CRR and SLR in glossary
2. 'Chronology of Bankrate, CRR and SLR Changes', *Reserve Bank of India*, https://www.rbi.org.in/commonman/English/History/Scripts/Bankrate CRR and SLR Changes.aspx.
3. Juhi Gupta, 'Seeds of debt: How loan waivers affect the farmers and the economy', *Forbes India*, 3 May 2024, https://www.forbesindia.

com/article/international-management-institute/seeds-of-debt-how-loan-waivers-affect-the-farmers-and-the-economy/92893/1.

4. Debashis Basu and Sucheta Dalal, *The Scam: From Harshad Mehta to Ketan Parekh*, Kensource Information Systems Private Limited, July 2014.
5. Claire Boyte-White, 'Bond Yield Rate vs. Coupon Rate: What's the Difference?', *Investopedia*, 9 June 2024, https://www.investopedia.com/ask/answers/051215/what-difference-between-bonds-yield-rate-and-its-coupon-rate.asp.
6. Debashis Basu and Sucheta Dalal, *The Scam: From Harshad Mehta to Ketan Parekh*, Kensource Information Systems Private Limited, July 2014.
7. Ibid.
8. *Handbook of Statistics on Indian Economy*, Reserve Bank of India, 2001.

Chapter 4: Growmore

1. Lekha Rattanani and Daksesh Parikh, 'Securities Scam: Harshad Mehta Throws Banking System, Stock Markets Into Turmoil', *India Today*, 31 May 1992.
2. Debashis Basu and Sucheta Dalal, *The Scam: From Harshad Mehta to Ketan Parekh*, Kensource Information Systems Private Limited, July 2014.
3. Special Correspondent, 'The Trees Minus the Forest, Janakiraman Reports on Banking Scam', , *Economic and Political Weekly*, 5 June 1993.
4. 'Off The Cuff with Rakesh Jhunjhunwala', YouTube: The Print, 20 January 2021, https://www.youtube.com/watch?v=rLxv5w-q68A.
5. Sudeep Chakravarti, 'The Scam Economy', *India Today*, 11 December 2015, https://www.indiatoday.in/magazine/cover-story/story/20151221-india-today-40th-anniversary-the-scam-economy-sudeep-chakravarti-820976-2015-12-09.
6. Prabhakar Sinha, 'NHB, ANZ Settle Scores Over Securities Scam', *The Times of India*, 14 December 2021, https://timesofindia.

indiatimes.com/business/india-business/nhb-anz-settle-scores-over-1992-securities-scam/articleshow/1598846996.cms.

7. Lekha Rattanani and Daksesh Parikh, 'Securities Scam: Harshad Mehta Throws Banking System, Stock Markets into Turmoil', *India Today*, 31 May 1992.
8. Committee to Enquire into Securities Transactions of Banks and Financial Institutions, Reserve Bank of India, April 1993.
9. Ibid.
10. Special Correspondent, 'The Trees Minus the Forest, Janakiraman Reports on Banking Scam', *Economic and Political Weekly*, 5 June 1993.
11. Shailesh Menon and Maulik Vyas, 'The Harshad Mehta Case: Where Time has Overtaken Justice by a Mile', *The Economic Times*, 5 July 2016, https://economictimes.indiatimes.com/news/politics-and-nation/the-harshad-mehta-case-where-time-has-overtaken-justice-by-a-mile/articleshow/53052771.cms?from=mdr.
12. Anil Penna, 'The Bid Deal about the Big Bull: 5 Things to Know about Harshad Mehta', *Hindustan Times*, 30 October 2020, https://www.hindustantimes.com/more-lifestyle/the-big-deal-about-the-big-bull/story-y30bro7jIxVTF4EhM0eH5H.html.
13. Debashis Basu and Sucheta Dalal, *The Scam: From Harshad Mehta to Ketan Parekh*, Kensource Information Systems Private Limited, July 2014.
14. Koustav Das, 'Story of Harshad Mehta, financial frauds and the lessons that were never learned', *India Today*, 3 December 2020, https://www.indiatoday.in/business/story/harshad-mehta-securities-scam-india-legacy-of-bank-fraud-1733374-2020-10-20.
15. Anupama Katakam, 'A Broker Behind Bars', *Frontline*, 1 September 2001, https://frontline.thehindu.com/other/article30161550.ece.
16. Swati Deshpande, 'Bhupen Dalal and 2 Convicted in Securities Scam of '90s', *The Times of India*, 19 January 2014, https://timesofindia.indiatimes.com/city/mumbai/bhupen-dalal-and-2-convicted-in-securities-scam-of-90s/articleshow/29024977.cms.
17. 'Hiten Dalal, five others get 2 yrs in jail in 1992 securities scam', *Business Standard*, 31 January 2019, https://www.business-standard.

com/article/pti-stories/hiten-dalal-five-others-get-2-yrs-in-jail-in-1992-securities-scam-119013101493_1.html.

18. Hamish Macdonald, *The Polyester Prince, The Rise of Dhirubhai Ambani*, Allen and Unwin, January 1999.
19. 'SC Upholds Conviction of Margabandhu in 1992 Securities Scam', *The Times of India*, 8 August 2009, https://timesofindia.indiatimes.com/business/india-business/sc-upholds-conviction-of-margabandhu-in-1992-securities-scam/articleshow/4868774.cms.
20. Debashis Basu and Sucheta Dalal, *The Scam: From Harshad Mehta to Ketan Parekh*, Kensource Information Systems Private Limited, July 2014.
21. 'Fairgrowth Financial's executives own up to company's involvement in securities scam', *India Today*, 2 January 2013, https://www.indiatoday.in/magazine/cover-story/story/19920831-fair-growth-financials-executives-own-up-to-companys-involvement-in-securities-scam-766796-2013-01-02.
22. Swati Deshpande, '25 Yeas On, Special Court Convicts 6 in Securities Scam', *The Times of India*, 7 July 2018, https://timesofindia.indiatimes.com/india/25-years-on-special-court-convicts-six-in-securities-scam/articleshow/64900664.cms.
23. Palakunnathu G. Mathai and Seetha, 'Narasimha Rao was totally opposed to economic reforms', *The Telegraph Online*, 11 November 2007, https://www.telegraphindia.com/7-days/narasimha-rao-was-totally-opposed-to-economic-reforms/cid/1534905.
24. 'V Krishnamurthy, the Public Sector Management Guru, is No More', *Moneylife*, 27 June 2022, https://www.moneylife.in/article/v-krishnamurthy-the-public-sector-management-guru-is-no-more/67579.html.
25. Shailesh Menon and Maulik Vyas, 'The Harshad Mehta Case: Where Time has Overtaken Justice by a Mile, *The Economic Times*, 5 July 2016, https://economictimes.indiatimes.com/news/politics-and-nation/the-harshad-mehta-case-where-time-has-overtaken-justice-by-a-mile/articleshow/53052771.cms?from=mdr. Harshad Mehta,https://www.harshadmehta.in/.
26. Harshad Mehta, https://www.harshadmehta.in/.
27. Harshad Mehta, https://www.harshadmehta.in/.

28. '1992: The Harshad Mehta Scam', *Frontline*, 15 August 2022, https://frontline.thehindu.com/the-nation/india-at-75-epochal-moments-1992-the-harshad-mehta-scam/article65730958.ece.

Chapter 5: The Pentafour Bull

1. Sucheta Dalal, 'Ketan Parekh: Delusions of Invincibility', *www.rediff.com*, 31 March 2001, https://www.suchetadalal.com/article/ketan-parekh-delusions-of-invincibility/657.html.
2. Neha Joshi and Varun Sood, 'Ketan Parekh: Inside SEBI's 30-month front-running probe', *Mint*, 5 January 2025, https://www.livemint.com/market/ketan-parekh-sebi-probe-stock-market-scam-motilal-oswal-nuvama-wealth-rohit-salgaocar-insider-trading-broker-scpl-11736079846015.html.
3. Lalatendu Mishra, 'Who's Ketan Parekh and why's he bad for the market?', *India Today*, 15 July 2012, https://www.indiatoday.in/business/india/story/ketan-parekh-stock-market-share-prices-sebi-k-10-stocks-109540-2012-07-14.
4. 'Indices: BSE Sensex', *BSE*, https://www.bseindia.com/markets/keystatics/Keystat_index.aspx.
5. Debashis Basu and Sucheta Dalal, *The Scam: From Harshad Mehta to Ketan Parekh*, Kensource Information Systems Private Limited, July 2014.
6. Ibid.
7. 'Off The Cuff with Rakesh Jhunjhunwala', YouTube: The Print, 20 January 2021, https://www.youtube.com/watch?v=rLxv5w-q68A.
8. 'RBI cancels licence of scam-tainted Madhavpura Mercantile Bank', *Moneylife*, 14 June 2012, https://www.moneylife.in/article/rbi-cancels-licence-of-scamtainted-madhavpura-mercantile-bank/26275.html.
9. 'Ketan Parekh gets one-year jail term for Canfina scam', *Mint*, 2 April 2008, https://www.livemint.com/Politics/1nLAOn7fUMHF61fhiON7IJ/Ketan-Parekh-gets-oneyear-jail-term-for-Canfina-scam.html.
10. 'Stock broker Ketan Parekh gets 2 yrs' RI', *The Statesman*, 4 March 2014.

11. Lalatendu Mishra, 'Who's Ketan Parekh and why's he bad for the market?', *India Today*, 15 July 2012, https://www.indiatoday.in/business/india/story/ketan-parekh-stock-market-share-prices-sebi-k-10-stocks-109540-2012-07-14.
12. 'How Ketan Parekh's wife's phone helped SEBI uncover his Rs 65 crore front-running scam', *The Economic Times*, 4 January 2025, https://economictimes.indiatimes.com/news/india/how-ketan-parekhs-wifes-phone-helped-sebi-uncover-a-rs-65-crore-front-running-scam/articleshow/116920346.cms?from=mdr.
13. Sai Aravindh, 'Tiger Global—The "Big Client" Behind Ketan Parekh's Front-Running Scandal', *NDTV Profit*, 4 January 2025, https://www.ndtvprofit.com/law-and-policy/tiger-globalthe-big-client-behind-ketan-parekhs-front-running-scandal.
14. 'Ex-Parte Interim Order Cum Show Cause Notice in the Matter of Extended Front Running by Rohit Salgaocar, Ketan Parekh and Others', Securities and Exchange Board of India, WTM/KV/ISD/ISD-SEC-7/31103/2024-25, 2 January 2025.

Chapter 6: The Ascent

1. My interview with Utpal Sheth, 11 February 2025
2. Nikunj Dalmia, 'The ruthlessness with which Jhunjhunwala exited his positions kept him afloat: Atul Suri', *The Economic Times*, 6 September 2022, https://economictimes.indiatimes.com/markets/expert-view/the-ruthlessness-with-which-jhunjhunwala-exited-his-positions-kept-him-afloat-atul-suri/articleshow/93987504.cms?from=mdr.
3. 'Tribute to Rakesh Jhunjhunwala | FLAME Investment Lab | 2012', YouTube: FLAME University, https://youtu.be/dzip7twG1qw.
4. Bombay Stock Exchange, www.bseindia.com.
5. Aseem Thapliyal, 'Rakesh Jhunjhunwala's portfolio: Titan Company zoomed 8,100% since big bull's entry', *Business Today*, 14 August 2022, https://www.businesstoday.in/markets/company-stock/story/rakesh-jhunjhunwala-titan-company-stake-rally-in-20-years-net-profit-sales-344624-2022-08-14.

6. 'Rakesh Jhunjhunwala: Making of the Legend', 6 July 2020, YouTube: ET Now, https://www.youtube.com/watch?v=x8-houvaP0s.
7. 'Off the Cuff with Rakesh Jhunjhunwala', YouTube: The Print, 20 January 2021, https://www.youtube.com/watch?v=rLxv5w-q68A.
8. Aanchal Magazine and Anil Sasi, 'Who is George Soros, the billionaire that India both attacks and partners with?', *The Indian Express*, 11 April 2023, https://indianexpress.com/article/explained/explained-economics/soros-the-man-his-activities-8452031/.
9. Larry Elliott, 'George Soros's indelible mark on UK runs deeper than Black Wednesday', *The Guardian*, 12 June 2023, https://www.theguardian.com/business/2023/jun/12/george-soros-indelible-mark-on-uk-runs-deeper-than-black-wednesday.
10. 'Profile: George Soros', *Forbes*, https://www.forbes.com/profile/george-soros/.
11. 'Tribute to Rakesh Jhunjhunwala | FLAME Investment Lab | 2012', YouTube: FLAME University, https://youtu.be/dzip7twG1qw.
12. *Rakesh Jhunjhunwala: The Man who Believed in India*, Ashoka University, 2023.
13. John Csiszar, 'If You Invested in Apple When Warren Buffett Did, Here's How Much You Would Have Made', 7 March 2024, https://finance.yahoo.com/news/invested-apple-warren-buffett-did-170010382.html.
14. 'Off the Cuff with Rakesh Jhunjhunwala', YouTube: The Print, 20 January 2021, https://www.youtube.com/watch?v=rLxv5w-q68A.
15. 'Rakesh Jhunjhunwala Lists Out 5 Qualities That Make a Multi-bagger', *The Economic Times*, 3 October 2019, https://economictimes.indiatimes.com/markets/stocks/news/rakesh-jhunjhunwala-lists-out-5-qualities-that-make-a-multibagger/articleshow/71418024.cms?from=mdr.
16. My interview with Utpal Sheth, 11 February 2025.
17. Ibid.
18. My interview with Amit Goela, 27 May 2025.
19. My interview with Amit Goela, 27 May 2025.
20. My interview with Rajiv Agarwal, 30 April 2025.

21. *Rakesh Jhunjhunwala: The Man who Believed in India*, Ashoka University, 2023.
22. My interview with Vishal Gupta, 20 May 2025.
23. My interview with Utpal Sheth, 11 February 2025.
24. Ahona Ghosh, 'Why low-profile Utpal Sheth is a perfect foil to Rakesh Jhunjunwala', *The Economic Times*, 24 August 2012, https://economictimes.indiatimes.com/news/company/corporate-trends/why-low-profile-utpal-sheth-is-a-perfect-foil-to-rakesh-jhunjunwala/articleshow/15624328.cms?from=mdr.
25. 'Remembering Rakesh Jhunjhunwala: Understanding His Belief in India | WizardsofTheStreet', YouTube: CNBCTV-18, 21 November 2022, https://www.youtube.com/watch?v=Tl4qo5px5Hs.
26. Shreya Shankar, 'Rakesh Jhunjhunwala was "investor with Midas touch" who never gave up on Indian markets', *The Print*, 6 July 2023, https://theprint.in/theprint-profile/rakesh-jhunjhunwala-was-investor-with-midas-touch-who-never-gave-up-on-indian-markets/1654819/.
27. *Rakesh Jhunjhunwala: The Man who Believed in India*, Ashoka University, 2023.
28. 'Ashoka University launches Rakesh Jhunjhunwala School of Economics and Finance', Ashoka University, 6 February 2023, https://www.ashoka.edu.in/ashoka-university-launches-rakesh-jhunjhunwala-school-of-economics-and-finance/.
29. 'EdelGive Hurun India Philanthropy List 2021', Hurun, https://www.hurun.net/en-US/Info/Detail?num=PVVW1DYHITVN.
30. 'I'm Rakesh Jhunjhunwala, I do what...: Big Bull on being called India's Warren Buffett', *Mint*, 19 August 2022, https://www.livemint.com/news/india/im-rakesh-jhunjhunwala-i-do-what-big-bull-on-being-called-india-s-warren-buffet-11660917088003.html.
31. 'Profile: Warren Buffett', *Forbes*, https://www.forbes.com/profile/warren-buffett/.
32. Berkshire Hathaway Annual Report, 2023.
33. Kathleen Elkins, 'Warren Buffett: "If I had been a female, my life would have been entirely different"', *CNBC*, 16 October 2018, https://www.cnbc.com/2018/10/16/warren-buffett-says-being-a-white-man-helped-him-succeed.html.

34. 'Rakesh Jhunjhunwala: Making of the Legend', YouTube: ET Now, 6 July 2020, https://www.youtube.com/watch?v=x8-houvaP0s.

Chapter 7: The Legend, The Myth, The Man

1. My interview with R. Balki, 17 June 2024.
2. *Rakesh Jhunjhunwala: The Man who Believed in India*, Ashoka University, 2023.
3. My interview with Rekha Jhunjhunwala, 6 June 2025.
4. 'BHK Voice | Sneak Peak into Billionaire Rakesh Jhunjhunwala's New Mumbai Home', YouTube: Moneycontrol, 29 March 2022, https://www.youtube.com/watch?v=bZqTrsfErZ8.
5. 'Late Rakesh Jjhunjhunwala's 70,000 square feet Mumbai Bungalow', YouTube: Business Today, 12 May 2023, https://www.youtube.com/watch?v=1RD7E7-WDaY.
6. My interview with R. Balki, 17 June 2024.
7. My interview with Bhaskar Bhat, 3 June 2025.
8. Simi Chandoke, 'Rakesh Jhunjhunwala Turns Fifty in Style', *The Times of India*, 18 July 2010, https://timesofindia.indiatimes.com/entertainment/events/mumbai/rakesh-jhunjhunwala-turns-50-in-style/articleshow/6180745.cms.
9. 'Godfather-themed 60th Birthday Bash for Rakesh Jhunjhunwala', *Bangalore Mirror*, 7 July 2020, https://mumbaimirror.indiatimes.com/opinion/the-informer/godfather-themed-60th-birthday-bash-for-rakesh-jhunjhunwala/articleshow/76826573.cms.
10. My interview with R. Balki, 17 June 2024.
11. 'Remembering Rajesh Jhunjhunwala, Ace Investor Madhusudan Kela's Ode to the Big Bull', YouTube: Moneycontrol, 14 August 2023, https://www.youtube.com/watch?v=pI_akL2BeSA.
12. 'Remembering The Big Bull Rakesh Jhunjhunwala', YouTube: ET Now, 14 August 2023, https://www.youtube.com/watch?v=wynHIe9SF94.
13. Mehak Agarwal, '"He was so angry": How Rakesh Jhunjhunwala had reacted to Tata vs Mistry saga', *Business Today*, 21 August 2022, https://www.businesstoday.in/latest/corporate/story/he-was-

so-angry-how-rakesh-jhunjhunwala-had-reacted-to-tata-vs-mistry-saga-345046-2022-08-19.

14. 'About Us: Values & Purpose', *Tata*, https://www.tata.com/about-us/tata-values-purpose.
15. Ashish Rukhaiyar, '"Right or wrong, keep harmony": When Rakesh Jhunjhunwala compared SEBI to spouse, *Business Today*, 20 August 2022, https://www.businesstoday.in/latest/corporate/story/right-or-wrong-keep-harmony-when-rakesh-jhunjhunwala-compared-sebi-to-spouse-345129-2022-08-20.
16. Association of Investment Bankers in India, 'You can't make money on borrowed knowledge', *Outlook Business*, 3 April 2015, https://www.outlookbusiness.com/magazine/business/story/you-cant-make-money-on-borrowed-knowledge-566.
17. 'Ramesh Damani Speaks to Market Leaders as Remember Rakesh Jhunjhunwala | Wizards of the Street', YouTube: CNBC TV18, 28 November 2022, https://youtu.be/luXeQzVawqg?si=krfxgJKMfmmF56cR.
18. My interview with Ramesh Damani, 4 June 2025.
19. 'Rakesh Jhunjhunwala: Making of the Legend', YouTube: ET Now, 6 July 2020, https://www.youtube.com/watch?v=x8-houvaP0s.
20. My interview with R. Balki, 17 June 2024.
21. 'Ramesh Damani Speaks to Market Leaders As Remember Rakesh Jhunjhunwala | Wizards of the Street', YouTube: CNBC TV18, 28 November 2022, https://youtu.be/luXeQzVawqg?si=krfxgJKMfmmF56cR.
22. *Rakesh Jhunjhunwala: The Man who Believed in India*, Ashoka University, 2023.
23. My interview with Ramesh Damani, 4 June 2025.
24. Malini Bhupta, 'Rakesh Jhunjhunwala: The Oracle of Dalal Street', Outlook Business, 14 August 2022, https://www.outlookbusiness.com/news/the-oracle-of-dalal-street-rakesh-jhunjhunwala-news-216304.
25. 'Rakesh Jhunjhunwala on Elections 2019 and More', YouTube: NDTV Profit, 7 February 2019, https://www.youtube.com/watch?v=PT0UQMhgpFc.

26. 'What Rakesh Jhunjhunwala Told PM Modi About India', *Outlook Business*, 14 August 2022, https://www.outlookbusiness.com/news/rakesh-jhunjhunwala-death-what-rakesh-jhunjhunwala-told-pm-modi-about-india-news-216318.
27. 'GDP per capita (current US$) – India', *World Bank Group*, https://data.worldbank.org/indicator/NY.GDP.PCAP.CD?locations=IN.
28. 'This is what caused Rakesh Jhunjhunwala's untimely death', *Financial Express*, 14 August 2022, https://www.financialexpress.com/market/this-is-what-caused-rakesh-jhunjhunwalas-untimely-death-2629416/.
29. 'Ramesh Damani Speaks to Market Leaders as Remember Rakesh Jhunjhunwala | Wizards of the Street', YouTube: CNBN TV18, 28 November 2022, https://youtu.be/luXeQzVawqg?si=krfxgJKMfmmF56cR.

Chapter 8: Lies, Damned Lies & Statistics

1. 'Rakesh Jhunjhunwala: A Perspective', YouTube: Moneylife News Bites, 1 September 2022, https://www.youtube.com/watch?v=3LIRy5_50nc.
2. *Rakesh Jhunjhunwala, The Man Who Believed in India*, Ashoka University, 2023.
3. 'World's Billionaires List: The Richest in 2025', *Forbes*, https://www.forbes.com/billionaires/.
4. My interview with Utpal Sheth, 11 February 2025.
5. My interview with Amit Goela, 27 May 2025.
6. 'Most of my Wealth is Invested in Equities: Rakesh Jhunjhunwala', YouTube: NDTV, 6 October 2016, https://www.youtube.com/watch?v=7cWtgYrv6YU.
7. *Rakesh Jhunjhunwala, The Man Who Believed in India*, Ashoka University, 2023.
8. Marc Rubinstein, 'Ackman's Pitch Shows Why So Few Hedge Funds IPO', *Bloomberg*, 6 June 2024, https://www.bloomberg.com/opinion/articles/2024-06-06/ackman-s-pershing-pitch-shows-why-so-few-hedge-funds-ipo.
9. My interview with Utpal Sheth, 11 February 2025.

10. 'What is the Difference Between Large Cap, Mid Cap & Small Cap?', *Kotak Securities*, 2 December 2023, https://www.kotaksecurities.com/share-market/difference-between-large-small-mid-cap-in-share-market/.

Chapter 9: Bombay House

1. Nilofer Haja, 'Bombay House: Inside the stunning transformation of Tata Group's global HQ', *Architectural Digest*, 30 July 2018, https://www.architecturaldigest.in/content/bombay-house-tata-group-mumbai/.
2. Rachna Tyagi, 'Tata Group history is also the history of Indian industry', *The Print*, 14 October 2018, https://www.theweek.in/theweek/cover/2018/10/05/tata-group-history-is-also-the-history-of-indian-industry.html.
3. R.M. Lala, *Beyond the Last Blue Mountain*, Penguin Random House India, 2017.
4. Vinay Kamath, *TITAN: Inside India's Most Successful Consumer Brand*, Hachette India, 2021.
5. 'Ford v/s Tata motors | Ratan Tata's $2.3 billion 'revenge': How a disagreement with Ford in 1999 led to acquisition of Jaguar Land Rover', *Financial Express*, 1 September 2023, https://www.financialexpress.com/life/lifestyle-ford-vs-tata-motors-ratan-tatas-2-3-billion-revenge-how-a-disagreement-with-ford-in-1999-led-to-acquisition-of-jaguar-land-rover-3199787/.
6. Michael Bradley, '25 Largest Car Companies: Gladiators Guiding Global Growth', *Luxe Digital*, 13 June 2024, https://luxe.digital/lifestyle/garage/largest-car-companies/.
7. 'RBI releases list of NBFCs in the Upper Layer (NBFC-UL) under Scale Based Regulation for NBFCs', 14 September 2023, downloaded from www.rbi.org.in.
8. 'Tata Sons pays ₹20,000 crore debt to avoid mandatory listing: Report', *Mint*, 26 August 2024, https://www.livemint.com/market/stock-market-news/tata-sons-pays-20-000-crore-debt-to-avoid-mandatory-listing-report-11724668803993.html.
9. Tata Sons Annual Report FY2024.

10. VSNL Annual Report FY2001.
11. 'Tata's Offer for 20% VSNL Stake Oversubscribed', *The Economic Times*, 10 May 2002, https://economictimes.indiatimes.com/tatas-offer-for-20-vsnl-stake-oversubscribed/articleshow/9394618.cms?from=mdr.
12. Rajan Gulati, 'How VSNL (Tata Communications) profited from privatisation', Value Research, 24 March 2021, https://www.valueresearchonline.com/stories/49162/how-vsnl-tata-communications-profited-from-privatisation/.
13. Tata Communications Limited, Rating Rationale, CRISIL Ratings, 29 May 2024.
14. Tata Communications Limited Annual Report, FY2020.
15. Tata Communications Limited Annual Report, FY2022.
16. Rachel Lopez, '10 things to know about the Taj Mahal Palace Hotel', *Vogue India*, 5 January 2012, https://www.vogue.in/content/10-things-know-about-taj-mahal-palace-hotel. 'Pioneering Spirit', *IHCL*, https://www.ihcltata.com/company/legacy/.
17. 'Pioneering Spirit', *IHCL*, https://www.ihcltata.com/company/legacy/.
18. The Indian Hotels Company Limited, Abridged Letter of Offer, 9 November 2021.
19. The Indian Hotels Company Limited, Placement Document, 25 March 2022.
20. Automobiles Industry Report, May 2024, India Brand Equity Foundation.
21. Transforming continually', *TATA Motors*, https://www.tatamotors.com/organisation/our-history/.
22. Tata Motors Annual Report FY2019.

Chapter 10: The Watch Project

1. 'Cancel broadband spectrum held by Reliance: CAG draft report', *Business Standard*, 29 June 2014, https://www.business-standard.com/article/companies/cancel-broadband-spectrum-held-by-rjio-cag-draft-report-114062900301_1.html.

2. Vinay Kamath, *TITAN: Inside India's Most Successful Consumer Brand*, Hachette India, 2021.
3. Ibid.
4. Harish Bhat, 'A Titan of Our Times', LinkedIn, 19 April 2020, https://www.linkedin.com/pulse/titan-our-times-harish-bhat/.
5. Titan Watches Limited Annual Reports, FY1987 and FY1988.
6. Vinay Kamath, *TITAN: Inside India's Most Successful Consumer Brand*, Hachette India, 2021.
7. 'Titan, Timex Wind Up Marketing Alliance', *Business Standard*, 23 December 1997, https://www.business-standard.com/article/specials/titan-timex-wind-up-marketing-alliance-197122301097_1.html.
8. Titan Industries Limited Annual Report, FY2002.
9. Titan Industries Limited Annual Report, FY2003.
10. Titan Watches, https://www.titan.co.in/shop/collections-edge?srsltid=AfmBOopXIfK3wzoLvBh2zLoEhdWiMxWW-vHTyp3hBqfn_RwVA7T_iJgn.
11. 'Titan Engineering & Automation Ltd.', Titan Company, https://www.titancompany.in/titan-engineering-%26-automation-ltd.
12. 'Titan Watches', https://www.titan.co.in/shop/collections-raga?srsltid=AfmBOopZMLvZl8Z5IL_lFkJ_q14UhaPtN1g9ysxyI-gYhkTfmw1qLm-G.
13. Titan Industries Limited Annual Reports, FY2004 to FY2007.
14. Sidin Vadukut, 'Finally, time runs out for HMT', *Mint*, 7 January 2016, https://www.livemint.com/Companies/YcaLPQBIKu8ZA5E3yHpITJ/Finally-time-runs-out-for-HMT.html.
15. Titan Company Limited Annual Report, FY2024.
16. Titan Watches Limited Annual Report, FY1987 to FY1988.
17. Titan Watches Limited Annual Report, FY1990.
18. One 97 Communication Limited Prospectus dated 11 November 2021.
19. 'One 97 Communications Limited IPO (Paytm IPO) Detail', *Chittorgarh*, https://www.chittorgarh.com/ipo/paytm-ipo/1128/.
20. One 97 Communication Limited Annual Report, FY2024.
21. National Stock Exchange, www.nseindia.com.

22. Neil Borate, Aprajita Sharma, Aditya Kondawar, , *The Big Bull of Dalal Street: How Rakesh Jhunjhunwala Made His Fortune*, Penguin Random House India, 2023.
23. Ibid.
24. 'Titan earns Rs126 cr from rights issue', *Business Standard*, 22 May 2006, https://www.business-standard.com/article/companies/titan-earns-rs-126cr-from-rights-issue-106052200029_1.html.
25. Titan Industries Limited Annual Reports, FY2007.
26. TIDCO Annual Report, FY2023.
27. *Rakesh Jhunjhunwala, The Man Who Believed in India*, Ashoka University, 2023.

Chapter 11: Banking on Banks

1. Rajesh Mascarenhas, 'HDFC Bank becomes world's 7th largest lender post merger', *The Economic Times*, 18 July 2023, https://economictimes.indiatimes.com/markets/stocks/news/hdfc-bank-becomes-worlds-7th-largest-lender-post-merger/articleshow/101840225.cms?from=mdr.
2. 'The world's largest banks by assets, 2024', S&P Global, 30 April 2024, https://www.spglobal.com/marketintelligence/en/news-insights/research/the-worlds-largest-banks-by-assets-2024.
3. 'Largest banks and bank holding companies by market cap', https://companiesmarketcap.com/sgd/banks/largest-banks-by-market-cap/.
4. 'Who is the world's best banker?', *The Economist*, 29 October 2020, https://www.economist.com/finance-and-economics/2020/10/29/who-is-the-worlds-best-banker.
5. 'Bank nonperforming loans to total gross loans (%)', *World Bank Group*, https://data.worldbank.org/indicator/FB.AST.NPER.ZS?locations=IN.
6. 'About Us: Our Founder', *Federal Bank*, https://www.federalbank.co.in/our-founder.
7. About Us: Milestones', *Federal Bank*, https://www.federalbank.co.in/milestones.
8. Federal Bank FY1997 and FY2016 Annual Reports.
9. State Bank of India FY2016 Annual Report.

10. My calculations based on Federal Bank's share price data published by Bloomberg.
11. 'Rakesh Jhunjhunwala Quizzes Federal Bank Mgmt || CNBC TV18', YouTube: CNBC TV18, 10 May 2018, https://www.youtube.com/watch?v=4AP1AwbV0GE.
12. 'Rakesh Jhunjhunwala Quizzes Federal Bank Mgmt || CNBC TV18', YouTube: CNBC TV18, 10 May 2018, https://www.youtube.com/watch?v=4AP1AwbV0GE.
13. 'History of Money Making in Chennai by V. Sriram', YouTube: V. Sriram, 20 April 2020, https://www.youtube.com/watch?v=mPGS8-VRsyI.
14. V. Sriram, 'An Unbeaten Century, Chronicling 100 Years of Karur Vysya Bank', 2016, https://www.kvb.co.in/about-us/history-kvb/.
15. Ibid.
16. Special Correspondent, 'The Trees Minus the Forest, Janakiraman Reports on Banking Scam', *Economic and Political Weekly*, 5 June 1993.
17. 'Canara Bank fined in UK for anti-money laundering breaches', *The Economic Times*, 6 June 2018, https://economictimes.indiatimes.com/industry/banking/finance/banking/canara-bank-fined-in-uk-for-anti-money-laundering-breaches/articleshow/64482077.cms?from=mdr.
18. 'About Us: Profile', Canara Bank, https://canarabank.com/pages/profile.
19. Canara Bank Basis of Allotment, 30 March 2017, https://canarabank.com/UploadedFiles/Pdf/canara-bank-basis-of-allotment.pdf.
20. Canara Bank FY2019 Annual Report.
21. Canara Bank FY2020 Annual Report.
22. Canara Bank Rating Rationale, CRISIL Ratings, 8 June 2024.
23. Adam Hayes, 'Value Investing Definition, How It Works, Strategies, Risks', *Investopedia*, 9 May 2025, https://www.investopedia.com/terms/v/valueinvesting.asp.
24. My Interview with Sriram Veeraraghavan, 27 November 2024.

Chapter 12: The Cash Machine

1. 'Mr. Pradip P. Shah', *BASF*, https://www.basf.com/in/en/india-investors/board-of-directors/pradip-shah.
2. CRISIL Annual Report, 1999-2000.
3. Pranati Deva, '5 stocks and key lessons learnt from the Big Bull - Rakesh Jhunjhunwala', *Mint*, 15 August 2024, https://www.livemint.com/market/stock-market-news/5-stocks-and-key-lessons-learnt-from-the-big-bull-rakesh-jhunjhunwala-11723714291982.html.
4. CRISIL Annual Report, 2003-04.
5. My interview with Uday Kotak, 11 October 2024.
6. 'S&P's Open Offer for CRISIL Sails Through', *Business Standard*, 26 April 2005, https://www.business-standard.com/article/finance/s-p-open-offer-for-crisil-sails-through-105042601005_1.html.
7. Yamini Sood, 'Why buying a home scores over investing in stocks', *The Economic Times*, 29 February 2016, https://economictimes.indiatimes.com/wealth/real-estate/why-buying-a-home-scores-over-investing-in-stocks/articleshow/51164932.cms?from=mdr.
8. 'How Rakesh Jhunjhunwala made 10000% return in CRISIL stock?', YouTube: Delta1Trading, https://www.youtube.com/shorts/JwGSo4pB-tw.
9. Aparna Iyer, 'Crisil's foothold in CARE sparks fears of a forced entry', *Mint*, 30 June 2017, https://www.livemint.com/Money/SffWzE4fXVSmq5HANpIAyH/Crisils-foothold-in-CARE-sparks-fears-of-a-forced-entry.html.
10. Mohit Bhalla & Reena Zachariah, 'Sebi questions CRISIL investment in CARE Ratings', *The Economic Times*, 14 August 2017, https://economictimes.indiatimes.com/sebi-takes-care-ratings-to-question-crisil-deal/articleshow/60050138.cms?from=mdr.
11. CareEdge Ratings Annual Report, FY2023-24.
12. ICRA Annual Report, FY2024.
13. 'Settlement Order No: SO/SBM/EAD-3/03/2018 on the application submitted by M/s CRISIL Limited', 31 January 2018, https://www.sebi.gov.in/enforcement/orders/jan-2018/settlement-order-in-respect-of-m-s-crisil-ltd-_37642.html.
14. IL&FS Annual Report, 2018.

15. IL&FS Transportation Networks Limited, CRISIL Rating Rationale, 25 July 2016.
16. Beena Parmar, 'IL&FS timeline: When and what happened so far', *Moneycontrol*, 2 October 2018, https://www.moneycontrol.com/news/business/companies/ilfs-timeline-when-and-what-happened-so-far-3005211.html.
17. CRISIL changed its financial year ending from 31 March to 31 December in 2005 to align its reporting with S&P's. The financial year ending for ICRA and CARE is 31 March.
18. CRISIL Annual Report, FY2011.
19. CRISIL Annual Report, FY2015.

Chapter 13: Potpourri

1. Pharmaceuticals, India Brand Equity Foundation, November 2024.
2. Kuldeep Sharma, 'Indian Pharma Industry – Current Challenges & Future Scope', 25 July 2023, https://www.linkedin.com/pulse/indian-pharma-industry-current-challenges-future-kuldeep/.
3. Lupin Ltd Annual Reports, FY2001 and FY2021.
4. Aurobindo Pharma Ltd Annual Reports, FY2013 and FY2017.
5. Kripa Mahalingam, 'Byte into this', *Outlook Business*, 12 April 2014, https://www.outlookbusiness.com/magazine/business/story/byte-into-this-160.
6. Aptech Limited Annual Report, FY2005.
7. Aptech Limited Annual Report, FY2010.
8. Kripa Mahalingam, 'Byte into this', *Outlook Business*, 12 April 2014, https://www.outlookbusiness.com/magazine/business/story/byte-into-this-160.
9. Aptech Limited Annual Report, FY2014
10. Ashish Rukhaiyar, '"Right or wrong, keep harmony": When Rakesh Jhunjhunwala compared Sebi to spouse', *Business Today*, 20 August 2022, https://www.businesstoday.in/latest/corporate/story/right-or-wrong-keep-harmony-when-rakesh-jhunjhunwala-compared-sebi-to-spouse-345129-2022-08-20.
11. Aptech Limited Annual Report, FY2022.
12. Escorts Limited Annual Report, FY2004.

13. Sumant Banerji, 'Back From the Brink', *Business Today*, 10 January 2021, https://www.businesstoday.in/specials/indias-best-ceos-2018/story/back-from-the-brink-282473-2020-12-24.
14. Escorts Limited Rating Rationale, CRISIL Limited, 22 February 2022.
15. 'Post Offer Advertisement in Accordance with Regulation 18(12) Of the Securities and Exchange Board of India (Substantial Acquisition of Shares and Takeovers) Regulations, 2011 (as amended)', 12 April 2022, https://www.sebi.gov.in/sebi_data/commondocs/apr-2022/Escort%20Ltd_POA_p.pdf.
16. V. Keshavdev, 'Rakesh Jhunjhunwala Makes a Killing in Escorts', *Fortune India*, 27 November 2021, https://www.fortuneindia.com/enterprise/rakesh-jhunjhunwala-makes-a-killing-in-escorts/106254#google_vignette.
17. 'A journey of benchmarks', *NCC Limited*, https://www.ncclimited.com/timeline.html.
18. NCC Limited Annual Report, FY2004.
19. NCC Limited Annual Report, FY2014.

Chapter 14: Jackpot!

1.. Renuka Ramnath, *LinkedIn*, https://www.linkedin.com/posts/renukaramnath_rakeshbhai-was-a-fine-investor-he-was-in-activity-6965181173044006913-PP_k/?trk=public_profile_like_view.
2. 'ICICI Ventures buys Tata Infomedia Stake', The Times of India, 1 September 2003, https://timesofindia.indiatimes.com/business/india-business/icici-ventures-buys-tata-infomedia-stake/articleshow/160278.cms.
3. 'Multiples, CPPIB and Jhunjhunwala's RARE to buy Cadila's Animal Health biz for Rs 2921 crores', *The Economic Times*, 12 May 2021, https://economictimes.indiatimes.com/news/economy/agriculture/multiples-cppib-and-jhunjhunwalas-rare-to-buy-cadilas-animal-health-biz-for-rs-2921-crores/articleshow/82568825.cms?from=mdr.

4. Krishna Veera Vanamali and Puneet Wadhwa, 'How did Rakesh Jhunjhunwala make his billions?' *Business Standard*, 16 August 2022, https://www.business-standard.com/podcast/current-affairs/how-did-rakesh-jhunjhunwala-make-his-billions-122081600056_1.html.
5. '13.4 Private Final Consumption Expenditure', *Ministry of Statistics and Programme Implementation*, https://www.mospi.gov.in/134-private-final-consumption-expenditure.
6. Baazar Style Retail Limited IPO Prospectus dated 3 September 2024.
7. Nazara Technologies IPO Prospectus dated 22 March 2021.
8. Concord Biotech IPO Prospectus dated 9 August 2023.
9. Inventurus Knowledge Solutions IPO Prospectus dated 16 December 2024.
10. James Chen, 'Unicorn: What It Means in Investing, With Examples', 27 April 2027, https://www.investopedia.com/terms/u/unicorn.asp.
11. One 97 Communications IPO Prospectus dated 11 November 2021.
12. Vidya Sreedhar, 'Warren Buffett's Berkshire books Rs 630-crore loss after holding Paytm shares for 5 years', *The Economic Times*, 24 November 2023, https://economictimes.indiatimes.com/markets/stocks/news/warren-buffetts-berkshire-books-rs-630-crore-loss-after-holding-paytm-shares-for-5-years/articleshow/105479535.cms?from=mdr.
13. Nandini Vijayaraghavan, *Unfinished Business: Evolving Capitalism in the World's Largest Democracy*, Penguin Random House India, 2023.
14. IL&FS Annual Reports.
15. My interview with Utpal Sheth, 11 February 2025.
16. Nazara Technologies IPO Prospectus dated 22 March 2021.
17. Metro Brands IPO Prospectus dated 15 December 2021.
18. Shampa Dhar-Kamath, *Rakesh Jhunjhunwala, The Man Who Believed in India*, Ashoka University, 2023.
19. My interview with Rajiv Agarwal, 30 April 2025.
20. Ibid.
21. My interview with Ramesh Damani, 4 June 2025.

22. Amit Mudgill, 'Half my private equity investment turned duds: Rakesh Jhunjhunwala', *The Economic Times*, 26 March 2021, https://economictimes.indiatimes.com/markets/stocks/news/half-my-private-equity-investment-turned-duds-rakesh-jhunjhunwala/articleshow/81686639.cms?from=mdr.

Chapter 15: Janus Stock

1. Berkshire Hathaway Annual Reports downloaded from berkshirehatahway.com/reports.html.
2. The New India Assurance Company Limited IPO Prospectus dated 6 November 2017.
3. *Handbook on Indian Insurance Statistics 2007-08*, Insurance Regulatory and Development Authority of India.
4. Shine Jacob, 'Star Health founder Venkatasamy Jagannathan resigns from company's board', *Business Standard*, 11 June 2023, https://www.business-standard.com/companies/news/building-star-health-from-rs-30-000-rent-to-rs-30-000-crore-market-cap-123061100473_1.html.
5. *Handbook on Indian Insurance Statistics 2021-22*, Insurance Regulatory and Development Authority of India
6. 'India Ratings Upgrades Star Health and Allied Insurance to 'IND AA'/Stable; Rates Additional Sub-Debt', *India Ratings & Research*, 20 September 2021, https://www.indiaratings.co.in/pressrelease/56166.
7. Star Health and Allied Insurance Company Limited, IPO Prospectus dated 7 December 2021.
8. Star Health and Allied Insurance Company Limited IPO Prospectus dated 7 December 2021.
9. 'V. Jagannathan quits from Board of Star Health and Allied Insurance Company', *The Economic Times*, 11 June 2023, https://economictimes.indiatimes.com/industry/banking/finance/insure/v-jagannathan-quits-from-board-of-star-health-and-allied-insurance-company/articleshow/100917832.cms?from=mdr.
10. 'About Us', *Star Health*, starhealth.in/investors/about-us/#board-of-directors.

Chapter 16: Mahalaxmi Race Course and Arthur Road Jail

1. Will Kenton, 'Reputational Risk: Definition, Dangers, Causes, and Example', *Investopedia*, 5 December 2022, https://www.investopedia.com/terms/r/reputational-risk.asp.
2. James Chen, 'Systematic Risk: Definition and Examples', *Investopedia*, 15 August 2024, https://www.investopedia.com/terms/s/systematicrisk.asp.
3. Will Kenton, 'Ring-Fence: Meaning in Finance Accounting and Legality', *Investopedia*, 9 February 2025, https://www.investopedia.com/terms/r/ringfence.asp.
4. 'RaRe Equity Private Limited, Rating Reaffirmed and Withdrawn', Acuité Ratings and Research, 7 October 2024.
5. Association of Investment Bankers of India, 'You Can't make Money on Borrowed Knowledge', *Outlook Business*, 3 April 2015, https://www.outlookbusiness.com/magazine/business/story/you-cant-make-money-on-borrowed-knowledge-566.
6. A2Z Maintenance & Engineering Services Limited Red Herring Prospectus dated 3 December 2010.
7. 'Spectacular Bust', *Outlook Business*, 11 May 2013, https://www.outlookbusiness.com/magazine/business/story/spectacular-bust-321.
8. 'A2Z Maintenance & Engineering Services Ltd IPO (A2Z Maintenance IPO) Detail', *Chittorgarh*, https://www.chittorgarh.com/ipo/a2z_maintenance_ipo/287/.
9. 'Spectacular Bust', *Outlook Business*, 11 May 2013, https://www.outlookbusiness.com/magazine/business/story/spectacular-bust-321.
10. 'A2Z Maintenance dips after Rakesh Jhunjhunwala resigns as director', *Business Standard*, 25 June 2013, https://www.business-standard.com/article/markets/a2z-maintenance-dips-after-rakesh-jhunjhunwala-resigns-as-director-112101600138_1.html.
11. Bilcare Ltd's quarterly shareholder filing dated 31 March 2004.
12. Bilcare Ltd Annual Report, FY2004.
13. Bilcare Ltd Annual Report, FY2011.

14. Rajat Ubhaykar, 'Let me explain it to you again...' *Outlook Business*, 6 March 2015, https://www.outlookbusiness.com/magazine/business/story/let-me-explain-it-to-you-again-597.
15. Bilcare Ltd Annual Report, FY2023.
16. Jason Fernando, 'How Investors Use Arbitrage', *Investopedia*, 21 May 2025, https://www.investopedia.com/terms/a/arbitrage.asp.
17. 'Beginner's Guide to Hedging: Definition and Example of Hedges in Finance', *Investopedia*, https://www.investopedia.com/trading/hedging-beginners-guide.
18. 'Rakesh Jhunjhunwala Talks About His Trading Style', YouTube: Yogesh Desai, 1 May 2017, https://www.youtube.com/watch?v=r8nl0NTQ0NY.
19. Ibid.
20. My interview with Utpal Sheth, 11 February 2025.

Chapter 17: The Show Goes On

1. Reena Zachariah, 'Rakesh Jhunjhunwala's wife, relatives and lawyer Berjis Desai to be executors of his estate', *The Economic Times*, 25 August 2022, https://economictimes.indiatimes.com/news/company/corporate-trends/rakesh-jhunjhunwalas-wife-relatives-and-lawyer-berjis-desai-to-be-executors-of-his-estate/articleshow/93762303.cms?from=mdr.
2. Santosh Nair, 'Radhakishan Damani to be at the helm of Rakesh Jhunjhunwala Trust', *Moneycontrol*, 11 August 2023, https://www.moneycontrol.com/news/business/markets/radhakishan-damani-to-be-at-the-helm-of-rakesh-jhunjhunwala-trust-9068351.html.
3. Reena Zachariah, 'Successor to "Big Bull" plays to her strengths', *The Economic Times*, 27 November 2024, https://economictimes.indiatimes.com/markets/stocks/news/successor-to-big-bull-plays-to-her-strengths/articleshow/115712844.cms?from=mdr.
4. Vipul Das, 'Rekha Jhunjhunwala bought fresh stake in this pharma stock in Q4: Should you buy?' *Mint*, 22 April 2023, https://www.livemint.com/market/stock-market-news/rekha-jhunjhunwala-bought-fresh-stake-in-this-pharma-stock-in-q4-should-you-buy-11682172933476.html.

5. Star Health and Allied Insurance Limited IPO Prospectus dated 7 December 2021.
6. Manish Pant, 'Maiden flight of Rakesh Jhunjhunwala-backed Akasa takes off', *Business Today*, 7 August 2022, https://www.businesstoday.in/latest/trends/story/maiden-flight-of-rakesh-jhunjhunwala-backed-akasa-takes-off-343983-2022-08-07.
7. *Handbook on Civil Aviation Statistics 2023-24*, Directorate of Civil Aviation, dgca.gov.in.
8. 'Akasa Air posts Rs 1,670 crore loss in FY24; CFO says performance will be better this fiscal', *The Economic Times*, 6 November 2024, https://economictimes.indiatimes.com/markets/stocks/earnings/akasa-air-loss-widens-to-rs-1670-crore-in-fy24-total-income-rises-to-rs-3144-crore/articleshow/114988442.cms?from=mdr.
9. Reena Zachariah, 'Successor to "Big Bull" plays to her strengths', *The Economic Times*, 27 November 2024, https://economictimes.indiatimes.com/markets/stocks/news/successor-to-big-bull-plays-to-her-strengths/articleshow/115712844.cms?from=mdr.
10. My interview with Utpal Sheth, 11 February 2025.
11. My interview with Ramesh Damani, 4 June 2025.
12. My interview with Rekha Jhunjhunwala, 6 June 2025.

Chapter 18: The Ten Commandments

1. *Rakesh Jhunjhunwala: The Man who Believed in India*, Ashoka University, 2023.
2. Securities and Exchange Board of India's Settlement Order No: SO/SR/EAD/09/2018-2019 dated 30 November 2018 on the application submitted by Mr. Rakesh Jhunjhunwala in the matter of Geometric Limited, downloaded from sebi.gov.in.
3. Securities and Exchange Board of India's Settlement Order No: SO / EFD-2 / SD/384/ JULY/ 2021 dated 14 July 2021 on the application submitted by Mr. Rakesh Jhunjhunwala, Mrs. Rekha Jhunjhunwala et al in the matter of Aptech Ltd, downloaded from sebi.gov.in.
4. 'Rakesh Jhunjhunwala Quizzes Titan Management | Morning Call | CNBC TV18 Exclusive', YouTube: CNBC TV18, 6 November 2017, https://www.youtube.com/watch?v=mSLvimTGiog.

5. 'About Rakesh Jhunjhunwala', *Business Standard*, https://www.business-standard.com/about/who-is-rakesh-jhunjhunwala.
6. Nikunj Dalmia, 'The ruthlessness with which Jhunjhunwala exited his positions kept him afloat: Atul Suri', *The Economic Times*, 6 September 2022, https://economictimes.indiatimes.com/markets/expert-view/the-ruthlessness-with-which-jhunjhunwala-exited-his-positions-kept-him-afloat-atul-suri/articleshow/93987504.cms?from=mdr.
7. My interview with Amit Goela, 27 May 2025.
8. Shilpa Phadnis, Mayur Shetty, Reeba Zachariah and Rupali Mukherjee, 'How a Rs 10,000 investment in these stocks grew over the decades', *The Times of India*, 23 January, 2021, https://timesofindia.indiatimes.com/business/india-business/how-a-rs-10000-investment-in-these-stocks-grew-over-the-decades/articleshow/80400114.cms.
9. Vipul Das, 'India's 75th Independence: 5 most valued stocks in the last 7 decades', *Mint*, 14 August 2022, https://www.livemint.com/market/stock-market-news/indias-75th-independence-5-most-valued-stocks-in-the-last-7-decades-11660489484242.html.
10. NSE's quarterly shareholder filing dated 31 March 2020, downloaded from nseindia.com.
11. Pavan Burugula, 'Radhakishan Damani Buys Stake in NSE', *The Economic Times*, 10 September 2020, https://economictimes.indiatimes.com/markets/stocks/news/radhakishan-damani-buys-stake-in-nse/articleshow/78004270.cms?from=mdr.
12. https://unlistedzone.com/shares/nse-india-limited-unlisted-shares/
13. 'NSE India Limited Unlisted Shares', *UnlistedZone*, https://unlistedzone.com/shares/nse-india-limited-unlisted-shares/.
14. Ibid.
15. Aswath Damodaran, 'A Viral Market Meltdown III: Pricing or Value? Trading or Investing?' 16 March 2020, https://aswathdamodaran.blogspot.com/2020/03/a-viral-market-meltdown-iii-pricing-or.html.
16. Nikunj Dalmia, 'The ruthlessness with which Jhunjhunwala exited his positions kept him afloat: Atul Suri', *The Economic Times*, 6 September 2022, https://economictimes.indiatimes.com/markets/

expert-view/the-ruthlessness-with-which-jhunjhunwala-exited-his-positions-kept-him-afloat-atul-suri/articleshow/93987504.cms?from=mdr.

17. My interview with Amit Goela, 27 May 2025.
18. My interview with Utpal Sheth, 11 February 2025.
19. Amit Mudgill, 'Half my private equity investment turned duds: Rakesh Jhunjhunwala', *The Economic Times*, 26 March 2021, https://economictimes.indiatimes.com/markets/stocks/news/half-my-private-equity-investment-turned-duds-rakesh-jhunjhunwala/articleshow/81686639.cms?from=mdr.

Chapter 19: Thus Spake RJ

1. 'Off The Cuff with Rakesh Jhunjhunwala (Originally published on January 20, 2021)', YouTube: The Print, 20 January 2021, https://www.youtube.com/watch?v=rLxv5w-q68A.
2. Cathy Scott, 'How to Think About Risk: Howard Marks's Comprehensive Guide', 13 September 2024, https://blogs.cfainstitute.org/investor/2024/09/13/how-to-think-about-risk-howard-marks-s-comprehensive-guide/.
3. '"Culture Eats Strategy for Breakfast" - What Does it Mean?', The Alternative Board, 26 February, 2020, https://www.thealternativeboard.com/blog/culture-eats-strategy.
4. 'Rakesh Jhunjhunwala in an Exclusive Interview with Alia Bhatt', YouTube: ET Now, 20 October 2017, https://www.youtube.com/watch?v=tDiWXG8sxno.
5. Ibid.
6. 'Off The Cuff with Rakesh Jhunjhunwala (Originally published on January 20, 2021)', YouTube: The Print, 20 January 2021, https://www.youtube.com/watch?v=rLxv5w-q68A.
7. 'Rakesh Jhunjhunwala: Making of the Legend', YouTube: ET Now, 6 July 2020, https://www.youtube.com/watch?v=x8-houvaP0s.
8. 'Off The Cuff with Rakesh Jhunjhunwala (Originally published on January 20, 2021)', YouTube: The Print, 20 January 2021, https://www.youtube.com/watch?v=rLxv5w-q68A.

9. 'Tribute to Rakesh Jhunjhunwala | FLAME Investment Lab | 2012', YouTube: FLAME University, 17 August 2022, https://www.youtube.com/watch?v=dzip7twG1qw.
10. 'Rakesh Jhunjhunwala Talks About His Trading Style', YouTube: Yogesh Desai, 1 May 2017, https://www.youtube.com/watch?v=r8nl0NTQ0NY.
11. Ibid.
12. Ibid.
13. 'Off The Cuff with Rakesh Jhunjhunwala (Originally published on January 20, 2021)', YouTube: The Print, 20 January 2021, https://www.youtube.com/watch?v=rLxv5w-q68A.
14. Ibid.
15. 'Remembering Rakesh Jhunjhunwala: Ace Investor Madhusudan Kela's Ode to the Big Bull', YouTube: Moneycontrol, 14 August 2023, https://www.youtube.com/watch?v=pI_akL2BeSA.
16. 'Wizards of the Street', YouTube: CNBC TV-18, 28 November 2022, https://www.youtube.com/watch?v=luXeQzVawqg.
17. 'Rakesh Jhunjhunwala To ET NOW | Mega Exclusive', YouTube: ET Now, 3 October 2019, https://www.youtube.com/watch?v=372xJdI5uKw.
18. 'The Spectacular Rise and Fall of WeWork', YouTube: Bloomberg Originals, 7 November 2019, https://www.youtube.com/watch?v=X2LwIiKhczo.
19. Ibid.
20. 'Rakesh Jhunjhunwala To ET NOW | Mega Exclusive', YouTube: ET Now, 3 October 2019, https://www.youtube.com/watch?v=372xJdI5uKw.
21. Matthew Frankel, CFP, 'What Companies Does SoftBank Own?' *The Motley Fool*, 19 March 2024, https://www.fool.com/investing/how-to-invest/stocks/what-does-softbank-own/.
22. Anton Bridge, 'SoftBank books $7.7 billion quarterly gain as Vision Fund finds its feet again', *Reuters*, 12 November 2024, https://www.reuters.com/business/finance/softbank-back-quarterly-profit-with-77-billion-gain-2024-11-12/.
23. Kana Inagaki, Katie Martin, Robert Smith and Robin Wigglesworth, 'SoftBank unmasked as "Nasdaq whale" that stoked

tech rally', *Financial Times*, 4 September 2020, https://www.ft.com/content/75587aa6-1f1f-4e9d-b334-3ff866753fa2.

24. 'Tribute to Rakesh Jhunjhunwala | FLAME Investment Lab | 2012', YouTube: FLAME University, https://youtu.be/dzip7twG1qw.
25. 'Off The Cuff with Rakesh Jhunjhunwala (Originally published on January 20, 2021)', YouTube: The Print, 20 January 2021, https://www.youtube.com/watch?v=rLxv5w-q68A.
26. 'Wizards of the Street', YouTube: CNBC TV-18, 28 November 2022, https://www.youtube.com/watch?v=luXeQzVawqg.
27. 'Rakesh Jhunjhunwala says "Stay Away" from IPOs; stock market may correct soon', *Financial Express*, 15 November 2017, https://www.financialexpress.com/market/rakesh-jhunjhunwala-says-stay-away-from-ipos-stock-market-may-correct-soon-933509/.
28. My interview with Utpal Sheth, 11 February 2025.
29. 'Off The Cuff with Rakesh Jhunjhunwala (Originally published on January 20, 2021)', YouTube: The Print, 20 January 2021, https://www.youtube.com/watch?v=rLxv5w-q68A.
30. Ibid.

Epilogue

1. My interview with Uday Kotak, 11 October 2024.
2. My interview with Ramesh Damani, 4 June 2025.

Also by Nandini Vijayaraghavan

Non-fiction

The Singapore Blue Chips: The Rewards & Risks of Investing in Singapore's Largest Corporates (Co-authored with Umesh Desai)

Unfinished Business: Evolving Capitalism in the World's Largest Democracy

Translations, Tamil to English

Kalki Krishnamurthy's *Parthiban's Dream*

Kalki Krishnamurthy's *Sivakami's Vow*

Savi's *A Wedding in Washington*